THE LETTERS OF ROBERT MACKAY TO HIS WIFE

*

ROBERT MACKAY
(1772–1816)
From the miniature by Edward Greene Malbone

THE LETTERS OF ROBERT MACKAY TO HIS WIFE

Written from ports in America and England
1795–1816

*

WITH AN INTRODUCTION AND NOTES BY
WALTER CHARLTON HARTRIDGE

*

PUBLISHED UNDER THE AUSPICES OF
THE GEORGIA SOCIETY OF THE COLONIAL DAMES OF AMERICA
BY
THE UNIVERSITY OF GEORGIA PRESS
ATHENS

Paperback edition, 2010

Athens, Georgia 30602
www.ugapress.org

Printed digitally in the United States of America

The Library of Congress has cataloged the hardcover edition of this book as follows:
Library of Congress Cataloging-in-Publication Data
LCCN Permalink: http://lccn.loc.gov/49010691
Mackay, Robert, 1772–1816.
The letters of Robert Mackay to his wife, written from ports in America and England, 1795–1816.
With an introd. and notes by
Walter Charlton Hartridge.

I. Mackay, Eliza Anne McQueen, 1778–1862.
II. Hartridge, Walter Charlton, 1870–
III. National Society Colonial Dames of America in the State of Georgia.
xxxi, 325 p. illus. ports. 24 cm.
CT275.M4347 A4
923.978 49-10691

Paperback ISBN-13: 978-0-8203-3538-4
ISBN-10: 0-8203-3538-X

IN APPRECIATION OF HER VALUABLE SERVICE
IN PRESERVING THE RECORDS OF GEORGIA'S PAST
AND IN AFFECTIONATE REMEMBRANCE OF A RARE SPIRIT
THIS VOLUME IS DEDICATED TO THE MEMORY OF
ELIZABETH MACKAY SCREVEN
AN HONORARY VICE PRESIDENT OF THE
GEORGIA SOCIETY OF COLONIAL DAMES

Foreword

The Letters of Robert Mackay to his Wife is the second in a series being issued under the auspices of the Georgia Society of Colonial Dames. The first of these, *The Letters of Don Juan McQueen to his Family*, appeared in 1943, and was so well received as to encourage the further publication during the next few years of the remaining letters in the valuable MSS collection presented in 1936 to the Society by Mrs. Franklin B. Screven and her cousin, Miss Phoebe Elliott. The collection comprises the related letters of the McQueen, Mackay and Cowper families, all well-known in the early history of Georgia's coast country.

It was Mrs. Screven, however, who made the gift possible. For many years she had been earnestly at work assembling various groups of old and partly forgotten family letters still in the possession of family connections, her desire being to make the correspondence, which she considered of potential value as source material, available for the use of students and writers interested in the social history of the South. With this in mind, she presented the majority of these private records to the Southern Historical Collection of the University of North Carolina at Chapel Hill, and others of a more formal nature to the Georgia Historical Society, while the letter groups that make up the Colonial Dames collection were selected by Mrs. Screven for the general significance of their Savannah background. The present volume bears witness to her good judgment, for its engaging letters, with their essence of age and their lively topics, bring to the imagination the currencies of the past in a period of Savannah history whose eventful days were giving shape to a new century.

Robert Mackay was a born letter writer, observant, informative, witty and caustic in turn, and at times solicitous and tender. His style is natural and forthright; he writes of trivial things entertainingly, and of matters of import with authority. Taken collectively, his letters offer a panoramic view of the times—1795–1816—as he writes from his sojourns in England, from ports of travel, or when at home in Savannah.

Our Society is doubly indebted to Mr. Walter C. Hartridge, who has long made a study of the social history of this region, for his evaluation of the historical quality of the letter groups of the Colonial Dames collection which stimulated interest for their preservation through publication, and for his generous offer to edit the Mackay letters as he did those of Don Juan McQueen. His Introduction, and the significance of his well documented notes, together with their unique genealogical data, give distinction to this second volume of the contemplated series. Without Mr. Hartridge's comprehensive knowledge of source material, the finer meaning of the letters, with their elements of human interest and contemporary gossip, would be lost, and references to people and places, little more than a processional of names. As it is, the explanatory notes give movement, purpose, and identity to the dim happenings of those far-off days, and create a perspective by which the realities of Robert Mackay's letters are brought into the seeing distance of the reader.

To the deep regret of our membership, Elizabeth

Mackay Screven died suddenly on February 11th, 1943. The present volume containing the letters of her great-grandfather, from whom she inherited so many zestful and appealing traits, is inspired by our remembrance of her and dedicated to her memory. It seems a fitting manner in which to recognize the accomplishments of an honored member of the Colonial Dames, whose modesty during her lifetime would have forbidden words of praise. And yet praise lives on in what she was and what she did, for in thinking of Mrs. Screven one does so in terms of the distinguished elements of her character, the vigor and charm of her personality, all of which gave such individual flavor to her long and constructive life.

Those who knew her like to look back with appreciation on her exhilarating qualities, her independence of spirit and freedom of action, her objectivity of thought, her liberal ideas and verve for humor. In reminiscing over the delightful informalities of her nature, one senses again those inner urgencies and their outward reflection. How readily she comes to mind! There was always that vivacity, the small swift gestures, so typical and expressive of her likes and dislikes, her opinions and decisions, yet in quiet moods, seeing her in repose was to behold her as a portrait of quality, the work of a distinguished artist. To dwell on Mrs. Screven is to recall the manifold ways in which she enjoyed the felicities of an active life. One likes in particular to remember her persistent preference for walking, those daily peregrinations on foot with their eager sense of dispatch that took her through the fulness of years to numberless destinations. It was all part of a liveliness of motion that seemed to act as pacemaker for her quick progression of ideas—all a happy rhythm of life that was to continue unabated to her last day. Indeed in the receding past Mrs. Screven becomes a memorable figure in the Savannah of her own times, in the city of her birth which she knew as intimately as one would a well-loved book, one whose tempered pages reveal her love of church and family, her friendships and charities, her perennial interest in the amenities of the present, her lively concern for the traditions of the past.

All such characteristics stood Mrs. Screven in good stead when she first assumed the task of extricating and later assembling the letters from their fugitive state, for most of these had undergone a precarious existence and been subjected to many hazards after lying secure for the better part of a century in the Robert Mackay house in Savannah, at what was once 75 Broughton Street (next to the southeast corner of Abercorn Street). The old house, built around 1800, survived the century, making way at last to business interests. Many pieces of the fine furniture which had given the interior such distinction and which today are valuable heirlooms, are still in the possession of Mackay descendants, none more prized possibly than the superb Sheraton breakfront secretary (made by the Early American cabinetmaker, J. Barry of Philadelphia) from which most of the letters were written, and where, in later years they were kept, safely returned from their many journeys. Today all that is left of the house is a much faded photograph that shows a simple wooden structure, large and rambling, with a pointed roof and dormer windows. Yet it remains rich in the annals of recollection. The substantial dwelling in its many stages of existence may well be said to have been the rallying point for the descendants of Robert Mackay. After his death in 1816, his widow continued to live there with her several small children, and it was there in the Thirties that Robert E. Lee, a classmate of young John Mackay at West Point, was a frequent visitor. During the carefree days of this period, one of the daughters, Margaret, was married to Dr. Ralph Emms Elliott, the wedding taking place in the drawing-room, young Lieutenant Lee being one of the groomsmen. Then as time went on, and with the death in 1862 of Mrs. Robert Mackay, matriarch of the household and, in years gone by, the Eliza of the letters, her two unmarried daughters became in turn the mistresses of the old dwelling, continuing to live there until the time of their death in the late Seventies.

The house served also as the birthplace of six of the children of Robert Mackay's grandson, Robert Mackay Stiles, one of these, born in 1866, being Elizabeth Mackay Stiles, who was first to marry Alfred E. Mills and later Franklin B. Screven. As a child her time was divided between the home of her parents, "Malbone," in Bartow County, and that of her great aunts in Savannah, where many a time she found herself listening to her Aunt Kate and her Aunt Sarah as they discoursed on The Past. Within the familiar walls of the now venerable house the great aunts would often reminisce over the halcyon days of their girlhood, when together with their older sisters they had enjoyed the friendship of Robert E. Lee. But now they were in the aftermath of the Confederacy, in their own austerities of age; only the house, with its sense of permanence, remained the same. It was in this atmosphere that the little girl would be shown the numberless letters which the elderly sisters had so piously preserved through the troubled times, among them being, of course, the letters written such a long time ago by young Lieutenant Lee to one of the fortunate Miss Mackays.

These memories of her younger days must have made a lasting impression on Mrs. Screven and very probably turned her thoughts to the historical interests which influenced her later in life. That she had a realistic attitude toward the past and respect for its traditions was always evident, while in like manner she held in frank contempt anything that verged on the sentimental or veered from the path of plain fact into the ways of exaggeration. For forty-seven years she was an influential and well-loved member of the Colonial Dames, unfailing in her cooperative spirit, and always active in the Society's undertakings. Now as we trace the influence of our organization upon the individual achievement to which this foreword pays tribute, one is impressed by how truly she took to heart the objects of the Society as defined in its constitution, words that she knew without benefit of the printed page: " . . . to collect and preserve manuscripts, traditions, relics and mementos of bygone days"; and again, " . . . to diffuse a healthful and intelligent information concerning the past." In thus preserving her family chronicles and making their contents available for study and enjoyment, it may well be said of Mrs. Screven that "through her aid the Past has become once more present and those vanished figures have again arisen into life."

The Society's grateful thanks are due to Mr. Walter C. Hartridge for editing the Mackay letters; to Mr. Charles

F. Mills of Boston, son of Mrs. Screven, for permission to reproduce the oil painting of the *General Oglethorpe* by Robert Salmon, and for several additional letters of Robert and Eliza Mackay especially recommended by Mr. Hartridge for inclusion, consisting of letters 1 through 8, and 12 (the courtship letters) and letters 13, 14, 16, 22, and 39; to Mrs. Clifford Carleton of New York, for permission to reproduce the miniature and pencil drawing of Robert Mackay by Malbone; to Mrs. H. Snowden Marshall and Miss Margaret Couper Stiles, sisters of Mrs. Screven, for helpful information and suggestions; to Mrs. Foreman M. Hawes, director of the Georgia Historical Society, for valuable assistance. The Society also extends its renewed appreciation to Mrs. Henry L. Richmond of Jacksonville, for having initiated the idea of publishing the Colonial Dames MSS collections. Her generous support has made it possible to establish the Richmond Fund, named in recognition of her kind interest, which assumes many of the expenses incidental to publication.

Elfrida DeRenne Barrow
Historic Activities Committee

Savannah, Georgia
December 15, 1948

Contents

Illustrations

The cover vignette, drawn by Christopher Murphy, Junior, represents the steeple of Savannah's old City Exchange. Built during Robert Mackay's lifetime, from the plans of a French architect, Adrien Boucher, the Exchange with its quaint steeple had a place in the affections of many generations of Savannahians, one of their favorite expressions being "as high as the steeple of the Exchange." From such an eminence Savannah merchants would scan the river for incoming ships, while sentinels of the City Watch kept vigil for signs of fire. The steeple bell, resonant and clear, was in a real sense the voice of the community, ushering in patriotic festivals, sounding alarms, and tolling the passing of civic worthies.

Introduction

The letters published in the present volume form part of the personal correspondence of a Savannah merchant, Robert Mackay. Written to his wife over a period of twenty-one years—1795 to 1816—and mostly concerned with social life in port towns and fashionable watering places on both sides of the Atlantic, they possess much interest to the modern reader. For Robert Mackay's vision was not bounded by the walls of his counting-room. His wit and keen appraisal of persons have a freshness that transcends the particular. Several of his most vivid vignettes treat of figures of national importance, while his descriptions of formal functions, whether in Savannah or in Liverpool, are alive with the texture of an exuberant era: an age dominated by the "merchant prince," whose type has passed from history into legend.

It is this delineation of the thought and way of life of a Southern merchant of the early nineteenth century that gives these letters significance. They provide a wealth of fresh material for students of American history, increasingly numerous, who are examining the common culture of North and South during the first decades of the new Republic. A solidarity of interests, rooted in the traditions of colonial times and sustained by trade, is known to have existed along the Atlantic seaboard; but its reality has become obscured and its memory dimmed by the later passions of sectional discord. To obtain a clearer understanding of the times, modern historians are devoting their attention to the seaport towns, particularly those of the South Atlantic. They are scrutinizing records relating to trade, such as bills of lading and merchants' ledgers, with as much enthusiasm as their predecessors devoted to politics and military campaigns. One result is that the romantic approach to Southern history has given way to more sober conclusions. The subordination of the ports to the plantations is now seen as a later development, and the broadly national role played by the merchants and professional men of Savannah, Charleston, and Norfolk is assuming a significance long denied.

These letters of Robert Mackay testify to the wide scope of a Southern merchant's interests. A citizen of Savannah, strongly loyal to its customs and institutions, Mackay was bound to the greater world by his business connections, his friendships, and ties of blood. His horizon, indeed, lay beyond his native America, for he was as much at home in Liverpool and London as in New York and Newport.

By ancestry and upbringing Robert Mackay was well fitted for this cosmopolitan life. He was born in Augusta, Georgia, on June 23, 1772, the son of an enterprising Scottish merchant and a New England mother. His father, for whom he was named, had left Inverness-shire at an early age for the New World. After sojourns in Jamaica and Cuba, he reached the American continent, and finally settled in Augusta, a small though important town commanding the trade of the upper Savannah River. There he married a widow, Mary Chilcott, daughter of Godfrey Malbone, that nabob of Newport whose memory is still kept alive by many a fabulous tale; and, acquiring an interest in an established mercantile firm, he soon made a fortune by trading with the Indian Nations of the Old Southwest. But this prosperity was of short duration. The elder Mackay died suddenly in 1775. His estate was dissipated in the turmoil of the Revolution, and his widow was hard put to support herself and young Robert.

But in a frontier town, far removed from the amenities of the coast, Mrs. Mackay and her son were sustained by that quality, always so desirable to the eighteenth-century mind: respectability. This was an asset that Robert Mackay was to cherish in his prosperous maturity. "Augusta was then a small town," he wrote in a memoir for his children, "the houses standing far apart from each other, being few in number, but principally occupied by very worthy and respectable people." He recalled his father's association in business with "a house of the first respectability." And having delved further into the family annals, he was pleased to note that his paternal grandfather had been "the Minister or Clergyman of Wick [in Scotland] which (although the income must have been very small) entitles him to the character of having been a very respectable man."

It was not until the last days of the Revolution that Mary Mackay gave thought to Robert's education. She had no confidence in the academies of Georgia, rudimentary at best and now disrupted by war; while the reputation of the Malbones as Tories kept her from sending Robert to New England. After much consideration, she decided upon Scotland. "Bob . . . is a puny Chap," she explained in a letter to her brother, John Malbone, "but I hope the change of Climate will mend his constitution, had the peace taken place a year or two sooner, he shou'd certainly have made you a visit before he went to Europe, as I believe never Child was possess'd of a more ardent desire for any thing, than he is to see his friends at Newport, but he's now eleven years old, & consequently no time to lose." Robert's schooling was entrusted to a Doctor Jackson of Edinburgh. Little is known about this gentleman, but a member of the Mackay family wrote that he imparted to his pupil "a love of study and of nature which contributed greatly to his happiness in after life." Young Robert remained six years in the household of Doctor Jackson, and formed friendships with his preceptor and his sister, Miss Jackson, that lasted until their deaths. A water-color sketch of Robert made at this time for his mother is owned by his great-granddaughter, Miss Margaret Couper Stiles. It gives the profile of an alert and attractive young boy, and in the words of a family memoir "shows traces of that beauty for which he was afterwards remarkable."

Robert Mackay was seventeen when he returned home in 1789. He found his mother practically destitute, for her husband's property had been scattered during the war: "all that he ever rescued from his father's estate," the family annals record, "were two negro carpenters and some old silver spoons." With the necessity of earning a livelihood thrust upon him, Robert made the rounds of Augusta seeking employment. But this town, though recovered from the war and now the state capital, offered no opening for him. It was with reluctance that he left his mother and went to Savannah, because of its maritime trade still the most important city in Georgia. There young Mackay was fortunate to obtain work in a store, "boarding in the house of the proprietor," according to his daughter's memoirs. This source is silent as to his activities over the next few years, but it may be inferred that he received from this nameless employer the thorough grounding in business that was to stand him in good stead the rest of his life.

From such humble beginnings Robert Mackay made a consistent advance in the mercantile world. He observed his majority by starting business on his own account. Renting a store in Commerce Row on the Bay, Savannah's center of trade, he advertised, in the customary phrases of the day, that he had for sale a "*STOCK of DRY GOODS*, Consisting of as good and fresh an assortment as any at present in the city." By way of confession Mackay added: "As a beginner he solicits encouragement, and hopes, as he will be regularly furnished with goods at the proper seasons, to give satisfaction" (*Georgia Gazette*, February 27, 1794). Mackay's success in his chosen field may be judged by the fact that within four years he was taken into partnership by two Scotsmen, Alexander and William Mein, whose foreign connections and local reputation placed them in the first rank of Savannah merchants. The new firm, under the name of Meins and Mackay, prospered to a degree undreamed of nine years before by Robert Mackay. Their advertisements in the newspapers show the wide scope of the "commodities" they sold. These included not only "Woolens and other Fall Goods" from London, and "Particular Madeira Wine" from Funchal, but also slaves brought from the coast of Africa.

That Robert Mackay's thoughts should now have

turned to marriage is not surprising. His choice was Eliza Anne McQueen, to whom he had been attached for several years. Family tradition states that Eliza was not distinguished by beauty; her letters indicate that she was literal rather than imaginative; but for Robert Mackay, she had an appeal heightened by a common background and experiences. For her childhood, like his, had been affected by the mixed loyalties of a family divided by the Revolution. Her father, John McQueen, was an ardent Patriot, a captain in the Navy of South Carolina, and on occasion the confidential agent of Washington and La Fayette; while her two uncles by marriage, Basil Cowper and James Wright, were strong in their allegiance to the Crown. She was born April 23, 1778, at the Grange, the Savannah River plantation of Basil Cowper. The ambiguous position of her family was symbolized by the insecurity of life at the Grange, which was raided by soldiers of both sides. As soon as she was able to travel, Mrs. McQueen brought Eliza to the comparative safety of her own parents' plantation in South Carolina. John McQueen, meanwhile, had been captured by the British, and when finally released on parole, turned to planting. He was joined by his family, and, with the coming of peace, it seemed as if their lives would fall in the quiet lines of their Low-Country plantation. But these were unsettled times. McQueen succumbed to the spell of land speculation. His property was seized by creditors; and, to escape further trouble, he sought in Spanish East Florida a refuge from the jurisdiction of American courts. His wife chose a less hazardous course. With her four children, she followed the Cowpers to London; and in the Margaret Street house of these exiled

Loyalists, the family enjoyed a security they had not known in America. When later Mrs. McQueen returned to South Carolina and Mrs. Cowper went out to Jamaica, Eliza was placed in school. She remained there several years, and it is interesting to note that her stay in England coincided with the period that Robert Mackay spent in Scotland.

In the summer of 1791, Eliza, then a child of thirteen, left England to rejoin her mother. She often told her own children in after years of the voyage across the Atlantic, made memorable by scanty rations and the fear of Algerine pirates. Mrs. McQueen was now living with her parents on a plantation near Savannah, and Eliza was to find this new life much to her liking. English accomplishments and manners assured her popularity in the gay society of a town that still measured values by British standards. When she tired of the round of balls and parties, Eliza would pay visits to her father in East Florida. The stately receptions at the Governor's palace in St. Augustine provided a novel contrast to the less formal entertainments of Savannah.

During this period Eliza McQueen and Robert Mackay saw much of each other. Casual interest ripened into friendship, courtship ensued, and on January 30, 1800, they were married: the groom, twenty-seven years of age, gay and exuberant; the bride, twenty-one, reserved and earnest. A full share of happiness was in store for them, even though their comparatively brief married life was interrupted by frequent separations when business affairs called Robert Mackay to distant ports. But they shared their experiences through letters that reflect joyousness and understanding to an unusual degree. This correspondence covers a period of fifteen years: from the first notes, written the year after their marriage, in which Mackay tells with boyish enthusiasm of his ship, the *General Oglethorpe;* to his last affectionate words written four days before his death, "God bless you My dear Eliza prays Yours ever & sincerely R. M."

Although Savannah was their home, Robert and Eliza Mackay lived for five years in England, that "delightful Country" as Mackay never ceased to call it. In 1811 they returned to America. Civic honors were tendered Mackay; his business prospered; and in 1813 he bought the Grange, possibly as much for the sake of sentiment as for the profits he hoped to make from its rice fields.

From now on, however, family letters and memoirs show concern over Robert Mackay's health. In the summer of 1816 he took the waters at the Northern spas, and believed himself benefited. That autumn he was in New York. On October 4 he engaged passage for Newport, intending to leave the next day to rejoin his family. But fate had decreed otherwise. The poignancy of Mackay's sudden death is conveyed in the memoirs of his daughter, Margaret Mackay Elliott:

He had made an arrangement with a lady friend to do some shopping the next morning, and went to bed apparently well, as he did not appear at breakfast a servant was sent to call him and found him quite dead in his bed, this was on Oct. 5th. He had friends in New York, his sons were sent for and arrived in time for their dear father's funeral. The sailing vessel which was to have taken him to his family carried the news of his sudden death, his wife saw the vessel enter the Harbor, she expected her husband, and had sent her children to church, it was Sunday, and awaited his arrival, instead of which letters came telling of her dreadful loss.

He was buried in the historic cemetery of Trinity Church in New York, far from the scenes of his life. There, but a few feet from Broadway, beneath Trinity's Gothic spire, itself overshadowed by skyscrapers, lies a flat stone with the simple inscription:

In memory of

ROBERT MACKAY Esquire

of Georgia

died 6th October 1816

aged 44 years

I. "Robert Mackay's Compt^{s} to Miss McQueen"

I. *"Robert Mackay's Compt.^s to Miss Mc Queen"*

With these words, written in the spring of 1795, a young merchant, recently come to Savannah, handsome and unattached, begins a correspondence with the daughter of a well-known family. The mode of address grows less formal as the century draws to a close and the courtship progresses. The event foreshadowed in these letters is duly announced in the Columbian Museum & Savannah Advertiser *of Friday, February 7, 1800:*

> MARRIED last Thursday evening, at Mrs. Smith's near this city, Mr. Robert Mackay, merchant, to Miss Eliza Macqueen, daughter of John Macqueen, Esq.

1: ROBERT MACKAY TO ELIZA ANNE MCQUEEN

Robert Mackay's compt^s. to Miss McQueen, has taken the liberty of troubling her with a letter for her Brother,[1] as she will in all probability be gone, before he returns from Charleston—

He sends p Bearer the Spanish Grammars,[2] which he hopes may be of service, though not so new as he thought they were—

April 1795 Wednesday*

* The date is in the handwriting of Eliza Anne McQueen.

2: ELIZA ANNE MCQUEEN TO ROBERT MACKAY

Miss McQueen took the liberty yesterday to trouble Mr Mackay with the care of a letter to her Father and at the same time intended to return the grammar now sent, but it slip'd her memory—The family unite in wishing Mr Mackay a pleasant voyage.

Cottage[8]*—Friday Morning*

Mr Mackay

3: ROBERT MACKAY TO ELIZA ANNE MCQUEEN

R. Mackay with compts: to Miss McQueen sends her the Exploits of Don Quixote—is sorry he could not procure a compleat Copy of Smollets translation, but hopes the only volume he has left of a sett by Jarvis, will make good the loss of the 3rd. by the former Translator.

Tuesday 21st. March 96

4: ROBERT MACKAY TO ELIZA ANNE MCQUEEN

If Miss McQueen is not engaged R. Mackay would be happy to dance with her this evening—

Wednesday
*March 1797**

* The date is in the handwriting of Eliza Anne McQueen.

5: ROBERT MACKAY TO ELIZA ANNE MCQUEEN

Savannah 3rd April 1799—

A letter from me will be matter of surprise, but handed by your brother will I trust be divested of the impropriety attached to my using so much freedom—

I have long wished for the power of declaring to you an affection which is now of five years duration, but my situation in life has hitherto precluded every determination on the subject—on arranging my present establishment in business[4] which has afforded every appearance of success I formed the resolution of immediately asking permission to pay my addresses to you, but the necessity of a voyage to Europe in the existing hazardous state of affairs, & the impossibility of foreseeing the difficulties which might, & did eventually attend me prevented—I have at length returned in safety, and now take the liberty which I beg you will pardon, of asking if you are without engagement, & if you are, whether or not my addresses will be acceptable—

It is almost unnecessary to mention (having already declared the early date of my attachment) that it is formed after a long acquaintance with your virtues on the purest esteem, & in the event of my being successful of its continuance with my life—Should this request not meet your immediate approbation, let me entreat of you not to be too hasty in forming a decision which may forever deprive me of happiness—

I shall wait with impatience your answer, and in the mean time remain

Your devoted
& very obed Servant
Robert Mackay

Miss M[c]Queen
Cottage—

6: ROBERT MACKAY TO ELIZA ANNE MCQUEEN

Should you want a horse and chair to carry you out, will you do me the favor to make use of mine,—& if there is not too much importunity in the request will you allow me to ride out with you tomorrow morning, if no other arrangement is made inform me of the hour you go & I shall be very happy to attend you—

Yours very sincerely
R: Mackay
Savannah 8th June 99—

7: ROBERT MACKAY TO ELIZA ANNE MCQUEEN

I send you the sashes to look at, they do not appear so handsome as when I opened them this morning—they are however new I believe in this place, having seen none like them before—

Am I at liberty to put you in mind of the request I made last Saturday of driving you out to the Cottage—if it will be agreable let me know the hour you go & I will call with a horse & chair—

Yours very sincerely
R: Mackay
Savannah 15th. June 99—

8: ROBERT MACKAY TO ELIZA ANNE MCQUEEN

I beg your acceptance of a few Books which I hope may add to your amusement on the passage—I also take the liberty of requesting you to receive as a trifling remembrance at your departure a watch—I am sorry it is not better worthy of being worn by you, but at present I could not procure one more suitable—I trust you will not think me forward in using this freedom—in the situation we now are, surely there can be no impropriety in the offer or in your receiving it—

The Captn. of the Dean informed me just now he will be ready to sail on Sunday morning—

Yours most sincerely
R: Mackay
31st. July 1799—

9: ROBERT MACKAY TO ELIZA ANNE MCQUEEN

Savannah 23rd. August 1799—

The lengthy letter enclosed must plead its own excuse—I should not have troubled you so much, but on a subject so interesting I wish you to know all that I do of it—in all probability Miss C.[5] will hear from S.[6] before I can receive an answer from you, but at all events you shall be regularly informed—

I saw M^rs^. Wright[7] & your Bro^r^. last even^g^. in Town—all well—I am sorry to say in Charleston a fever has appeared which carries off sixteen to twenty daily—the intercourse is not yet prevented but talked of—Yrs ever

R: Mackay

Miss M^c^Queen

10: ROBERT MACKAY TO ELIZA ANNE MCQUEEN

[*Savannah, September 3, 1799.*]

I had really promised myself the pleasure of a letter from you ere this—I did not however consider when I made you the request there could be any impropriety in it, and as it is a principle with me that you can do nothing but right, you certainly have reasons satisfactory to yourself for withholding what would have been productive of so much happiness to me—I must therefore be content to receive information from the Cottage, and rest thankful to know that you are well and happy.

This will be handed to you or forwarded by M^r^. W: Mein[8] who after many revolutions in opinion, has at length resolved on the necessity of going to New-York, with the determination to return here within a month—Should you see him, I think Miss Margarets threat of not speaking to him, ought to be put in execution, for allowing your party to go on without an escort—but if any extenuation can be admitted of, I would tell you that business could not a month ago allow of his absence, and that some particular arrangements makes his presence now necessary in New York and Philadelphia—Your Brother says you may place yourself and Sister[9] under the care of this *Old Gentleman* to come home, provided M^rs^. Cowper[10] leaves you in the Northern States—how much pleasure would it give me to accompany the ladies to Jamaica, and were they here now & M^rs^. Cowper could trust the hurricane Season, I should certainly enjoy the satisfaction very soon, as I am to sail for Kingston in the William on the 15th, and to induce such agreable passengers to favor me with their company, I should most readily agree to run down to Rio Bueno & put them ashore —this unexpected trip of mine will astonish you a little, but the cause will convince you of the necessity—to meet the Cotton contracts M & M have made, the Iron-Chest must not be allowed to be empty, & as disappointments in money matters are not infrequent here, we have resolved to run no risk, I therefore go to Kingston to negotiate Bills on London and return with Dollars—I shall be here again by the 25th October, as my stay in the Island will not exceed eight days—and, should the usual ill luck of long passages attend me, I have every hope to be at home at least as early as you

I acknowledge to you I have felt very anxious to go somewhere since you left this, & the variety that occurs in a West India voyage will in some small degree supply the vacancy your absence occasions—in active business and a continued change of scene, the mind is employed & leaves less room for the recollection to wander—But how much more happy should I have been to exchange trips with M^r^. Mein, this however could not be done, circumstances require his visiting the Northward, which he must be there himself to execute—I cannot help flattering myself with the hope of seeing you in two months from this—and when we do meet, I am sure you have too much goodness to deny me any longer the happiness of being united to you forever—

I wrote you by the Two Sisters inclosed to J. & B. Forbes[11] not long after you sailed, & since that a long letter by post under cover to my Sister M^rs^. Chilcott[12] in Newport—the first you must have received early, & the last you will soon, I was exceedingly anxious to know before I leave this the event & effect of my advice to Scarbrough, & still hope to hear something of it—I have had nothing from him since I wrote you—

Doct^r^. Wilson[13] paid Natures debt a few days ago, the victim I fear of too free a life—few men have died in Savannah more generally lamented—his last complaint was a nervous fever—This is the only death since you went away, & at present I know of nobody sick—*except* M^rs^. Sampson Neyle[14] who is fast recovering, having presented a young Lady to her friends a few mornings ago.

I am truly sorry my short stay in Jamaica will prevent my visiting M^r^. Cowper[15]—the very high esteem I have for the Ladies and himself, and the obligations I am under for the civilities & attention received from him when in the Island before, are certainly great inducements—but with so expensive a Vessel as the William, and the nature of the business that carries me, dispatch is requisite—and as I hope to compleat everything in eight days, a journey across the Island will be utterly impossible—I shall however do myself the pleasure to write M^{r}. Cowper, & reserve the visit to Rio Bueno for some future day, to experience more happiness in going there with you to accompany me—indeed your Mamma says she intends to see Baron-hill herself some of these days—& we will astonish them, when they don't expect us, with quite a Georgia party—

I have this moment a Letter from Baillie,[16] he says " 'Tis a cursed ill wind that blows nobody good—& if he had *eight* days passage to St. Simons,[17] the Celestials must have arrived at New York in less than five or Six—so that he is contented, but perhaps a little more so, because this Southerly wind served his purpose as well as yours, by keeping him two days at Montgomery[18]—where the lovely blue eyes of Miss Eliza gave the *coup de grace* to his already wounded heart—and he now wanders a sighing Strephon among the woods, thinking only of his love" —These Live-Oaks on St. Simons, or the Cotton-fields, or the Quarter-Cask of Madeira (I don't know which) have so many attachments that he does not mean to come to Town for Six weeks yet—

M^{r}. Phineas Miller[19] came up a day or two ago, & brings an account of the capture and destruction of the Spanish post & Galley at Amelia,[20] by two Providence privateers[21] who were in search of Henriques' Ship & Cargo—fortunately for him however a contrary wind had forced him into Tybee,[22] & he is now here—so that he may well repeat with Baillie " 'Tis an ill wind that blows no good"—

I cannot help still entertaining some hope that I may be gratified in hearing from you yet before I sail—but whether I am disappointed in this pleasure or not, believe me my dear Miss McQueen

ever faithfully Yours

R: Mackay

Savannah 3rd. September 1799—

11: ROBERT MACKAY TO ELIZA ANNE MCQUEEN

[*Savannah, September—, 1799.*]

The William has just fired her signal Gun for getting under way, & in less than half an hour I shall be on board —a part of the short space of time I have left I owe to the duties of friendship in running hastily over a few lines to each of my Sisters,[23] who will expect at least a farewell—the other part I devote my beloved friend to you, in begging you to accept an apology for not answering yours of 17th. August earlier, & to assure you the continued hurry I have been in with Books & accounts preparing for my departure has prevented my writing you untill this late hour—What happiness would it have given me instead of this trip to Jamaica to have been with you in New-York—I know as strangers in a place like that, how many inconveniences you must have been subjected to, and am glad Mr. Forbes has been attentive—a pleasing task to him certainly—By your last letter to your Mother, John informs me of your determination to go on to Connecticut about the 1st. of this month—a circumstance which I assure you afforded me much satisfaction, for while you remained in a spot where there reigned even a symptom of contagion I could not be happy—I regret more than I can express that I am forced to leave Georgia without knowing where you remove to—however I am pleasing myself with the fond hope that on my return I shall find you safe here, & that all my anticipation of happiness will soon after be realised—

I have heard no more from Scarbrough, which would surprise me much, but that I know his business must lead him far into the interior of North Carolina, where probably he may be out of the way of Post-Offices & my Letters may not have reached him—I however hope to hear eventually that he has acted towards Miss Cowper as in his situation he ought to do—& that whether a reconciliation is ever effected or not, her feelings may in some measure be gratified—

It has been for these few days sickly in the eastern part of Savannah, & I find several have died, but principally persons who from their occupations in life have been much exposed to the Sun—I am however truly sorry to add that the 18*th* proved fatal to Mrs. Sampson Neyle[24]—she had nearly recovered from her confinement, but exposing herself too soon to the air, she caught a cold which it seems her friends thought lightly of, but which terminated her existence about 3 O'Clock the day before yesterday—Mrs. W. Neyle[25] visited her immediately on knowing of her danger & continued the duties of a Sister untill she breathed her last—indeed she has been constantly in the house since & acts a motherly part towards the children—Your Brother came in yesterday to the funeral & talks of another trip to Tybee with me this morning in the William—

However reluctantly—I must bid you adieu—beg the

Ladies to accept my best respects—and that Heaven may protect and bless you is the pray'r my Dear Eliza

of your ever faithful

Robert Mackay

Miss M^c^.Queen
Care of Messrs. J. & B. Forbes
Merchants
New-York—

12: ROBERT MACKAY TO ELIZA ANNE MCQUEEN

I have just been informed that you dine to day at James Johnstons[26]—pray do you go out of Town this evening? —if you do I shall beg for the pleasure of driving you out—let me know by the bearer, who will bring your answer to me at M^r^. Youngs,[27] & I will wait upon you when you please—Yours very faithfully

R: Mackay
Friday 2 O'Clock

II. Concerning the Ship General Oglethorpe

II. *Concerning the Ship* General Oglethorpe

With the increase of their overseas trade, Robert Mackay and his partners felt the need of acquiring a sailing vessel of their own to carry their goods across the Atlantic; and as ship-building had become a recognized industry of coastal Georgia, it was natural that they should seek a shipwright of the region to build one for them. From a wide choice, they selected John Patterson, a skilled ship-builder of Philadelphia, who now worked at St. Mary's, the southernmost port of Georgia.

The vessel was finished early in 1801. Eager to be present at her launching, Robert Mackay abandoned the comforts of Savannah and made his way by stage and open boat to the primitive township that he described to his wife in unflattering terms. But his privations were rewarded "with a view of the most beautiful & superb object I ever beheld in my life." This eulogy describes the General Oglethorpe, *a ship "of 530 tuns burthen," named in honor of Georgia's founder. Nor was Mackay's pleasure in her to diminish. "She looks more & more beautiful every day as the rigging becomes more compleat," he informed Eliza in his next letter. When all was in readiness, William Patterson, the builder's son, was engaged as captain, a cargo loaded, and the ship* General Oglethorpe *went on her maiden voyage to Savannah with her proud owner aboard.*

The General Oglethorpe, *however, was not to fulfil*

Robert Mackay's high expectations. Under Captain Patterson she made several trips to England, on one of which an oil painting of her was done by the celebrated marine artist, Robert Salmon. But within a year of her completion, having left Georgia for Cuba with "some Slaves to insure our admittance into the Havana," as Mackay wrote, the General Oglethorpe *was wrecked in a storm off the Bahamas. Mackay, a witness of the end of his beloved ship, was rescued after enduring many privations. The memory of these experiences was so vivid that on his return to Savannah he prepared an account of what had happened. This has since been published* and because of its succinctness and effective understatement has achieved a place in the narratives of adventure at sea.*

13: ROBERT MACKAY TO ELIZA ANNE MACKAY

St. Mary's 20th Feby 1801—

My Dear Eliza

On arriving here this day about 1 O'Clock—I was presented with a view of the most beautiful & superb object I ever beheld in my life—in fact words are entirely out of the question to describe the new Ship; to form any idea you must see her—She was launched at little before 12 O'Clock on Wednesday, & went in the water without sustaining the smallest injury, although her weight was so great as to crush the ways to atoms as she passed over them—I have yet had no settlement with Col[l]. Patterson[1]

* "Wreck of the Ship *General Oglethorpe*—1802," edited by Charles F. Mills, *The American Neptune*, II, 1 (January, 1942), 44–55.

THE *GENERAL OGLETHORPE*

From the painting by the British artist, Robert Salmon

but hope to get over things more easily than I at first expected—should this be the case I will leave this on Monday in the Alective, but if not I must wait for the next Mail—Of my passage here I must avoid as much as possible attempt at description—it beggars my abilities so I am not anxious to expose them—let me however say that it was the most fatiguing journey that I ever had in my life—I walked about eleven miles after breaking down the Stage up to the knees literally in mud, & was two nights on the water in a little open boat—We had however not much bad weather, or our case would have been truly pitiable—I got to Mr Nightengales[2] last even^g. at the Plumb-Orchard where I remained one Tide, Catherine[3] is sick, I left your Letter for Cornelia[4] there, but could gain no information as to her accepting your offer of invitation—Littlefield[5] who happen'd to be there says he thinks not, as he is trying hard to obtain permission for her to accompany him to the North[d]—I have thoughts of going tomorrow to see them at Dungeness[6] if I can spare an hour or two, but of this am doubtful—I regret my being so much hurried as it will not be in my power to visit your father[7] who I wished very much to see, he did not attend at the launch—

This is the most miserable starved place in the coast—nothing to eat but [letter torn] & such a thing as milk has not been seen within the limits of the Township[8] for these four months—their drink is as poor as their meat—nothing but rum, in one house excepted, where I was handed just now a miserable Glass of Sherry, which even when of the best quality is barely drinkable—

Believe me when I declare the strongest anxiety to return to the endearments of your society & to fondle our darling little boy[9]—& that you are both well is the continued prayer of My dear Eliza

Yr. unalterable

R. Mackay

M[rs]. R. Mackay
care Mess[rs]. Mein & Mackay
Mail) Savannah

14: ROBERT MACKAY TO ELIZA ANNE MACKAY

St. Mary's 12th March 1801—

I am waiting with anxious impatience the arrival of tomorrows post to hear again from My Dear Eliza, & which I fondly hope will convey the pleasing intelligence of the welfare of her & our darling little boy—The Box & Letter by the Alective arrived safe on Saturday—I am truly thankful for your remembrance of me, the nice things you sent were all rarities in this odd corner of the World & I have been very choice of them—You would be astonished at neither seeing or hearing from me by last Mail—it seems a new arrangement had taken place in its departure, & I only knew of its arrival a few minutes before it went away, so that I had only time to scrawl a line to Mein to acknowledge the receipt of some money he sent me—

Capt. Patterson[10] has had a serious time of it—he is now thank Heaven out of danger & this morning for the first time has been helped out of bed—his illness has been a sore evil, for having no Office to conduct matters on board during his absence the Men have not exerted themselves as they might have done—the Ship is however in a considerable state of forwardness & on monday I shall begin taking in the cargo—She looks more & more beautiful every day as the rigging becomes more compleat—I am in hopes to settle accounts with Col^{l}. Patterson this day, so that I shall have no hindrance to prevent my return home next week—never was there a poor Devil so home sick since the creation—

I inclose you a Letter from your father—in answer to it I guarded him against Suares,[11] who I am convinced is laying a plan in this Negro business to take him in, & furnished what I conceived staunch reasons for his having nothing to do with him—as to securing the Negroes for you—I threw cold water on the proposal—

I see Nightengale or Littlefield once a week up here, but I have been but once at Dungeness—indeed Capt. P's. illness & the business of the Ship keeps me pretty close here—I however made out to go down to Point Peter[12] one evening with Mr Seagrove[13] & returned next day after an unsuccessful attempt to shoot a Deer—13th The hour for the departure of the Mail is come, & that from Savannah not yet arrived, so that I have been in anxious suspence all day & yet no Letter from my darling Girl—when it does come the boat will not stop here 5 Minutes so that I cannot answer your Letter—but you must this by return—Capt. Patterson recruits fast & I have settled acco^{ts} at last with the Col^{l}. so that I shall leave this next friday & will be with you on monday at 3 O'Clock—it appears to be an age till then—Kiss the little boy a thousand times for me—kind regard to all at the Cottage & accept for yourself all the Love & fondness of Your ever affectionate

R. M.

M^{rs}. R: Mackay
Savannah

15: ROBERT MACKAY TO ELIZA ANNE MACKAY

St. Mary's 17th March 1801

Yours of the 10th by post I received & felt as much gratified as usual at hearing from my darling Eliza from whom I now trust I shall not be long absent, as I have determined on going on in the next mail at all events—Captn. Patterson recruits very fast & is now walking about, but I am in dread of a relapse for in spite of all I can say I cannot prevent his exerting himself too much, [letter torn] he will & yesterday in hawling at the end of a rope it broke & he fell over the Wharf & from his being so excessively weak it was not without some trouble we got him out again—The Ship is half loaded & will be ready to sail the moment the Alective returns here from Savannah by her we expect some necessaries which cannot well [letter torn] obliged to M [letter torn] Hunter for her kindness in staying so much with you, without some such friend you must have been at a great loss—

I have another Letter from your father, I am sorry to say his Cotton machine so long in completing has turned out to be worth nothing—

Remember me affectionately to all friends kiss the dear little boy for me & believe me My D^{r}. Eliza

ever yours

R Mackay

16: ROBERT MACKAY TO ELIZA ANNE MACKAY

Nassau New Providence 18th. feb^{y} 1802

Here I am My dearest Eliza once more the Child of misfortune—The Genl. Oglethorpe was cast away on the night of the 5th Inst^{t}. on one of the Bahama Keys & Twenty three souls perished[14]—C^{n}. Patterson, M^{r}. Putnam, Mr Broadfoot John, Archy Atkinson, seven Seamen & two Slaves with myself were saved in the Boat, in which we have dragged out a miserable existence of twelve days, but were yesterday picked up by a Charleston Schooner & arrived here about two hours ago, I have just heard of this opp.^{y} & can say no more at present, in the mean time be assured that a few days good living will restore me, I feel much refreshed by rubbing with Brandy & putting on Dry clothes which our friends here have supplied us with, as we saved only what we had on our Backs—I shall write or come myself in a Vessel to sail next week—

I have agreed to go to a dance tomorrow night—this to convince you I am not very ill—only reduced a little in flesh & weak from want of refreshment—

Remember me very affectionately at the Cottage & kiss our darling Boy a thousand times for My dearest Girl

Yrs ever faithfully

R Mackay

III. *From Savannah*

III. From Savannah

No American city greeted the nineteenth century with more optimism than Savannah. Founded in 1733 as the southern outpost of Britain's continental empire, it had known for the greater part of the intervening years disasters and insecurity. But conditions were now changed and the future held promise. For Savannah was the seaport and commercial center of a state fast emerging from the turbulence of the frontier to an eminence that was to evoke the tribute: "Empire State of the South." In 1800 the Census officials counted but five thousand persons within the municipal limits (half of this number were Negro slaves); even so, Savannah ranked as the fourteenth largest city in the nation; and the older residents predicted a substantial increase in population over the next decade, pointing to the many Northerners and Europeans who were attracted to Savannah each year by the expanding export trade.

This commercial activity led to the growth of an influential group of merchants and factors. According to the estimate of a British visitor at the turn of the century, these gentlemen enjoyed an aggregate annual income of half a million dollars, an opulent sum for those days and one which enabled them to live in a lavish manner. Fine dwellings in the prevalent Regency style were built for them by talented architects; and these "little palaces," as they were called by the exiled Neapolitan prince, Achille Murat, provided appropriate settings for the round of entertainments in which the Savannah merchants sought relaxation from the tedium of their counting-houses.

Of this circle, Robert Mackay was an acknowledged leader. Wealthy, personable, often assuming the role of a bachelor during his wife's absences from town, he was much sought after by ambitious hostesses. It is evident, from his letters, that Mackay enjoyed this life to the fullest, an occasional half-jesting protest to the contrary: ". . . as usual in this place," he wrote one summer to his wife, "pleasure & dissipation are either crammed down our throats whether we will or not . . . there has been no less than three balls . . . in this charming of all Seasons for dancing when the Thermometer rises occasionally to 96°." The picture that he gives of such urban diversions, supplemented by "fêtes champêtres" beside slow-moving tidal streams, is alive with the texture of a youthful society, confident in its strength, sure of its goal.

Yet Mackay could be also a severe critic. His opinion of the flat Georgia landscape was given in a letter from England: ". . . the fact is we are all pleased beyond expression with the first place we see after leaving Georgia, the lofty Welch Mountains appeared like a spot in Paradise to me as we approached this Coast & they are not more fertile than our Pine Barren, but certain it is with all its local advantages Georgia sinks in the comparison with most other places I have seen. . . ." And "this direful Climate" he blamed for the death of his first-born son.

In spite of these drawbacks and the contrasting charms of English life, to which he was always much attracted,

Robert Mackay remained a Savannahian. "I like Sav^h: very well," he wrote to his wife when the question of living in England was being discussed, "I hope it will not be displeasing to you, the health & education of the Children is the only objection. . . ." One spring his feeling for Savannah was sufficiently strong for him to exclaim: "The weather is most delightful . . . , & the alterations in the squares so great an improvement, that Savannah is quite fascinating."

However it is apparent that Robert Mackay's affection for Savannah was not caused by the physical aspect of the town, "fascinating" as he might think it in moments of enthusiasm. Instead, it was the human kaleidoscope that held him to the spot. His capacity for friendship found wide scope in the group of close-knit families who arbitrated on matters of social precedence; and his delineation of their foibles, ironic yet affectionate, preserves in warm terms the values of that world he knew so well. He makes of lively interest to the modern reader such recurrent themes as the solecisms of Mrs. Scarbrough ("the Countess" of many a caustic anecdote), whose ambition was to become the leader of Savannah society; the splenetic outbursts of Thomas Gibbons, famous in American legal history as the plaintiff in the case of Gibbons *v.* Ogden; *or the star-crossed love affairs of the vivacious Margaret Cowper, who finally "when neither party was young" yielded to the importunities of her cousin, John McQueen.*

Robert Mackay occupies a special place in the circle of early Savannahians whom his fellow-citizens like to recall. His claim to remembrance rests not so much on his career as a merchant, eminent though that was, nor on the number of civic offices he held; but rather on the distinguished quality of these letters to his wife.

17: ROBERT MACKAY TO ELIZA ANNE MACKAY

Savannah 22nd. June 180[1]

Col^{l}. McIntosh[1] was polite enough to hand me my Dear Eliza's Letter immediately on his arrival in Town, by which I was rejoiced to find you were safe on your way as far as Frederica,[2] I have little doubt but you were at Fort George in two days after, & I hope you found your Father[3] well & glad to see you—I was afraid the confinement in the boat would not be particularly pleasing to our young traveller,[4] but if he has suffered no other inconvenience than the bare confinement I think he will have little cause to regret his expedition—Savannah has been little alive for this fortnight past, on the day you went away we all dined with Caig[5] on Turtle, in the Evening there was a Wedding at Waynes[6] & party after party has been the consequence almost every day since in that circle—but as usual in this place pleasure & dissipation are either crammed down our throats whether we will or not, or there is a total stagnation & we all become as dull as Stockfish—there has been no less than three balls—at Waynes, Noels[7] & Andersons[8]—in this charming of all Seasons for dancing when the Thermometer rises occasionally to 96°. —You & I were invited to the Parties but as I am a very great enemy to making myself uncomfortable I declined accepting—The day we were at Caigs, Mein & I received as a present the finest Turtle I ever saw in Georgia, it weighed 80*lbs* & was literally fat as butter, we dined on it a week after & made a sit of [letter torn] my *good & much respected friend* Mrs. Pooler[9] furnished me a Cook & I never saw more justice done a Turtle, Gibbons[10] was delighted & swallowed green fat in platefulls—Woodruff[11] looked charmed & confessed approbation by inarticulating silence, Nichols[12] thought he had the Calipatch to serve out, took good care to serve himself very plentifully & as to Caig, as Burns says in his Poem of the Haggis "He was like to rive"—in case you don't know Scotch enough to explain this you must be informed that *rive* means *burst*—Our dinner altogether was good, well dressed & well attended—every body was happy or apparently so, & Gibbons having sent us a batch of his oldest wine which had ample justice done it, some of the party I believe reeled home without knowing there was even an alloy to happiness among mortals—

The Marquis de Montalet,[13] James Houstoun[14] tells me sets out with himself this afternoon for Fort George, on a visit to your Father—it is also said Mr. & Mrs. Harris are going to Cumberland & may possibly go also to St. Johns—

I was at the Cottage on Thursday, found Mr & Mrs. Smith[15] there who went out for the benefit of change of air, Archy having as they supposed got the hooping cough—Bell Hunter,[16] E. Zubly[17] & Mary Williamson[18] were also there—& all very happy to hear you were well—Catherine Bourke[19] sailed on the 14th. for N York—

I assure you my dear Eliza I feel your absence most forcibly & believe I shall never be induced to admit of another trip unless I am of the party—this Bachelors-hall after having had a Mistress to it so long will never do—the house appears vacant & lost without you—no cheering smile to welcome me home when I return from the labours of the day, nobody to hearken to & soothe ones little cares—hasten to return my dear Girl to your ever

affectionate & fond

R: Mackay

[letter torn] membrance to Your Father,
[letter torn] & many many Kisses
[letter torn] sweet little fellow—

18: ROBERT MACKAY TO ELIZA ANNE MACKAY

[*Savannah, September 19, 1803.*]

My dear Eliza

Baillies boy brought me the inclosed last even' & went out early this morn' I sent the old Gentleman[20] some Gloves & Segars—& wrote him that although John was hobbling about the house on crutches, I should endeavour to persuade him to accompany M^r. Mein on a visit to Belleville[21] on wednesday morning—While Mary Anne[22] continues so unwell I have no great disposition to go to Sapelo[23] & I think it would be a good plan for John to take my seat in the chair with Mein—it might be proper for him to see his father at present—Meins intention is to set out at 4 O'Clock in the morning & go through in one day which with the relieve of horses we have could be easily done—M^r. Clay[24] made his debut yesterday afternoon as a Babtist Preacher & I must confess I was never more mortified or disappointed—His Pray'r was undoubtedly a very excellent one, but delivered in the full perfection of Methodistical Cant—even this however did not entirely drown the musick of his voice, which in spite of himself some times shone forth, with all the beauty of eloquence & persuasion I have often admired in it at the Bar—At the close of the Pray'r he informed the congregation of his intention to read a Sermon from some famous Babtist preacher—saying that his own mind was not yet sufficiently strengthened in the true light, to take upon himself to reason from his own imperfect idea's, but that he found this light encreasing daily in strength, & that with the Blessing of his Heavenly Father he would ere long pos[s]ess the power of gratifying the most ardent wish of his heart—I think M^r^. Toblers[25] application of the opinion of Festus is not amiss—it may be *learning—something* at all events has made him *Mad*—

Stephen[26] carries you the things you wanted let me know by him how Mary Anne is this morn^g^—it is cold & raw she ought to be kept within doors—

Remember me affectionately to your Grand Mother
& all at the Cottage
& believe me ever yours
R: Mackay

Sav^h^. 19th. Septr. 1803—

M^rs^. Mackay
Cottage—
p Stephen.)

19: ELIZA ANNE MACKAY TO ROBERT MACKAY

Cottage 14th Sepbr 1804

When in Town last week I wrote a few lines to you my Dearest Friend just to say that we were well & longed to hear from you—the next day we came out here which I considered very fortunate for soon after we had a most violent Storm or rather hurricane[27]—& I should have been more frightened tho' perhaps in less danger at home than here where my good Grandmothers[28] example of composure extended itself to all around her—On the morning of the eighth the wind blew high from the North East but we apprehended nothing uncommon & past our time in the usual way—at ten oClock we perceived the tide to have covered the whole of the marsh between this & Jacksons at twelve it should have ebbed but to our great disappointment & surprise it continued to rise—the wind at the same time encreasing till it became so loud we could scarcely hear ourselves speak—it was with great difficulty we kept the doors & windows shut for the salt spray dashed against them with great force—& so much came through the cracks that we were obliged to bail it out—the Stable & every tree fell to the ground also part of one Chimney—this little dwelling shook with such violence we were in great dread of being crushed—I will not attempt to discribe our feelings—you can imagine what they were—I thought perpetually of what you must have suffered in the Oglethorpe & proposed your activity & resolution as an example to myself—but here there was nothing to be done but to remain quiet & endeavour to bear with resignation the evil whatever it might be & it has kindly past off without injury to any one of us—the Children were unconscious of the danger & in as good spirits as usual—every thing looks dreary—the bluff washed away almost up to the doors the small trees that remain withered & many without a single leaf—the accounts from our Neighbours & the plantations are dismal many lives lost but none among our people—I have not yet heard from richmond[29]—but the crops in general have suffered extremely at some places I fear entirely destroyed —at Oatlands[30] there is scarce any thing left—no appearance of a garden or fence—they say if the water had been two feet higher there would not [have] been a spot of the Island uncovered by the flood—We hear from town that much damage has also been done there[31] the particulars I suppose you will hear from Mr Scott[32] & many others—I have taken the first opportunity of telling you how well we have fared in this general calamity as I know you w^d^ be anxious about us—there is no Vessel in a condition to sail from this port but I dare say Mr Scott will find a way of sending this—I hear Mr Mein is still in Charleston & that the storm has not been near so bad there—I have had two letters from Anne Mine[33] since you went if you are with her give my best love & say I will write soon—The Eliza cannot be very far from here now by her perhaps we may hear from you indeed I expect that pleasure & shall be disappointed if I do not receive the congratulation of our friends on your safe arrival—Robert continues to be troubled with boils Mary Anne & him often speak of you & say you have been gone long enough & it is time you should come home—Adieu believe me always

Yours affectionately

E Mackay

Mr Robert Mackay

20: WILLIAM MEIN TO ROBERT MACKAY

[*Savannah, October 10, 1804.*]

My Dear Mackay

You must prepare your Mind to bear up under a most severe affliction for I never took up my Pen to address you with so heavy a heart And how to disclose to you the Cause of my distress when it must affect you more severely My hand shakes, my Pen trembles And I want language to impart to you My feelings Would to God I could take you by the hand & mingle my Tears with yours for the Loss (how shall I name it) of your oldest & Darling Son Yes! my dear friend Poor Robert is no more[34] & you are bereaved of the finest child I ever beheld—He was the pride of our City And I had flattered myself would long have been spared as a Comfort to his Parents and an ornament to his Country But alas! it has been otherwise decreed by Providence And We must bow with Submission to the omnipotent hand who gives & takes away—His Mother your amiable & affectionate Wife bears the Loss with more fortitude than I could have expected Every thing is doing & will be done by your friends & her own family to Solace her Mind so as (if Possible) to mitigate this severe affliction till your return which I trust is near at hand And Time & Good Sense with the attention which the other Children daily require must be the blunter of feelings & regret for him that nothing in this World can bring back to us—Poor little fellow It was soon over with him but it was a severe fever while it lasted—About eight days previous to his being attacked Mrs Mackay came to Town from the Cottage for some medical assistance to Mary Anne & William[85] who were rather unwell And Robert had been Complaining for some time previous but on the Wednesday before his Death he was uncommonly playful & to me appeared in the finest Health—I did not call the next day for you must know I had Just got out of bed from a little attack that I had on leaving Charleston On Thursday he was taken & Dr Jones[86] was sent for but no Danger was apprehended till Saturday Morning when D^r^. Cuthbert[87] was sent for—He was not at home & not to be found—Dr Irvine[88] was called in but neither he nor Dr Jones could avert its Progress It was a case allmost as violent as *Penns* And I do not think it was in the Power of the faculty to save him—On Sunday Evening his little Soul left this earthly Abode for Mansions of Bliss where I hope we shall one day Join him—You must my Dear friend bear up under this most severe affliction It is the first of your Trials in the Relation of a Parent but such as all who are blessed with a family must lay their account with—If it can give you any Consolation I do assure you all your friends share & have partaken in your distress—The Inclosed from your Dear Wife I once thought of ordering to be sent to Liverpool but on second thought, I considered, it was too cruel in me to be the forwarder of News that was to distress & dwell on a Mind during perhaps a long Passage where there were few objects to divert it & more particularly as on your Meeting with Mrs Mackay the whole Scene of affliction wo..^d^ be renewed—This is my excuse if I have erred My Dear Mackay it is the error of a friend who most Sincerely loves you & yours—

W: Mein

21: ROBERT MACKAY TO MISS JACKSON

Savannah 27th Feby. 1805—

My dear Miss Jackson[39]

I should have announced to you my safe arrival some time since, but that my mind has not been sufficiently at ease, or reconciled to the severe shock it has sustained, to communicate its unhappiness to even you, who I always have, & always shall consider one of my dearest & most beloved Friends—I had an unpleasant passage of fifty days from Liverpool, & was highly gratified at meeting, a few days after I sailed from thence, one of our own Ships, the Captain of which gave me the pleasing intelligence, that at leaving Savannah only 25 days before I spoke [with] him all my friends were well, elated with his account I landed here on the 25th of last month, & found a dreadful blank indeed—my darling little Robert was no more, in the bloom of health on the 5th October, he was seized with one of the fatal fevers of the Climate & on the 8th became its victim—a friend who I met as I step'd on shore gave me the first information—on entering the house my little Mary Anne was the first of the family I saw, she knew me immediately & was scarcely in my arms before she told me "Her dear Brother Robert was gone to the Skies" —You can readily imagine what a meeting with the other parts of the family was—to describe it is to me impossible —The unbounded affection I possessed for this sweet little fellow, & the hope I had of presenting him to you in person before he was much older, had prevented me from mentioning him very particularly to you, you must have accused me of a Fathers partiality & that in its strongest sense, had I described him to you as he was—But alas! it has been the Almighty's Will to deprive me of this great Blessing, & could I now do it, I should certainly be forgiven—I find it however out of my power, & shall only tell you that he was within two months of being four years old—that he had a most beautiful & engaging face, his little person was almost symmetry itself, his frame stout & firm—his manners far above one of his tender years & more winning than you can imagine—Manly in his idea's & the opinions he entertained of things, & the ingenuity of his argument where he met with opposition, & his pretty mode of expressing himself frequently astonished us all—He was by no means what is so often met with here—a spoil'd Child—he was never permitted to persist in anything that his Mother or myself knew was wrong, & when it was necessary he was corrected, but without going so far as to break his spirit, or do away that *Will* which he had of his own, & which ought secretly to be allowed to all children as far as is found necessary after studying their temper & disposition—He had had the Smallpox & Measles, which with the sickness incidental to the Climate (& of which he had his share) prevented his being so much improved as he would otherwise have been, when I left him in July he was spelling words of three syllables—It was strange that shortly after the disorder seized him he entertained a presentiment that he was to die—he repeated his pray'rs, told his Mother he was going to leave her, beg'd her to keep him & not to let them dig a hole to put him in—took his medicine most willingly; indeed asked for it before the periods arrived that it was directed to be given—impressed upon his Mothers mind over & over again to tell me, that he was a Good Boy & had taken his physick—said often, Papa & Mamma have three Children now, but will soon have only two—And used many of those little expressions—heart-rending indeed to the affectionate Mother who heard them, & at the same time witnessing the excruciating torment, that he who utter'd them underwent from the application of Blisters, administering nauseous medicines & the burning heat of a highly inflamatory fever—But why have I entered into a detail distressing beyond measure to me, & why tell you of what you know I must feel?—I wished to write to you, I have delayed it as long as I could & now that I make the attempt nothing but this mournful subject presents itself—No longer would I risk lives so precious in this direful Climate as the rest of my family are to me, but that I am arrested by the tremendous effects of the Hurricane, & the loss of crops of Cotton, destroyed by an Insect which untill last season has never done so much injury—these circumstances have so much altered the face of my affairs, that God only knows whether I shall ever be able to take up my abode in your happy Island, be this as it will we must not remain here another Fall, & as

I cannot spare time for an European voyage, I shall pass the sickly months in some of the Eastern States & perhaps (with successful crops this Season) pay you a visit next Year—Dreadful have been the effects sustained from the Hurricane all over the Country & the acco[ts] I rec[d]. in England far from being exaggerated—the sufferings of the Planters & their Slaves from the total loss of their provision crops, as well as the means of buying at the exorbitant price the scarcity has risen corn to—are beyond conception distressing—

I can give William Hamilton no encouragement to come here at present, instead of making money this year, we must live at a heavy expence—indeed I most heartily advise his fixing upon something in his own Country, which is at all events free from the vicissitudes we are so liable to here—neither sickness nor Hurricanes to fear—Remember me affectionately to Peggy & her daughter, & receive from M[rs]. M & myself all the good we can wish you—I hope I shall be able to write you in better spirits ere long, in the mean time it will give much pleasure to us to hear from you—Believe me always My dear Miss Jackson with sincerity & truth your friend

Rob[t]: Mackay

22: ELIZA ANNE MACKAY TO ROBERT MACKAY

Cottage 29th March 1806

My Dearest Friend

Your last letter expresses so much uneasiness about William that I am sorry I did not write on Thursday to satisfy you that he continued better—but as I had nothing new to say & had told you the post before that you might be easy about him I thought there was no occasion—

I suppose from what you say I may expect you about the middle of next week I am delighted to hear that you and Cousin Malbone[40] are prepareing a present for me I am impatient to see it—last night I dreamed you imposed a profile on me for it that I did not think like you & you were just going to shew me the right one when I awoke—I shall not tell Mary Anne that she may expect her cup when you return & we shall see if she remembers herself that you promised them to her—the Scissors too remain as yet a secret to be divulged on the first little misfortune to restore her temper—I hope you will have time to pay your compliments to Mr Bowmans[41] family—Yesterday we spent very pleasantly at Oatlands the weather was delightful & the orange blossoms were in the greatest profusion we employed ourselves very industriously for you in gathering them—as the boat was small I left the two Children with Aunt Betsy & only took the little one who improves every day—When we returned in the evening we found Mrs Nightingale & Mr Goodrich here Mrs M —[42] is better & intends going next week up the Country with Louisa[43] & Mr G—the other two girls are to stay & return home with Mrs N—who expects her husband in a week to stay here a few days—& then all go together to Cumberland—if all this takes place I think there is a delightful prospect for us—Mr Goodrich is about buying my brothers Carriage for the expedition & I dont think it unlikely that they will apply for Stephen as they are in search of a driver—you perhaps had better write Mr Mein in case of this what is the lowest price you will take for him—I scarcely think you will get as much as you gave—as it is certainly above his value & they all think worse of him than we do—My Mother and all the family send you their affectionate regards the Children send their love & I am as always Dear friend

your affectionate
Eliza Mackay

Robert Mackay Esqr
Care James Broadfoot Esqr
Charleston

23: ROBERT MACKAY TO ELIZA ANNE MACKAY

Savannah 18th December 1806—

My dear Eliza

I am afraid your not hearing from me for so great a length of time will make you very uneasy, & I am happy I was able to get a line on board the Mary to M^{r}. Davison[44] merely to let you know I was safe—We arrived here[45] on the evening of the 15th after 57 days passage, the first 15 of which the weather was so extremely bad we lost all our live stock except eight small pigs, & the man who laid in our stores in Liverpool not having done us the justice we were entitled to many of the articles were of a bad quality & we consequently had but indifferent fare, we went to the Southward & soon got into very warm weather, & caught some fish which helped out a little—Our party was a very tolerable one & upon the whole we made out pretty well—M[r]. Scott & Capt. Stookes had just come in from dining at the Cottage the even[g]. I came up & Mein who had been at Coleraine[46] came in half an hour after me, we had had a very tedious passage from Tybee in a pilot boat with nothing to eat on board, & almost perished with cold, so that with my friends about me & a very good supper I passed a very pleasant even[g]., it was however considerably alloyed at missing you & the Children from the group for everything conspired to keep you constantly in my remembrance, indeed My dear Eliza the house though quite alive from the Countinghouse being kept in the Cowpers room, seems to me quite deserted without you, I never enter the parlour or drawing room, but am in expectation of seeing you, this I suppose will wear out a little from the frequency of the disappointment —I went the next morn[g]. to the Cottage & surprized them not a little, Betsy Hunter saw me first as I entered the Piaza & really I believe took me for a Ghost, I was happy beyond measure to find them all alive & in such good health, Aunt Betsy[47] excepted who looks miserably, John is almost quit of his headach & has quite a Northern complexion, I have seen of course but little of William as yet, but he is I think a fine smart Boy & not half such a Yanckie as I thought he would be—Sally looks very well & Williamson[48] is almost as fat as Sandy Mein, indeed I was surprized to see them all look so well as they do—It has been what they call a very healthy fall, but I still find there have been many deaths, though not among our acquaintance, poor Fisher was drowned last week in crossing a Creek some where up the Country—Williamson was civil enough to call & I have already been twice there—Last

Even^{g}. we had a grand Ball at Scarbrough's,[49] we danced upstairs & Madams bed was taken down to make room for us, the party was very pleasant & particularly so to me, as they all seemed glad to see me, the enquiries after you were of course more numerous than I can relate to you, I danced twice with a North Carolina Cousin of the Countesses,[50] who was pretty well—The things sent by Stookes have given most unlimited satisfaction, the Gown is said to have created the jealousy of the whole Town, though only two ladies have hitherto been allowed to look at it—it is carefully locked up out of sight to astonish the Natives at the first Concert, which it seems is to be soon—I breakfasted this morn^{g}. with Taylor,[51] Miss Jackson is prettier than ever, to day I dine with Gibbons where I am to meet the celebrated M^{r}. Kollock, the great Jersey preacher,[52] said to be the first in America; in consequence of his Wife's[53] ill health he has been induced to come here for one Season, Gibbons took me to see him this morn^{g}. he is a most agreable man & his Wife I think quite a fine & elegant woman—They must prove a great acquisition to this society—20th After writing the foregoing I went to dinner & passed a most agreable day, I am exceedingly pleased with both M^{r} & M^{rs}. K. & tomorrow shall hear him in the Pulpit—We had a lady party which you know is quite a new thing at Gibbons', it consisted of M^{rs}. Stites, M^{rs}. Taylor & Miss Jackson, M^{rs}. Gibbons[54] enquired very kindly for you & I believe was really glad to see me, the plate & pearls they are quite pleased with, though he says as usual I am too extravagant for him & he will never give me another memorandum—His old wine is as good as ever, & meeting with that & other old friends we kept it up so late, that instead of attending to business yesterday, Mein, Mitchel[55] & myself went to the plantation—You would see by Mr. Meins letters to me the loss sustained again at Coleraine, it is fully Six hundred Barrels, however there will still be 600 made & there will be 100 Bales Cotton from the Bluff, I don't know yet how collections will turn out, though I believe the Sea Island crops are generally good, however we shall do all we can to reduce our debts in England & make us easy there—All the Cottage folks have made bad crops, John does not exceed 22 Bales—Red Bluff[56] does not seem to be the Lottery his Prize is to be drawn from, he is removing to Sedgefield[57] (having accepted Sir James's[58] offer) where I sincerely hope he may be more successful—I am very sorry to tell Miss Cowper our Lottery[59] ticket is a Blank, as is also Scarbroughs present to Mary Anne & William, I have been rather more fortunate in my own having drawn 108 Dols. which deducting the cost of the tickets leaves a gain of 53 Dols this will buy half a ticket in the next English Lottery & I hope will turn out well—I long to hear how our English tickets have turned out—Mein has as you may suppose been very inquisitive as to his affair with Miss C.,[60] having no instructions I could of course give no information whatever, I recd. a letter from her the morng. I left Liverpool, she there tells me she intended to write other Letters to Georgia than those for John & Miss H. but circumstances had come in the way to prevent, one of these circumstances might you know be a change of opinion as to a residence in Georgia—Mein will certainly go to England with me next Summer & will no doubt lay himself at her feet (or in any other pleasing situation that she may admit of) & between this & then she has time to make up her mind, which betwixt you & I, appears to be very luke warm on the subject, & should it ever be a match, will as far as it has already progressed look more like a match of convenience than any I have known—I should have answered her letter but don't know how to direct, as she says they would leave Cheltenham on the 18*th* Oct. but for where she could not tell—it however appeared decided that Kensington would not do for them—I hope Miss Margaret is better—I have invited all the old set to the Christmas dinner & Juno has promised to give us as many good things as she can, but here again you will be much missed—Capt. Stookes will sail in four or 5 days by him you will receive some Sweetmeats from your Mother, Corn flour & a half Bbl Rice, with respect to ground Rice John is to consult your G. Mother as he thinks it will mould on the passage—We have resold the Lucy & E. to Taylor & C. who are highly delighted with Mr. Davison as a correspondent, Stookes does not return here but carries the little ship to New York to sell her & there a larger Vessel is to be bought for the London trade which I have agreed to take one half of—We have received dreadful accots. of the French successes on the Continent,[61] I fear our produce will be down to nothing & our losses will be great—I can of course say nothing of future arrangements to you, whether we shall or not return next fall to Savh. I can't tell, but I shall endeavour if possible to get fixt in Liverpool—

Mein has insisted upon my occupying our old Bedroom in which his best furniture & drawing room Curtains are hung, I am glad of this as it alters the appearance of the room a little, your Wardrobe stands where it did & is this day to be filled with my Goods & Chattels, I had thoughts of bringing Lucy to Town to wash for Charles Roberts & myself, but Sophy says she will undertake it for me & indeed insists upon it, which upon the whole is as well as I understand Lucy is "in the way that Ladies like to be who love their Lords"—I hope you may receive this letter safe as it is a kind of Journal of my passage & arrival, by Stookes I shall write you again & of course by frequent opportunities & God knows my dear Eliza I cannot describe to you how anxious I shall be to hear every day from you were it possible—I am dreadfully afraid the Children will get the Measles & Hooping Cough & perhaps the Small Pox—if anything ails either of them employ the best medical aid instantly—Doct. Myers is recommended by Mr Davison & he will give you his address that you may keep it by you to send an express by a porter to him at a moments warning—How is Johns[62] eye, & how is your own situation, is it as was suspected? Adieu my Darling Wife & Children may Heaven protect & bless you prays your ever

faithful & affectionate

Best remembrances to all friends) *R. M.*

24: ROBERT MACKAY TO ELIZA ANNE MACKAY

Savannah 29th Decemr. 1806—

You & the Children are now My dear Eliza I suppose pinched with the cold, I hope however you find the house snug & comfortable, & that Mrs. Opie continues to please you, in addition to good fires the Children should have woolen stockings & warm clothing of every kind, the weather here since my arrival on the 15th has been very warm, so much so, extraordinary to tell, I have been sleeping with the windows open & the musquitoes have been troublesome, but this day ends all this, for the wind is at Northwest & I think in my life I never felt a colder day—Capt. Stookes sailed a few days ago & the Hamilton also, by both of them I wrote you & I hope they will have good passages, as I fear you would be uneasy at not hearing from me—We had a party as I wrote you we intended on Christmas day, all the old set, we were invited to attend at Doct. Jones's in the even[g]. w[h]ere there was a fiddle, but unfortunately some of our guests liked the wine better than dancing & Mein at a very early hour slip'd away & left me the care of them, the consequence is that Miss Campbell[63] is quite offended at me & says she will never invite me to another hop, I met them all at the Concert on friday (the first this Season) where we had a very pleasant party indeed, I danced till 1 O'Clock in the morn[g]. with one of the Wallace's[64] & Scarbroughs No: Carolina Cousin—I have been also at a Junior Bachelors Ball, to escort Sally & the Bourke's,[65] I danced with Harriet Campbell, there was a very large collection of Ladies & things went on very well—So you see I have been quite gay in spite of your absence, & shall continue to be so as long as I am satisfied that you & the children are well and happy—I have however been as attentive an attendant at Church as at the Ball room, on Christmas day I went to hear M[r]. Kollock & again yesterday, he continues to please me as much as ever & I think I shall not miss a Sunday while I am here—I met him at dinner at old Youngs the other day & Mein & I intend giving him a Ham & Turkey some day next week—We had quite a pleasant dinner at Williamson's, I call there very often & am quite a favorite with Jane[66]—Among other news, the All Saints Club is likely not to be revived, Mein & Nichols being the only members here during the Summer they neglected the Meetings & now that they have all returned, the little schism between Gibbons & Nichols seems not to be quite healed, & a most irreconciliable quarrel has happened betwixt Gibbons and Mein, so that unless we were upon our former footing the pleasure of the thing is done away—In the absence of Gibbons last Summer several of his drivers & leading Negroes formed a plan of an insurrection, they invited all the sensible Drivers on the River to a meeting & laid a plan before them for their adoption, among them were two of Meins drivers, who instead of entering into advised against it, the others fearing these two might discover their plot waylaid them, they say with an intent to murder them, they however did not fall in with them & afterwards hearing of the risk they had run, came to Town & informed Mein of all the circumstances, he made some enquiry into the thing & had all the leaders apprehended, they were tried & upon the evidence produced by M^{r}. Mein, three of Gibbons' most valuable people were condemned to be hang'd—G. arrived in the interim betwixt condemnation & execution, & had interest enough with the Justices to suspend the execution untill he could go to the Legislature then in Session to obtain their pardons, he went up & was successful in his application, they were pardoned, but little Welcher[67] who was one of the Members from this County wrote down to the Justices, that unless they ordered the execution immediately, the pardon would be obtained, they met & three out of the five signed the warrant, & they were instantly carried to Cherokee hill[68] at the end of the Avenue to Coleraine & there suffered the final penalty of the Law—Gibbons swears the people were innocent, that Mein has been the cause of their deaths & consequently they are involved in a quarrel which I don't think even time can do away—I am very sorry for this, for Gibbons is a most excellent companion, & his weight & influence in society make him a valuable intimate, I have been a good deal with him but he has never opened the subject to me as far as Mein is interested, he has only regretted the loss of his people & the illegal manner in which they were executed—I have heard within a day or two of several deaths that happened during the Fall, particularly Mr. Nightengale[69] & your Aunt McQueen,[70] which really shocked me, the letters you would receive after my departure would furnish you with all these—Williamson tells me it is his intention to go to England in the Spring with his family, & Scarbrough & Wife are to go also, Caig says he believes he must be of the party—I was at the Cottage on Saturday your Mother looks very well, William has spent one day with me here, I think him a very fine boy, what they are going to make of him I don't yet know, John still talks of going to France next year, but I suppose without any fix'd intention—Mr. Petit[71] has just come up from St. Mary's where he has been for some weeks, he saw a great deal of your father who he says is very well & looks very young—I begin to be very impatient for some arrival that I may hear from you, your last letter was the 18th Octr. & am very anxious to know how you all stand the Winter, I have so much dread of Measles, Hooping cough & Small-pox that I shall not be easy if you don't get Doct. Myers's address from M^rs^. Davison & keep it by you, so that you can send a porter as an express at any moment that you may want him—I shall write Sir James one of these days, I beg you will always remember me kindly to them, to M^rs^.[72] & Miss Hunter,[73] the Bishop,[74] the Grayhursts &^c^ and with the most sincere love & affection to yourself & the Children I remain My dear Eliza ever faithfully Yours

R. Mackay

25: ROBERT MACKAY TO ELIZA ANNE MACKAY

Savannah Jany 1. 1807—

This Ship being detained a few days longer gives me an opp^y^. of wishing you a happy new year, would to God I had the power of doing it in person, however as this is impossible I can only write that I hope we may pass many happy future ones together—There are several other Vessels ready to sail it is probable I may drop a line by each, but you must put up with this as the only long letter this week, I have now written you three & am very impatient to hear from you—This you know is Taylor's feast day I am to dine with him & I believe all the Town will be there—John dined with me yesterday says they are all well, I am glad to see him so much so—Hannahs[75] husband has been heard of, he is skulking somewhere in the neighbourhood, consequently our fears of his having gone to England are quite unfounded—Your Mother talks of sending William next week to see your father, which I daresay will be highly gratifying to both parties—I yesterday was astonished with a present from Miss Charlotte Scarbrough[76] of a Topaz Breast Pin handed by her Father, I happened to praise it in her Mothers Handkff. the other day, meaning the praise to be ironical, for it is coarser & uglier than my prize topaz which you laughed at me so much for wearing—it is impossible to wear it so I fear I shall be obliged to give offence—If you see Owens[77] tell him his Father dined with me yesterday, he looks remarkably well—

God bless you My dear Eliza with many happy returns of the day & with every other good prays your own ever faithful

R. M

Mrs Mackay
Care of Messrs Simpson & Davison
Merchants
London—
p Magistrate.)

26: ROBERT MACKAY TO ELIZA ANNE MACKAY

Savannah 3rd. Jany. 1807—

My dear Eliza

When I wished you a happy new year the day before yesterday I promised to drop you a line by this Vessel, I believe she is just going & as I have had a good deal to write my time is limited—I can only hope that it will find you & our little darlings well & happy—This is the 4th letter since my arrival & the only short one—

The Hunters are come in to spend a fortnight at M^{r}. Woodruffs I am just going to call on them, your Mother is gone to the Island & John to Redbluff, I understand William has been two days in Town but he has not called on me—Doct. Cuthbert came in yesterday from the Cottage, he is pretty well again, but as he is gone to Richmond I suppose he will soon knock himself up—The Golf club[78] goes on very well & I have attached to it an Evening Whist Club, we have rented a room at the Exchange[79] where such Members as feel inclined go every Even^{g} at 7 O'Clock, the club closes at 9, but we stay later if we chuse, it is very well attended, & now that I am a Bachelor I think it one of the best establishments that could have taken place, as it is sure to break us up from the dinner table at 7—A Tumbler of Porter & a biscuit are the only refreshments admitted—We had it in contemplation last week to give a Golf Club Ball, it was carried, & Nichols, Scarbrough, O'Donnell[80] & myself were appointed Managers, we met to make arrangements for it, but from the smallness of our numbers, we found it would cost us about 25 Dol^{s}. each, which thinking too large a sum to throw away, the thing has drop'd—Le Roy[81] has established what he calls the "Savannah Assembly" at the Exchange last night began them, in passing to & from our Club room, I looked in & saw only seven ladies, among whom were Mrs Scarbrough & Miss Gibbons,[82] who beg'd me to send for their carriages, it was ½ past 9 & I did so, this would break it up for the night, & seems to be an unfortunate beginning—

I begin to weary very much at not hearing from you, there has been but one arrival & I am looking out most anxiously for another, the America must soon be in & I hope she will have a letter from you—The Martha Washington sails next week for London by her I will drop you another line, for I know a little Sav^{h}. news will be interesting to you in the long winter even^{gs}. I fear you will so often pass alone—The house occupied by Mein & Scott when we left this is now rented to Burroughs & Sturges,[83] and Scott is moving into old Clays house which he has bought in consequence of its contiguity to the Wharf—

Mitchel continues to have the Blue devils as bad as before he went to France, we however have a little more of his company in the Bank square[84] than formerly—I rather think he will go to England with Mein & I next May—I should like to know where your Aunt & Cousins have fixed themselves for the winter, as I wish to answer Miss C^{s}. letter—Caig looks rather younger than he did & still talks of getting married next year—

Pray remember me to all friends & believe me ever My dear Eliza yours most faithfully *R: M*

Mrs Robert Mackay
at Mrs Opie's
N°. 7 High Row
Kensington Gravel Pits
p Boston.) Middlesex—

27: ROBERT MACKAY TO ELIZA ANNE MACKAY

Savannah 10th January 1807—

My dear Eliza

Still we are without any arrivals & consequently I am yet without hearing from you, several are expected & I am hourly watching the wind, certain that every breath from the Eastward brings your letters nigher to me—The fortune of affairs in Europe also creates a vast deal of anxiety for political news, we are completely at a stand here in point of business, no sale for any article of produce & not a planter paying an acco^{t}., I don't know what all will end in, but I fear our collections will be very small this winter & the disappointment of course very great—Our late Vice president Col^{l}. Burr is at present making a great deal of noise, he has headed an insurrection in Kentucky & with about 7000 men is now on his way to take possession of New-Orleans, which with the whole of the Western Territory it is said he intends to wrest from the American Republick & form into a separate Government, it is also believed that it [is] his intention, at least he has held it out as a bait to gain recruits, that after seizing all the treasure to be found in New Orleans he means to continue on to Mexico, which he is to deliver up to his followers for plunder—Others think this all groundless so far as respects Mexico, & assert that Burr is leagued with the French Empire, which has given him funds to carry on the insurrection, so as to deprive this Country of Mr Jeffersons favorite purchase, Louisiana, the papers are full of this matter & say that many people of consequence throughout the Union are concerned with Burr & even some Members of Congress—God knows how it will end, but from the progress already made, it will cost the Gov^{t}: an immense sum of money to quell the Insurgents, & must at all events bring disgrace upon the present Administration, who to make themselves popular have been ever since they were in Office counteracting the measures of the late presidents, Washington & Adams, who saw the necessity of keeping up a respectable standing Army & a navy sufficiently large to keep in awe & respect at least our own Citizens—these M^r^. Jefferson has done away & he of course has nothing but Militia to oppose to this lawless force, who are more likely to join them, than prevent their successes—So much for politicks—thank God we are far removed here from the scene that is likely soon to be displayed at New Orleans—I was at a very pleasant hop at Gibbons's on tuesday last, after dining with Scarbrough, I danced with M^rs^. S. & Martha Campbell[85]—Last night went to the Concert, about 40 Ladies there, the Hunters & Bourkes with the Jones & Campbell concern—I intended to dance with Bell H. but she would not, so I sat still as long as I staid—Miss G. sported her Pearls for the first time at her own hop & they were vastly admired—So did M^rs^. S. her Gown, I assure you Mein & I are in high favor with the *Countess*, she sent us three days ago from the remains of her Twelfth day feast, more Jelly, Pyes & Tarts than served us for two days desert, though we had Caig, Nichols & several other of the Sweet Tooth Gentry to help us destroy them—I have had all Hector's[86] secret from his friend & Confidant M^r^. Weir, On Christmas night just as I was going to bed after the party had left me, Weir who had a party at his own house, came over when they went away to see what we were about, he was pretty well in for it, & not only told me of Hectors application to our fair Cousin & her refusal, but also confessed himself an Admirer, assuring me that nothing but his friendship for Hector who was earlier smitten than himself had prevented him from making a declaration, & I think he said that H. was not yet at rest, but meant renewing the attack whenever he had an opptʸ.—I think as we are on the subject, our other Cousin is playing a curious game with Mein, she will neither write, nor suffer him to write her, he feels confoundedly sore at this kind of distance & certainly with much reason, I think this & the condition of his living in England, appear so exceedingly like making him a husband of convenience & not of choice, that it is too gross & I suspect he sees it a little in that light, at all events why so much romance & fustian at their time of life, they can't be looked upon now as Lovers of 20 & 17 when the follies & nonsense of a favorite Novel must be copied & nothing but hairbreadth escapes & a pleasant catastrophe end in a marriage—This stuff ought to be abandoned, it is out of fashion & her own sense ought to inform her that at their age this is silly & trifling, Mein will see her in a few months & the matter must then off or on—

12ᵗʰ Janʸ. So far I wrote you on Saturday since which there is an arrival from Liverpool & I have not a line by her from anybody, which I attribute to the carelessness of A. Mein, other vessels are daily expected, by some of them I hope to hear—I had a visit yesterday after Church from Miss Campbell & Miss Telfair,[87] they sat half an hour in the drawing room, & were quite low spirited at the deserted appearance of the house, they have insisted upon drinking tea with us one day this week—Parson Kollock was out of Town yesterday & I went to hear Dʳ. Best[88]—After gallanting the Ladies & making several calls, found John at Sally's, he came home & dined with me, picked up Mitchel & Nichols to join him, Mein was in the Country, saw the Hunters & Bourkes, nobody else in from the Cottage—Jaˢ. Broadfoot[89] called at Arundel Stᵗ. the very morn^{g}. we left it for Chelt^{n}: it is said he is just about to be married to one of D^{r}. Percy's daughters, who came out in the ship with him, he has said nothing of it to me as yet—God Bless you My dear Eliza, Kiss our sweet little children over & over again for your ever faithful & affectionate

R: M—

Mrs Mackay
at Mrs Opie's
N° 7—High Row
Kensington Gravel-Pits
p Huron) near London

28: ROBERT MACKAY TO ELIZA ANNE MACKAY

Savannah 24th January 1807—

My dear Eliza

My last letter to you was by the Huron & I most sincerely hope by this day you are in possession of my first by Capt. Stookes on the Hamilton as it is now almost a month since they crossed the Bar, & I know untill you hear of my arrival you will not be happy—My patience is almost exhausted at not hearing from you, what can keep vessels from arriving is quite incomprehensible, when I think that upwards of three months have elapsed since I have heard a word of or from my darling Wife & Children it really makes me miserable, but surely some ship will soon be in & I trust bring me the welcome intelligence of your being quite well & getting agreably through the

Winter—Since the commencement of the present year the weather has been colder than I ever experienced it here before, for so long a continuance, & at the North[d]. it has been exceedingly severe, but as it has been clear we cannot complain, at Augusta the Snow has been laying 4 inches thick & all hands have been using slays, I have a letter from William[90] in which he enquires particularly after you, I am told he is getting on pretty well in his profession, & had very nearly been married to Miss Hammond, but that Capt. Barnes who perhaps had been more assiduous, carried her to the Altar while William too confident, was riding the Circuit—Our fellow passenger M[r] Gardner[91] has been down here for a week, he really speaks affectionately of you all & begs to be particularly remembered—I was at Sallys yesterday for a minute, Miss Bourke was there, they are all well at the Cottage, John over Ogechee,[92] he begins to be low spirited at his ill success as a planter, & if things do not get better now he has taken Sedgefield, I suspect he will become so disgusted as to be induced to sell his property & turn his attention to something else for a living, he seems quite sick of Georgia & would do anything to be clear of it, I shall endeavour to persuade him to accompany me to England & if he makes a good crop of Rice he will take fresh courage—I have heard it surmised that Williamson is about buying the Cottage to join to Placentia,[93] if so that establishment will be broken up & relieve John a good deal, for he is always grumbling about it—However I have no direct information on the subject —I was invited to a Tea party at Sallys last even[g]., but it was Golf Club dinner day & I did not leave the Tent untill late, & after getting home Mein, Nichols & I dressed &

went to the Concert, we had but little musick as Petit is down at St. Marys, but a very agreable dance after it, my first partner was Miss Campbell[94] the daughter in Law of Parson Kollock, as nice a little Girl as I ever saw, she is very young & like her namesakes very small, but has more sense than the whole of them, & knows a vast deal better how to behave, the latter part of the even^{g}. I danced with "the little Sally" as Caig calls her so that you see I was quite among the Campbells—Peter Henry Morel & his Son have made friends with Roe & wife,[95] the reconciliation took place three days ago at the request of the Son, the old fellow sent for them & when they arrived he threw his Will into the fire before them & shook hands, I met Roe last night at the Concert, he took me aside & told me of it & I never saw a poor Devil more elated, he said they had dined with him yesterday & I suppose he sent them both drunk home—He has the worst of it, for necessity has driven him to be industrious, he has commenced a Grocery Store & I am told is doing tolerably well, these two bears will eat & drink him out of house & home, & what he has for some time thought the summit of his happiness will eventually in all probability prove his ruin—

The Ladies are still insisting upon Mein & I giving them a tea party, but I must first hear that you are all well before I think of it, M^{rs}. Taylor & M^{rs}. Scarbrough insist upon making all the Jellies & trifle, Cake &^{c}. &^{c}., & will not be said no to, but I have a letter from Lee[96] who says M^{rs}. Cruger & him are coming here next month, & I think if we do call a hot water club together, it must be when they are here—I intended this letter to go by Capt. Parrott who sails in a few days, but Scott has just called in & says the

Robert Bolton a fine new ship is just going so I shall close it as quickly as I can & send it by her, & if anything worth communicating turns up I shall write again by Parrott, but really there is so little going on, it is nothing but a dull journal of ones daily transactions that I have to furnish you with—Lee begs to be kindly remembered to you—

26th After finishing the last page I found the Bolton would not sail untill this day, therefore I stop'd & went to dine with Caig & Mitchel, in the evening the latter gave me a very long letter which he had written when in france but never forwarded, it is really so amusing I should like you to see it, & were it not that its postage would come too high from its bulk I should now send it to you, but you shall see it when you see me—Yesterday being Sunday I of course went to hear Mr. Kollock, who pleases me more & more, I saw the Bourkes & William after Church at Williamsons, your Mother could not come in as John had the Chair at Ogechee, he came in yesterday afternoon & I have just seen him, he is getting things in order by degrees —I finished yesterday again at Caigs Mein being at Coleraine, we had the old set there, with the addition of Campbell, and Hogarth & Tubman from Augusta—William Bulloch[97] is to be married to Miss Young on thursday next, & this seems to be the only news of that kind at present going on, except Charles Howard[98] to Jane Wallace which is to take place very soon—Lucy has added a daughter to our stock, this happened the day before yesterday & I understand is doing very well, Moore the owner of her husband has offered to purchase her & John wishes me very much to part with her, I have however not yet determined upon it & should like to know your opinion first—As to Stephen I have only seen him twice since my return, I understand he has set up as a Farrier somewhere in Town & is doing well in his profession—I am about making a bargain with Mendenhall[99] for him, but Stephen keeps so much out of my way that I fear he will not act his part in the transaction, I shall however get rid of him I am resolved, even if I give him away—Sally thinks her little boy Bower[100] is getting the Hooping Cough, he is a very fine child, I hope ours will keep clear of it untill the weather is warmer & the Measles also—God bless & protect you My dear Wife & Children, Prays your ever faithful & affectionate

Pray remember me to all our friends— *R M*

Mrs Robert Mackay
Care of Messrs. Simpson & Davison
Merchants
p Robert Bolton.) London—

29: ROBERT MACKAY TO ELIZA ANNE MACKAY

Savannah 18th. May 1807—

I have just wrote you My dear Eliza a long letter by the William acknowledging yours by M^r. Moore & should not write again to day having a good deal to do, but that I could not reconcile it to myself to let Capt. Stookes go without a line from me, he came here last week in the Lucy & E. & has taken the command of a new Ship of Taylor & Scarbroughs in the Greenoch trade, he sails tomorrow morning & M^r. & M^rs. Scarbrough are his passengers—Their stay will not be long in Scotland, you will therefore soon see them in London & you will of course be as attentive to M^rs^. S. & my little God-daughter Charlotte as your own situation will admit of—I hope & trust my beloved Eliza that this letter will find you safe through your trouble, & that our little Stranger[101] is excelled by neither Brother or Sister in anything but a superior knowledge of the World—Oh how anxious I am to be with you, & how uneasy I shall be untill I arrive in England to hear how you are—I console myself with the reflection that you will have kind & attentive friends about you & I flatter myself with the hope of finding all well—I hope Miss Mein remains with you, though you will feel less the want of her from your Cousins being in her place, I do envy them the happiness of being with you & our darling Children—

I have only time to add that I saw your Mother & all the folks well at Church yesterday & she & Sally just now rode through the square,[102] John has been here all the morning & is in very good health though he looks thin—

William[103] is still in Florida & M^rs^. Miller tells me is quite delighted with it, I don't know what your father means to do with him, I believe he has not written to any of us lately—

God bless & protect you all prays your ever
faithful & affectionate
R M

Mrs Mackay
7 High Row
Kensington Gravel Pits
p Mary } near
Capt Stookes. } London—

30: ROBERT MACKAY TO ELIZA ANNE MACKAY

Savannah 18th. May 1807—

Since writing you My dear Eliza p the Alexr. Hamilton on the 12th & 13th I have received yours by Mr. Moore, forwarded from Petersburgh, by which I am truly sorry to hear of the bad health of Mrs. Davison & Elizabeth, Stookes tells me they were looking out for a place in the Country which I hope will restore them; the heart of London must be an unhealthy situation for a constant residence to anybody, & particularly so to Children—Stookes came here last week & has taken the command of a new ship of Taylor & Scarbrough's called the Mary in the Greenock trade, he sails tomorrow morning & Scarbrough & Wife go with him, I am dreadfully mortified that I cannot go with them, I was always in hopes of managing so as to go at the same time, but it is impossible, I do not think I can get away for a Month to come—By the time this reaches you I suppose my dear Eliza you will be confined, may God of his infinite goodness & mercy bear you through in safety, would to Heaven I could have been with you, however as your Aunt & Cousins are to be in the same house & having Hannah by you, I rest satisfied that you will not want for care or attention, the Ladies are no doubt with you before this & after the Winters seperation you must feel very happy to be all together again, you don't know how much I should like to be of the party—but I ought not to say so, for I am sure you do know as well as I can tell you—Stookes has told me so much about the Children & about you that if possible since

I have seen him my impatience to be with you has increased—M^rs^. S. no doubt will expect you to shew her all the fine things in London as she goes there a perfect stranger, but your situation is a good excuse, & will save you a vast deal of trouble, however you will of course be as civil & attentive as circumstances will admit of, though Miss Cowpers being in the same house will make matters a little awkward[104]—for God's sake don't ask the Countess to sing, or she will frighten the good people of England—you will see my little God-daughter, poor thing it has been very sick from being weaned so young & cutting teeth together, but change of air may bring her round again, I gave her a frock & cap for her christening, made by M^rs^. Gilbert, but her Godmothers frock (Miss Giekie) was so much handsomer that it was used for the occasion—If the Countess happens to be in a chatting humour she will give you all the Sav^h^. news, though there is not much worth hearing—The weather is getting exceedingly warm, the Thermometer has been in our passage (the coolest place in the house) at 92° for three days past, but I feel none other than the immediate inconvenience from it, for I am sure I never was in better health in my life—John is sitting by me reading his Democratick Newspaper he looks thin but makes no complaint & eats his allowance, I saw all the family at Church yesterday & chatted with your Mother at Sally's after service, the Hunters & Bourkes were there, I never saw your G.Mother looking better than at present—

We have had M^rs^. Miller, Louisa & Letitia in Town for a few days & I believe they left it the day before yesterday, I saw them several times at M^rs^. Melvins & danced with

Letty at the last Concert, they were to have gone up the Country but the old woman found herself so much better that the jaunt was laid aside, she appears to me to look younger every year, though she says she is in miserable health—this however is all conceit—I intended this letter to go by Stookes, but as I have mentioned the Countess I believe I will send it by the William, which sails also to-morrow & I shall write a single line by the Mary to say we are all well—We had a very pleasant party a few evenings ago at Gibbons's, neither of the old folks appeared, John, Betsy Hunter & the Bourkes were there, we were treated with a great abundance of Strawberries & real cream, with many other nice things, Ann sent over for ODonnels fiddle without any of us knowing it, not even himself, & when it arrived she insisted on his playing, he did so & we danced reels untill 11 O'Clock—

Montalet has left his Diamonds with me to dispose of in London for him, they cost him a great deal of money but I fear they will fetch far short of his expectations, he calculates on getting half price which will be about A thousand Guineas for him—I intended to have written Miss Cowper by this opp^y^. but really I have not time, you must apologize to her for me & also to the Baronet,[105] out of whose good Books I fear I shall get by my silence—You must say a great many kind things to them all for me in the mean time, & I will try my hand at apologies when I arrive—Your Mother & Sally have just rode past on the opposite side of the square, I see them from my seat where I am now writing in the parlour & they have not given the house one look, not even turned their heads towards it—I shall write M^rs^. De Cadignan[106] in a few days, there is a

Ship going from Charleston to France—I have exhausted all the subjects I can muster at present & to your satisfaction I daresay that they are finished, for I am sure some of my letters must puzzle you to read & there is so little amusing to send from this barren soil, that they are scarcely worth the trouble—However I can conclude with assuring you that I am as usual your ever faithful & affectionate

I long to hear Mary Anne read & the rest Chatter—I shall be too happy when I am with you all again— *R. M.*

M[rs] Mackay
7 High Row
Kensington Gravel Pits
near
p William) London

31: ROBERT MACKAY TO ELIZA ANNE MACKAY

Savannah 24th May 1807

Only a few days have elapsed since I wrote you My dearest Eliza by the William & the Mary in which last Ship M[r]. & M[rs] Scarbrough went passengers, they did not get to Sea I believe untill yesterday as the wind has been a head—We have had a few days of severely hot weather, but it did not last long, & latterly I have never known it more pleasant, a continued breeze & the Thermometer not above 70° or 75°—M[r]. Lee has been here on a visit for his health which has been bad for some time past, but he is recruiting fast, he begs to be most particularly remembered to you—He went with us last evening to a party at Caustons,[107] the Hunters, Bourkes & Sally Campbell were the ladies, John gave us a feast of Blackberries & we had a glass of our oldest wine, which I assure [you] relished exceedingly well—Mrs Moodie arrived here on thursday last & I went to see her next morning, she is just as per last —James a fine Boy, says he remembers Mary Anne, she put up at Caigs, but since that M^rs^. Woodruff has taken her home—All the Island folks are to be at Church this morning except your Mother & John swears she stays at home merely to keep from calling on M^rs^. Moodie—there is nothing going on whatever to amuse you with, & to sit down merely to give you a letter of assurances of love & affection, is only to repeat what you know so well already that it is needless to repeat them—but I cannot help saying I would give the World to be with you at this particular period, & I shall always lament the hardship of the fate which prevents me, but I hope My dearest Wife all will be soon & well over & that in a short time I shall meet you quite recovered from your illness & a sweet little Addition to the family to welcome me home—There have been no late arrivals therefore I have no letters since those by Capt. Stookes & Mr Moore, but I look out anxiously every post for the Two Friends arriving at Charleston, by which I have no doubt I shall have letters from you & I trust informing me of you & the Children having quite got over your colds, and of the safe arrival of your Aunt & Cousins with Miss Margaret in better health—

Boltons new Ship was launched on thursday even^g^ last, & went off most beautifully,[108] all the Town & Country too was collected to see the sight & I did not think Sav^h^.

could produce such a multitude, your G.Mother & the family took their stations on the edge of the Bluff opposite Ja[s]. Wallaces Wharf & had a fine View, the Old lady was quite delighted & told me it was just 35 years since she saw a large Brig of her Husbands[109] building launched from the same spot—the new Ship is called the "*Gossipium*" the latin word for Cotton—Which by the bye is the most stupid name I have yet heard—I can't persuade this fellow Lee to go to Church & out of civility I must stay at home with him, as Mein & John are just going up to Coleraine to spend the day with Gen[l]. Read[110] & Rutledge[111]—This is the second Sunday only since my return to Georgia that I have missed Church & I really regret it exceedingly—I fear I have put off writing too long for Bob Scott[112] says the Vessel that this is intended to go in is now under way —therefore may God bless & protect you is all I can add to My dear Wife & Children from their ever faithful

R M

Single }
Sheet }
M[rs]. Rob[t]. Mackay
7 High Row
Kensington Gravel Pits
near
William & Henry—
London

32: ROBERT MACKAY TO ELIZA ANNE MACKAY

Savannah 29th May 1807—

Again I sit down to address you My beloved Eliza without a possibility of saying with any kind of certainty when I shall embark, surely there never was a state of more distressing perplexity, so much delay is met with to retard our arrangements that I sometimes feel disposed to wash my hands of the whole business & go immediately to be with you, however a little patience & perseverance now, may save a great deal of trouble hereafter, & however terrible the seperation, we had better submit with cheerfulness than suffer at another time longer inconvenience— We are using every exertion to make our remittances as large as possible, so as to insure a pleasant reception on the other side, for I hate to encounter grumbling or angry looks, & though our payments must fall short of our hopes, yet they will not be so despicable either, Mein still talks seriously of going with me, but really our concerns here are of such magnitude & so much depends upon their being carefully attended to, that I do not know whether he will or not, & to all this I may also add the very great uncertainty of his determinations, for as he himself says, he does not always ride when he puts his Boots on, he is however very desirous to go this Summer & will be very much disappointed if he does not accomplish it—I have been looking out for the arrival of the Two Friends to receive another Letter from you, I want to know how your colds are & how you have got through the Winter, we have had a few days of very warm weather, but latterly it has been extremely cool & pleasant, the crops are beginning to look better, the late Spring & the Cut Worm together have been of some injury, but I hear no complaints now, Johns Cotton at Caustons looks remarkably well—Sally & the Hunters are gone to the Island, & I have made a promise to spend two or three days there this week, but I don't know whether I can accomplish it or not, I missed a fine party at Gibbons's yesterday in the Country, Rutledge, Gen[l]. Read, Woodruff & Caig were with him, I had a piece of business to attend to in the Afternoon & could not go, I am sorry that Mein & him are still at variance, I see no prospect of accomodating it & have given up any farther attempt—Mein thinks he did his duty in bringing the Negroes to trial, Gibbons thinks otherwise, & indeed so widely do they differ, that he says Mein must pay him for them or they can never be friends, this Mein will of course never do, so I suppose they will be enemies, or at least the thing must remain as it does, as long as they live—I wrote you on the 24th by the William & Henry & on the 18th by the William & the Mary, in which last went Scarbrough, Wife & Child for Greenock, I find they are to go through Edinburgh & visit Liverpool before they do London, in which case I hope to be with you before them, for I imagine the Countess relies a good deal upon your friendship & attention, in which case I shall save you some trouble, but I have told her of your situation, & therefore she ought not to calculate on having you much with her, she is cursed coarse sometimes—I hope she may sink North-Carolina when in the presence of any of our acquaintance—in her principal sitting room wherever it may be, you will be sure to see

Charlottes Cradle & *chair*, unless some kind Soul may give her a hint, for *he* has not sense enough or she too much obstinacy—

I wrote you that Lee was here, he has been very ill but the trip here has been very serviceable to him, I never saw anybody recruit faster, he is gone home & talks of spending the Summer at the Sweet Springs, but I rather think him too fond of Charleston—Before his departure he told me a secret of Miss Caroline Villepontoux,[113] which she herself communicated to him—She is very soon to be married to a young Frenchman a M^r^. Belleanse—The crop looks famously at Coleraine & the Overseers letters from Sutherlands Bluff[114] are very flattering, I hope this good appearance may continue, for a thousand Barrels of Rice and One hundred & fifty Bales Cotton will help to reduce our debts in England very much—I am really distressed to hear of Mrs Davison's & Elizabeths bad health, I hope they have removed into the Country before this—Williamson talks of living at the Cottage this Summer, in which I think he is wrong, for I cannot divest myself of the opinion that it is a very unhealthy place, Jane is really a fine little Girl, but a mere Button, I do not think her a bit larger than John was when I left you, she is gifted with a tongue for I never heard such an incessant little Chatterbox—Would to heaven I could hear some of the chatter of our little Darlings, my patience is completely exhausted—I want very much to charter a Ship to load with Rice & Cotton to Cowes & a Market, but such is the scarcity of Vessels that we cannot procure one either here or in Charleston, could I succeed in this I should either take my passage in her, or follow by the first good opp^{y}—after her, indeed by being detained here so long I shall loose all the best of the Ships from here & shall be obliged to go to Charleston for a passage—You must remember me affectionately to your Aunt & Cousins who by this day I suppose are with you—I should write Miss Cowper but I know nothing pleasant to communicate, there is nothing immediately interesting but acco^{ts}. of her friends & you can give her on that score all that is necessary—Your last letter is now so old that I am quite anxious for some arrival to tell me how you all are, one more letter must satisfy me, for I suppose after the Two Friends you would not expect me to be here, you may be assured I shall be off as soon as I possibly can, Would it were tomorrow, a week or two however must produce something decisive—May this find you perfectly recovered from your confinement, & the Children in good health is the fervent prayer My beloved Eliza of your ever faithful & affectionate *R. M.*

Mrs Mackay
7 High Row
Kensington Gravel-Pits
near
p Missouri) London—

33: ROBERT MACKAY TO ELIZA ANNE MACKAY

Savannah 11th. June 1807—

My last to you My dear Eliza was by the Missouri on the 29th. May since which I have nothing from you, the Two Friends is not yet arrived, by her I calculate on a letter & a truly welcome one it will be, as it is now a long while since I have had one, it is the only happiness I can enjoy at such a distance from you, therefore you cannot but suppose me a little anxious—I suspect it will puzzle you to read what I now write for I have had an ugly Bile on my wrist which has given me great pain & is yet far from easy, though it has been lanced by Dr Irvine & is in a fine state of suppuration, it will be well in a few days & my next will be more legible—The weather is becoming very hot which is an additional spur to getting away from this but we have not determined in what Ship we are to embark, I shall be obliged to go to Charleston for I do not think there will be any opp^y^. from hence that I should like much to go in, however a very few days must determine our plans, Mein is so indecisive he puts me out of all patience, he never thinks alike two hours in succession, & if this week does not bring him to some conclusion I will go to Charleston & embark without him—it is not the pleasure of having him for a companion on the passage, be assured that has detained me untill now, but the short remittances & disappointments we have rec^d^. here at all quarters

William has returned from Florida grown very tall & quite a Spaniard, at present is determined to live no where else—He brought me a letter from your father, saying that as his promise was out to Lady W. to let William go to England for a few years, he wished me to take him with me & do what was necessary; to defray his expences he sent me an order on Petit for a Spanish Lebranza of a thousand dollars, which in the present depreciated state of that paper is not worth fifty pounds, indeed a hundred

Dollars Cash could not be got for it on the Continent of America, & how the good old gentleman could calculate on this as a fund, is to me a little incomprehensible—Had our collections placed it in my power to make the advances necessary, with the utmost cheerfulness would I have step'd forward, but I find my own expences an unpleasant load while so much money is due, & we must put every shoulder to the wheel to get clear of the difficulty—It is totally out of Your Mothers or Johns power, for you know they have made no crops, & what little is saved will not more than carry them to the Northward & back, for it is proper your Mother should go, she has had another attack of her usual complaint & with difficulty she has consented to go, she now rides out every day & is recovering fast—It will be a sad disappointment to poor William, for he is exceedingly anxious to visit England & they will be very much at a loss how to dispose of him this Summer—

I have nothing but one dull sing song to write you from here, everybody is going away the packets carry 40 & 50 passengers, Parson Kollock & family sail on thursday next, Miss Gibbons goes under their protection, as her father can't get away so soon & in a few weeks the Sandhill[115] will be quite deserted—Davis the father-in-law of Mrs. Leval has been detected in the act of stealing Negroes from different people here & conveying them to Florida, the facts are so clear against him that he must be hanged to a certainty, he is now in Jail loaded with irons to wait his trial—Your G. Mother & all the other folks are well, they came in on monday last from the Island—The Town continues to be very healthy, I hear of nobody sick but

Mrs Geo: Anderson who has had a pleurisy but now recovering—Remember me to all our friends, Kiss the dear Children over & over again & in the full hope My Dear Eliza that by this day you are safe through your trouble I remain ever faithfully & affectionately yours

R. M.

Single)
M[rs] Mackay
7 High Row
Kensington Gravel pits
near
p Edward) London—

34: ROBERT MACKAY TO ELIZA ANNE MACKAY

Savannah 17th June 1807—

The Two Friends has at length brought me My dear Eliza's letter of 3rd. April, which though of an old date is the latest account I have of My dear Wife & Children & was of course most truly welcome—Miss Meins having been with you all Winter has really been a comfort to me, she is a good Soul for staying so long, but I wish she could remain with you untill I arrive, however you will have your Cousins with you & I hope you will be quite happy—You must have suffered amazingly from your violent cold, I was exceedingly anxious to hear of your being better, & your letter has been a great relief, I hope in God you have had no return, & indeed that you are safe through all your troubles & almost able to go about the house again—It is truly hard that I have not been able to be with you, &

that at this late hour I have not fixed upon a Vessel to go over in, but my anxiety to rake & scrape everything together to send before me has been such that I have been kept much longer than I expected—We have also been trying to settle the affairs of M. M. & C°. so as to dissolve the Copartnership this Summer, but we find it cannot be done while the debts in England remain so considerable—It is the intention of M^r^. Mein & myself to continue in business together, & I hope next years collections will enable us to put this intention in execution—I have however every year been promising myself the prospect of being easy from Collections, but this is a broken staff I find to rely on, the Country has really been unfortunate & the planters could not pay—all this makes it necessary that we should return here next Fall, much as I shall regret the necessity of bringing our darling Children to this most dreadful Climate, but necessity hath no law, & we must just take our chance like other people, we must go to the Northward to avoid the Fall & do all we can to bear up against difficulties—I am quite sorry that Mary Anne & William disgraced themselves so much before M^r^ & Mrs Davison, I was in hopes the former had got over that ugly habit of bashfulness, & as to Will I had no idea that he ever possessed it—however it will all wear off in time—the dear little Souls what would I not give to be with them—

Your Mother has been ill but is better, she has lost her fever & rides out twice a day, John had prevailed on her to promise to go to the North^d^. with him, but now she is better she has recalled her promise & seems determined not to stir, he talks of going next week, the Parson & family sail tomorrow, with a packet full of passengers, among them old Mr Williamson,[116] I told the old Gentleman the other day he would have an agreable fellow passenger in Mr Kollock, he said, "he was no acquaintance of his, he did not like Parsons"—I have endeavoured to get a passage for Liverpool in a fine Brig that is loading here, but the Captain says he can make more money by carrying Cotton, so that I fear I shall be obliged to go round to Charleston to look out for a Vessel there which will be very trouble-some indeed, I never knew Ships so scarce here before at this Season—I have at last written a few lines to Sir James, I did not know what to say, they go by this oppy. & will pave the way for my arrival—John is trying to manage matters so that I may take William with me to fix him at School, but I don't know whether he will accomplish it or not—I am still in hopes that Mein may accompany me but it is by no means certain, I hope he may for I wish him to face Davison & his Brother as well as myself, & I have also some distant hope if he goes that I may be enabled to spend next Winter in England—You say nothing of Miss Margarets health, whether or not their *charming Winter residence* has been favorable to it or not, I sincerely hope it has, for to be always sick must really make one tired of life, her friends are very anxious to hear of her—

You never saw a place so stupidly dull as this is at present not a single occurrence have I to inform you of at all interesting, or to fill up a letter with—18th The Bile on my wrist is quite well, but I have suffered a great deal from it, for the Doct. gave me a dose of Jalap & without telling me added a large quantity of Calomel, the consequence was from not being guarded against it I caught a severe cold, which made me very sick indeed, I am now recovered & as well as ever, but might have had a severe bout, & indeed last week I did not think I should have got so well off—I went last even^g to see the folks near the fort,[117] they are all well I found Sally there, William has got a bile on his knee, Little Jane is the most complete chatter box I ever saw—Remember me affectionately to all friends & believe me ever My dear Eliza faithfully & sincerely Yrs—

R: M

Mrs Mackay
7 High Row
Kensington Gravel Pits
near
p Gossypium) London—

35: ROBERT MACKAY TO ELIZA ANNE MACKAY

Savannah 3rd July 1807—

My dear Eliza

My letter intended for the Gossypium was too late for her, Nichols having called in & misled me as to the time of her sailing, however it followed in a day or two after by the Minerva & I hope will get safe to hand, you will there see that I had been a little unwell from an unlucky dose of medicine the Doctor gave me, & I then thought I had got over it & made a lucky escape, but it did not let me off so easily, for I had another attack which laid me up for several days, during which I was really very sick, but the application of a Blister to my side, where the seat of pain seemed to be, removed it, & upon the whole I think the thing has been of service to me for I have got clear of a most immoderate quantity of Bile, & though I am of course rather thinner than I was, I have not seen my complexion so clear for many years, I was very fortunate in having very little fever, indeed what I had was so slight, it was only perceptible from a little quickness of pulse, & all the Bash I had occasion to take was one Phial of decoction, which I finished the day the doctor sent it—

This goes by the Pallas the Brig I was pushing to get a passage in, & had other things been ready I should have gone in her though her Cabin is full of Cotton, but the fact is we have not settled our affairs, day after day have we been from morning to almost night shut up in the drawing room endeavouring to make some arrangement that would be satisfactory to all three of us, but as yet nothing conclusive has taken place, Mein is dilatory & makes long calculations, & Scott is grasping at more than he is entitled to, so that God knows when we shall close, I really could not have thought there was anything in Human affairs that could possibly have taken up any such time or given such trouble—these things of course all to yourself—we have however concluded to sell the Wharf & when this is effected it will enable us to make farther remittances to England which at present I am most anxious about—I am happy to say that Doct. Jones has at last persuaded your Mother to consent to a trip to the North[d] it will be of great service to her, & it is full time John was off for he has fever & ague every now & then, they are waiting for one of the Packets to arrive in which they have a choice of berths, & if our matters could be brought to any kind of point in time, I would step on board with them &

take my passage immediately from New York to London, I had at one time made up my mind to go round to Charleston to go with M^{c}.Neil, but he sails this day week, & that is now out of the question, so that if I can't get away with your Mother & John, who I have offered to nurse, I must take my chance in some of the Vessels from here for Liverpool, there are two or three very good ones loading, but they fill their Cabins so full that they can't be very comfortable—Your Mothers plan is to spend the Summer at Morristown in Jersey recommended by Judge Jones as a cheap place & one of the healthiest in America, I believe Miss Jones[118] will go with her, as she has been unwell & the Judge has expressed such a wish—This John will have no objections to, for it is whispered about town that he is quite her humble serv^{t}.—I have nothing new to tell you from this dullest of all dull places, M^{rs}. Swarbreck[119] poor Woman is dead of a cancer in the Breast, & I believe I forgot to mention to you that little Tom Tatnall died some time ago,[120] he went off so suddenly that I had been speaking to him as he passed our corner, & two or three days after as we were sitting at dinner I saw a funeral passing through the Square, & on enquiry found it was his, though so near I never knew a word of his being sick —What a state of suspence shall I be in untill I see you, I cannot hear from you again, as I do not think you would write after the Two Friends, & indeed it will be impossible for me to hear the event of your illness before I leave this—God Almighty avert all evil & bring us soon & happily together, & may we may never seperate again while it is his Will that we remain on Earth—I shall scarcely know the Children they will be so grown—Oh that I was with them—Pray remember me affectionately to your Aunt & Cousins & all other friends & believe me My dear Eliza ever faithfully & affectionately yours

R: M

Mrs Robt. Mackay
7 High Row
Kensington Gravel Pits
near
Pallas) London—

36: ROBERT MACKAY TO ELIZA ANNE MACKAY

Savannah 9th July 1807—

My last to you My beloved Eliza was on the 3rd & was just sent to the Letter-bag when I was handed your two letters by the Georgia & Miss Margarets of 25th April, giving the welcome & truly pleasing intelligence of the appearance of another little daughter & of your being very well after it, nothing could have been more unexpected to me than receiving this account before I left Georgia, & consequently nothing could give me more heartfelt joy, or be more satisfactory, I shall continue to hope & trust that you went on as well as Miss Margaret says you set out, & that you were soon able to stir about again, it was really fortunate that your Aunt & Cousins arrived in time —as to Anne Mein she seems always to make her escape before our Girls appear, this being the case now, as well as when Mary Anne was born—It is really hard upon me that I should be far from you, & I see no prospect of getting away before the end of the Month & then I expect

I shall be obliged to go to New-York to look for a passage—A long spell of Southerly winds have kept the Northern packets from arriving & your Mother & John are consequently still here, he is now pretty well again but your Mother still continues weak & has slight fevers, though she rides out twice every day, all the rest of the folks are well, Williamson has bought the Cottage for 2000$. & he & Sally & Jane have furnished the house & moved out for the Summer, they went out ten days ago, he seems quite fond of it for I believe he has been in town but once since—Mr. Burrs trial[121] has been going on for some time & has made much noise, the Grand Jury have at last found Bills against him for Treason, high Crimes & misdemeanours & as Jeffersons party is very violent against him, I have now very little doubt but they will hang him, he is in close confinement in the common Jail at Richmond where the trial is held—I am sorry to say some very respectable characters are implicated with him in different parts of the Union—But the whole Country is now agitated from each extreme to the other, by an outrage committed on our frigate the Chesapeake[122] by the British Ship Leopard of 50 Guns, it seems four Mutineers & deserters from an English Sloop of war, were enlisted on board the Chesapeake, while they lay in Hampton roads, immediate application was made for them & refused (in March last), the Admiral on the station then issued orders to any of his Ships meeting the Chesapeake at Sea to demand the men & if refused to take them by force, she went out last month & the Leopard falling in with her, her Captain wrote a polite note to our Commodore Barron & inclosed his Admls. orders, Barron was obstinate in his refusal & the other immediately fired a few Broadsides into him which killed three of his men, & wounded himself & 11 others, he then struck his Colours & the Englishman came & took away his four Mutineers, & told Barron to go on his cruise as he had no more to do with him—You never heard of so much violence as this has been received with, & War seems to be the cry of every voice, however I hope our Philosophical Pres^{t}. is too peaceably inclined for that —I assure you M^{rs}. Marshall acquitted herself in presenting her Colours to the company most admirably,[123] she was quite undaunted, not so the Officer who received them, he absolutely trembled & for a long time could not remember a word of his speech—I have a copy of her address to shew you—I have now given you everything that is going on here & can only add that I shall follow myself as soon as possible, Remember me affectionately to all about you, Kiss the Little ones for me & believe me ever faithfully & affectionately your *R M*

Mrs Mackay
7 High Row
Kensington Gravel Pits
near
p Mount Vernon.) London

37: ROBERT MACKAY TO ELIZA ANNE MACKAY

Savannah 22nd July 1807—

I sit down at length in good spirits to tell My dearest Eliza that I have taken my passage for Liverpool in the

Georgia, the Captain says he will sail on the first of August, but this being only the day talked of, I suppose we may allow him a few more to get ready in, I shall hurry him as much as possible you may be assured & I still hope that I shall see you in a fortnight or three weeks after you get this letter—On Sunday the 19th your Mother, Miss Hunter & John accompanied by Delory embarked for Boston, they went at 8 in the morng. with as fine a breeze as they could wish for, & it has lasted ever since, so that I hope they will have a good passage, your Mother was rather better when she sailed, & I have no doubt but she will recruit fast when they reach a cooler Climate—As to John his health seemed quite restored, but I can in some measure account for this, for the last two months he has lived with us, & I may say entirely, for within that space, both before & since my illness, we have not dined out more than twice, nor had company once, so that we have lived quietly & regularly, taking enough to do us good & no more, riding out or walking every afternoon, the weather however has been confoundedly hot sometimes & keeps me from getting as much fat as I lost, so that I shall not appear before you in a pair of Meins pantaloons, which I have been wearing all the Spring, but a little good Roast Beef & cool Climate will soon remedy this evil—Your Brother William accompanies me in the Georgia to be placed at School for three years & he seems quite delighted with the thoughts—

The unfortunate affair of the Chesapeake I am very much afraid will lead to a War betwixt this Country & England, you cannot imagine with what violent resentment the people all along the Continent are agitated—

nothing is talked of but war, & the most extensive preparations are making for it—here we are quite a Garrison Town, the Volunteer Corps & Militia are paraded every day, & defaulters are posted up as "enemies to the Country, & their characters hereafter to be held infamous"—Should a war take place our prospects are all knocked in the head, & a most ruinous step it would be to this part of the Union, at all events we must be here if it does happen, & I think you may make up your mind to return here very soon after my arrival—I wish you had some of the fine Fruit we are enjoying here every day, the Peaches & Figs are very good & abundant, I breakfast on them constantly, & the Musk-Melons are this year very superior—however I daresay in turn you are wishing me some of your fine Strawberries, Cherries &c. &c.—Your Grandmother & the family are all quite well, they are going over to the Island this morng. I believe for the Summer—Williamson sticks close to the Cottage, however they have been to Town to see your Mother away—

I forgot in my former letters to tell you, that on my recovery from my fit of sickness Lady Houstoun[124] very politely called to see me, & beg'd that I would go & stay at White Bluff to recruit, & promised to take a great deal of care of me, her kind offer I of course declined as I had not time to spare, but I shall always remember it most gratefully—

You will suppose from my leaving Georgia that we have settled all our affairs & dissolved the Copartnership,[125] but it is not so, nothing is concluded upon, & there is such a diversity of opinion that I really don't know when the thing will be brought to a close, I see no likelihood of it before I go—Mein who has been all along determined to go to England with me has at length declined, it was impossible to get away earlier, & the Season is now too far advanced for him to be back in time to attend to the crops & the collections, which circumstanced as we are it is absolutely necessary he should do, & another thing—it would scarcely do at this time for him to leave the Country in its present agitated state, for should they find two of us in Great Britain at once, there is no telling but they might seize the property—

There have been some curious preaching concerns formed here since M[r] Kollock left us, a number of the Ladies of his flock formed a plan of praying & reading a Sermon in Church every wednesday, & subscribed their names to some paper, obliging themselves to hold forth in turn, it commenced with (I believe) M[rs]. Taylor, but the thing was so talked of & so laughed at, & such multitudes were determined to go & hear out of curiosity, that it went no farther, I was mortified beyond all description to hear that your Sister[126] was one of the Subscribers to this Bedlamite piece of extravagance—But as if madness was not to be confined to the female part of the flock, the Bell rang last wednesday & on the people assembling, who the Devil should appear in the pulpit but his Type old Tom Young[127]—He gave a long pray'r & having given out the Psalm left the pulpit, & his Nephew young Tom ascended it, & read one of Logans Sermons—M[r]. Holcombe[128] & M[r] Clay are both gone away & Tom Williams, of the house of Dennis & Williams, exhibits to crouded audiences every Sunday in the Babtist Church—There are two vessels daily expected from Liverpool, I sometimes flatter myself I may get a line by them, but I think it is to[o] late, you would scarcely calculate on finding me here on this day, & yet it would be an immense gratification to hear how you were a few weeks after the 25th April—I can only hope that all was well—Pray remember me affectionately to all about you & in the hope of soon seeing you & our darling Children I am My D^{r}. Eliza

ever faithfully Your *R: M*

Mrs Mackay
N° 7 High Row
Kensington Gravel-Pits
near
London—
p Cotton Planter—)

38: ROBERT MACKAY TO ELIZA ANNE MACKAY

Savannah 5th feb^{y}. 1810—

My dear Eliza

My last to you was from Charleston where I was detained untill the 28th. Ult^{o}. with a contrary wind, on that day I sailed & arrived here on the 30th (the anniversary of a day I recollected with the most heartfelt satisfaction)—M^{rs}. Gadsden[129] & two daughters came round with me & I found them very agreable, but their spirits consequently much depressed from the recent intelligence of Mrs Judge Jones's death,[130] which happen'd some day last week, & only three days after the confinement of Mrs Noble Jones (little Sally)[131] who has presented her friends with a fine bouncing Girl—I found our friends here all in the old way, Mein as well & as young as ever, though he says & *thinks* he was very ill last fall & saved his life with difficulty, but they all laugh at him & say that he was only frightened—Caig is grown quite fat & as funny as ever—Mitchel very ill at New York & never expected to recover—James Wallace[132] thinner than a lath—Petit still our neighbour & the same good creature, lost his Wife[133] in the Fall, but seems to have recovered his spirits—very proud of his boy William & truly grateful for the Sponsorship—I see no change in Nichols, & indeed almost everybody look very much as they did—Sally is soon to be confined & at present is very well—Mrs Scarbrough & Mrs. J. Hunter[134] similarly situated—I dined at Williamsons the other day & met the old man, Houstoun, Mein, Caig, Petit & the Hunters—had a pleasant day, & finished at the Whist Club—I have been at Coleraine & am much pleased with the new Mill which will be at work in a few weeks, it is an immense thing & I hope will succeed, dined yesterday at Caig's & had all the old set to meet me, & this morning being Sunday have been occupied for an hour shaking hands with the numerous complimenting visitors from the different plantations—Old Phillis so delighted to hear of you, that she almost danced, says she must stay here untill tuesday to hear all about you—Jemmy is quite well & says he is very anxious about his wife, wants much to see her—Kelso has just appeared with a Calibash of Eggs as a present, says he has a Son called Hero in compliment to my right hand man—& Lucy has just made her curtsey & very kind enquiries, with as fine a Child (her second) as I ever saw, Thompson is grown amazingly, they are all well & appear to be very happy, which is certainly grateful & pleasant—The boat is preparing & the day after tomorrow I push off for Florida, to look after things there, I don't know how we shall come on, but shall do the best we can—From Florida shall write you again, as I doubt not there will be opp^{s}. from thence—The streets of Sav^{h}: are completely crouded with Carriages, & most of them the neatest you can imagine, we far surpass Liverpool I assure you—Miss Gibbons it is said is about to give her hand to a Mr Trumbull of Connecticut, a little fellow who as far as I have seen of him, has not much to recommend him, I was rec^{d}. by the family with the usual civility, the old Lady quite glad to see me—they have M^{rs}. Cruger with them at present & a Miss Dayton from Jersey a great Belle & much admired—The widow Oliver is setting her Cap at *Old Massa*, but I don't think she will succeed, he has not forgot his last love, for he sighs when she's mentioned, & Caig makes a rule of giving her as a Bumper toast, whenever Mein is present—God Bless you all prays yrs ever

R M

M^{rs}. Williamson has a Son[135] & is doing very well—

Mrs R. Mackay
Stanhope Street
p Edward) Liverpool

39: ROBERT MACKAY TO ELIZA ANNE MACKAY

Savannah 2nd April 1810.

I have the pleasure to address you My dear Eliza once more from this place, where I assure you I am very happy to find myself, after having been an Exile for eight weeks in that Country of Robbers, Sandflies & Musquitoes—I assure you Sav^{h}: has the appearance of something very superior when compared with Amelia Island—The improvements going on are very great, Bolton[186] is beautifying the Bay with ranges of most elegant & extensive warehouses—Commerce row is pulled down & a superb edifice with a Steeple as high almost as the Exchange has suddenly been rear'd in its place—every square in town is now enclosed with light cedar posts painted white & a chain along their tops, trees planted within, & two paved footpaths across., the remainder of the ground they are spreading Bermuda grass over,[187] & upon the whole the Town looks quite another thing & very enchanting—I arrived here the eveng. of the 30th: & met with the usual hearty welcome from our friends, who are all quite well, I have been twice at Williamson's, Sally looks very tolerably, the Boy I have not yet seen, but he is said to be a fine fellow—Williamson exerted himself so much as to call upon me yesterday morning to invite me to a seat in his pew to hear Mr. Kollock, (it being Sunday), I went of course, & though the Church was so crouded that we were almost suffocated, & the whole almost of this croud, were loud in their praises of this (as they still call him) incomparable Preacher—I was by no means pleased—a part of his doctrine I thought detestable, & he has acquired since last I heard him a harsh monotonous tone of delivering that is very disagreable—he has now—not the least alteration of note when reading a Psalm, Chapter in the Bible—or repeating his pray'r or Sermon—it seems all a heavy harsh song—but his language is still very superior

& the people absolutely adore him[138]—I called after Church to see the two married couples at Gibbons's[139]—they all appeared very happy, young M[rs]. Gibbons (Miss Dayton that was) is truly an elegant woman, & what the devil could induce her to marry such a Savage, is to all the world a thing incomprehensible—At Scarbrough's I saw Miss Lucy who has turned out a very charming Girl, M[rs]. S. is invisible expecting to be confined every moment, I sent her up word to make haste, as I had betted a suit of clothes upon another boy before next Sunday[140]—I dined at Caigs where we got one bottle of Gibbons's P P wine, as a *bonne bouche*, & Eben[r] Jackson[141] called in to help us drink it—I saw the Miss Bourkes at Williamson's but missed Betsy Hunter, she was in Town but had gone to dine with her Brother—Nancy W. is at Oatlands, with the Miss H[s] & has got the whooping cough—I stopt at Cumberland a day & was storm bound two days at Spaldings—he was from home, but M[rs]. S.[142] really did the honours of the house to admiration, Sands[143] & Whitney were with me, we rode the length of the Island & met the boat at Montalets, where I was delighted with the situation & a most elegant Garden[144]—Spalding is building an immense large house on the South end of Sapelo, 74 by 50 feet—with three large Bow windows[145]—I forgot to mention that I found your letter of the 19th. Dec[r]. here on my arrival, this is the one I was afraid was lost—though old I was very much delighted & highly thankful for it—I expected to have found something more about John's matrimonial scheme, but you have never hinted at it in any way but once & then only to awaken curiosity—I suppose we shall know all about it by & bye—Mein & the Widow Oliver are the talk all over town at present, *they have had* her wedding clothes ready for a fortnight past & kept *her waiting my arrival* to witness the ceremony—All that he says on the subject is "let the d—d fools talk on—if they would mind their own affairs, they would think less of his"—whether there is anything in it, I cannot say certainly—but I believe there is—she looks very handsome, considerably improved in appearance by her northern trip—G. Baillie is getting better & expects to come on next month, M^rs^. B. is also better—Remember me to all around you—God bless you my darling wife & Children prays your ever affectionate

R M

Scarbrough has made an elaborate apology that Madames situation has prevented his offering me a bed in his house, which but for *that* he expected I was certainly to occupy —this is kind enough, but might have been spared, for I could scarcely be expected to stay anywhere else than where I am—So disjointed is correspondence at present that Mr Hamilton still thinks his wife alive, & Mr Gibson Who is now here asserts most positively that Moffat is not married—

Mrs Mackay
Care of Mess^s^. Alex^r^. Mein & Co
Mercht^s^
Liverpool

40: ROBERT MACKAY TO ELIZA ANNE MACKAY

Savannah 15th April 1810—

Yesterday brought me my dear Eliza's letter of the 30th Jan^y^:—I am happy to know you are all well & pleased that you had heard of my arrival—I wrote you a fortnight ago to say I had returned from the South^{d}. & met with things here pretty much as I left them—the Non-intercourse act still in existence & I am afraid not likely to be immediately removed, but all depends upon acco^{ts} from Europe, upon the movements there will our Government be influenced—I have had some correspondence with Mr C. Simpson[146] on the subject of the settlement he made last year with M. M. & Co, which Mr Davison refused to confirm, I don't know how the thing will end, but I suspect there will yet be some trouble, I am in hopes he will bring an action as I wish the matter settled by a legal descision, they cannot undo what they have done, & the sooner this is understood the better—No day is yet fixed I believe for making Mein & the widow *one*, but it is likely to take place either at the North^{d}. this Summer or immediately on their return, I am however not yet fully acquainted with the plans, it is the only time Mein has ever restrained himself from telling me everything, I don't know the cause of his being so silent on this occasion, but there is no doubt (I think) that they are to be married—this you must consider altogether as *secret information*, which though I have no authority to communicate, my "*discreetness*" cannot prevent my telling you—I am sorry *yours* obliges you to shew that you have not the same confidence in me—a circumstance I never untill now doubted—but if "the News you are to surprise me with when you next write" is your Brothers marriage with Miss Margaret, I can only (after the way you express yourself) be surprised at the fact—and not at the *news*—for on my arrival here from the South^{d}. I found such a report in current circulation, but which the veil of mystery you have thrown over your communication to me in two letters, (& your entire silence on the subject in several intermediate ones) in my mind flatly contradicts—From your manner of writing I do not think she is the happy fair one—but if the report here is true, I confess you have succeeded in your intention of making me think otherwise, & if there is gratification in it yours must be complete, however relying upon your letters I shall never be convinced it is her, untill the fact is confirmed—If in the end it proves so, & that you were afraid to trust me with what is on every tongue here, I shall certainly be much mortified at your want of confidence in me, & in an event which will give me so much pleasure, for surely I need not tell you at this day that the interest I feel in Johns happiness does not spring from idle curiosity, but goes hand in hand with my own—I could be angry with you that others sho[d] know what you are afraid to trust me with, & I wish you had said nothing about it, untill your fears were at an end, by the Newspapers announcing the event to the world at large[147]—

The Georgia is now nearly loaded & might sail this day week if the ports were open, it would however be much too soon for me to go in her, the time I would have used in arranging my matters here has been taken up at the South[d]: & I hope will be attended with beneficial consequences to your Brothers affairs, I neither spared my time or my exertions for his interest there, his lumber contract will I think do well, & his other matters in Florida are so much narrowed that he can soon put a finishing hand to them himself next winter, I wish he was entirely clear of that Province, Delany is perfectly honest, but very indolent, & the sooner everything is settled there, the better, to prevent future impositions—Williamson & I are I think on more intimate terms than we ever were, we went to Oatlands together last wednesday & dined with the Hunters, the Miss Bourkes & Aunt Betsy were also there—Nancy has been over with them for some time, with the whooping cough, but is now recovering—we spent a very pleasant day, it is certainly a charming situation & capable of being made a beautiful place—

As soon as I have come to some understanding with Mr Simpson I shall determine what our future plans are to be, at present I think it likely we shall fix here, I like Sav^h: very well & hope it will not be displeasing to you, the health & education of the Children is the only objection, but we must do the best we can—Should any thing like a rupture betwixt the two Countries take place I have requested John to take charge of you & bring you out, either to N. York or here according to the Season, in which case I would meet you there, but even if peace is preserved, unless I come to some settlem^t with Simpson & Davison it is doubtful whether I can return to England this Summer, I may probably pass it among the Mountains, but I shall of course keep you regularly informed of all that occurs, for there is nothing that *I know that I should like you to be a moment ignorant of*, but it must necessarily be some time before any arrangement can take place as a letter this morning from Mr Simpson says it will probably be six weeks before he can come round here from Charleston—Maj^r. Butler[148] is at present here & looks much broke, he dined with us a few days ago, he has declined selling his property & is about purchasing more Negroes—Mr Scott is talking of going in the Georgia, but he does not always ride when he puts his boots on—You will be surprised when I tell you that though I see Tom Young every day he has never said that he has a Knife & fork in his house—Pray tell Hannah that I saw her Mother at Oatlands, she is well & made many kind enquiries—I send this by the packet & shall write you by every other conveyance that offers—I have not wrote John since I came up from the So: ward but shall soon, though there is nothing of consequence to communicate respecting his affairs, I hope long before this he is happily married, & that it will soon be no secret *even to me*—I have to beg my affectionate remembrance to all around you, M[rs]. M[c]Queen among the number, let her be who she will, I shall look upon her as a Sister—Kiss the Children for me & be assured my darling Girl that although your *discreetness* has punished me with suspence, I am ever most unalterably and faithfully your

R M.

M[rs] Mackay
Care of Mess[rs] Alex[r]. Mein & C[o].
Liverpool
p British Packet } England—
Via New York— }

41: ROBERT MACKAY TO ELIZA ANNE MACKAY

[*Savannah, May—, 1810.*]

Your last letter my dear Eliza is dated the 30th Jan[y]. so that I am without any acco[t]. of you for three months, I have no doubt but you have wrote me often since, & fear your letters have miscarried, M[r] Davison however mentions your being well as late as the 10th Feb^{y}:, I look anxiously every mail in the hope of arrivals at the North[d] or by way of Amelia, there have been several at the latter place but I had letters from nobody—The weather is most delightful as yet, & the alterations in the squares so great an improvement, that Savannah is quite fascinating; I am rather better pleased with Parson Kollock than when I last wrote, but I do not, by any means like him so well as when I first knew him, there is something stiff & austere in his manner that does not comport with my idea of what a Man of God ought to be—instead of tempting one to be religious, it looks as if he would force or frighten one into it—I have come to no resolution as yet, as to the time of my departure from here, or what my future plans are to be, Mr Simpson is not come round, but is expected soon, when I shall immediately decide whether I can go to England this Summer or not, we expect tomorrows post is to bring the news that our trade is again open, in which case Capt. Stookes will go to sea directly for Liverpool, & I prepare this letter for him to carry to you—I dined yesterday at Scarbrough's & saw Madame & the little Girl upstairs—a very fine stout child, Charlotte is the most perfect little beauty I ever saw, & I cannot imagine how they manage to keep her always in full dress, & her hair exactly as if she was from under the hairdressers hands, she is grown very tall & her shape is elegance itself—Elizabeth Taylor[149] is taller & bigger than our Maryanne & though a little spoilt, (which the Mother confesses,) is a fine Girl, grows pretty, & plays astonishingly well on the Piano—Mr Robt: Scott goes in the Mary on business, he will tell you all that's going on here, Stookes has a half Tierce of best Rice for you—The new machine at Coleraine is to be at work next week, & the

Town report is that Mein is to marry the widow on that day—but I don't think it will happen before the Fall, I understand one day has actually been appointed & the preparations were making, but something put a stop to it, & if I mistake not it was the report of John's marriage with Miss M. Cowper, which was then in common circulation, & furnished a hope that this might bring Miss C. once more to Georgia—however as I am not in the Liverpool secrets I could of course say nothing—William M^c^Lean staid a week with us, & went up much improved in his appearance, & he said he felt much better, Mr Pell has been at Augusta, merely to see the place, he is returned much pleased with it, but not with the journey, he carried Mary Anne's rug to her Aunt Course, who is quite delighted with the present—The non-intercourse[150] has kept everything very dull, there is little doing, but people's spirits seem to be good, I lost all the dancing, there has been none since I came up from Florida & the Season is now over, M^rs^. Oliver gave two grand routs the week before last, almost the whole Town attended at one or the other, they were considered as farewell parties & her wedding has been daily expected since—I was asked to the first, but was engaged to meet some strangers at a late dinner at Carruthers's[151] & could not go—Petit is constant in his attentions, he has got a most beautiful assortment of Geraniums, Heliotropes &^ca^. &^ca^., keeping in high order for Mrs Mackay—the moment you arrive they are to be sent over to you, he has also some remarkably fine Grape vines which produce most abundantly, these are to be transplanted in an harbour wherever you may direct—He is also preparing what he calls some of his delicious Cordial, Vinegar & Sauces all for you—I have not seen the Miss Hunters for some time,

Nancy's cough is better, & they are all coming to Town tomorrow—

We have just got the dreadful acco^{t}. of the fall of the Old Church in Liverpool,[152] most aweful & distressing indeed, I will not suffer myself to think that any of you are involved in it, it is not at all likely, that you would be there, but to think for a moment that curiosity or any other cause might by accident have carried you there on the fatal day —surely I cannot be so unfortunate, but it will increase my anxiety to hear of you—

So far I wrote yesterday—this mornings post brought me yours of the 8th Feby. in which I find you have broken your promise of "surprising me in your next, with something your discretion would not admit of your communication in your last"—May 9th I had got to the end of the last sentence, when I was interrupted, & the intercourse being still continued, another week has elapsed, during which Mr Simpson has come round, but as yet we have come to no conclusion about things—M^{r} & M^{rs}. Belcher[153] are here on a visit from Boston, he has recovered his health & spirits entirely, they went up to Coleraine yesterday with us & dined, & the Miss Hunters accompanied us, we pressed Williamson & Wife very much to be of the party but without avail—Robert Mitchell who arrived on Sunday & very much recruited in his health went also with us, the rest of the party was, Simpson, Nichols, Petit, & M^{r}. Gibson,[154] we had a very pleasant day, & did not keep it up all night as the last lady party did there, (We were in Town by 7 O'Clock,) & had one of Juno's usual good dinners—Mitchel's appearance is not at all alter'd by the Stroke of the Palsy he had, but he has some little difficulty of pronunciation & though not very lame, cannot handle his right leg or arm very nimbly, he consequently does not walk much, he is very cheerful & seem'd to enjoy himself as much as he ever did, though he limited himself to three glasses of Wine—One of his eyes feels very weak though it does not appear so, but it obliges him to wear Green spectacles—There have been English letters down to the 13*th* March in Town for three weeks, but I have nothing from anybody, I am quite in despair at not hearing from you—I cannot think what is the matter with Mein, surely you must have rec*d* some of the many letters I wrote you all from Amelia, & you would know from them that I would be here—Remember me affectionately to all around you, kiss the Children & believe me my dear Eliza

ever faithfully yours *R M*—

12th: May—J. G. Forbes is arrived at New-York after a short passage, but I have not a scrape of a pen from anybody by him—truly strange—dates are to 24*th* March—everybody in town has letters but me—14*th* The Collector this day has rec*d* permission to clear Ships for where they please—thank God—& this days mail has brought me your & John's letters confirming the report we have had these Six weeks in circulation, of his happy union with Miss Margaret Cowper—May Every good attend them—Bob Scott carries you a small package of Tea from Yrs Ever

R M

M*rs* Mackay
Care of Mess*rs* Alex*r*: Mein & C*o*.
Merchants
p Mary
Capt. Stookes } Liverpool—

42: ROBERT MACKAY TO ELIZA ANNE MACKAY

Savannah 18th May 1810

The winds have detained the Georgia since I closed my dispatches by her, untill this day, I think there is every prospect of her getting out at daylight tomorrow, her detention affords Mr Pell an oppy. of going direct instead of making his intended passage to New York—The Essex frigate came here the day before yesterday (that is to Tybee) & Capt. Smith[155] one of the finest fellows in the world, who I became well acquainted with at Norfolk has been in Town, he & his Officers dined with us yesterday & left us this morning, they were strangers here & have occupied my time very much for the last two days—but extraordinary to tell—Capt. Smith never drank in his life anything but Water—though a South Carolinian born, & been regularly brought up a Sailor—So that it is not his being a *Bon Vivant* that has attached me to him—I have nothing to add since my last by both the Mary & Georgia, but that I am likely to close things in an amicable way with Mr Simpson (though not yet arranged)—should this event take place I shall embark from this in the first good oppy. direct for Liverpool, or go on to Boston & take my passage from thence—however I would rather go from here, as it is very probable we shall return here in the fall altogether—

Say to John that I have been doing all in my power to fix a contract with Bacon & Malone[156] to supply timber to load the vessels Logan & Co. may send out—Bacon is gone up the Country to make the arrangement, I could not get it under 6½ Dols.—the present price, & in great demand, is 8 Dols—I hope Bacon may succeed in this—for really I have not time to attend to establishing a new settlement to cut with the hands now at St. Marys, & as to keeping them at St. Marys, it is quite out of the question, for Pickitt will eat the whole up—John I know is very sanguine as to this Lumber business, & I daresay if he was fairly fixed at it in Georgia & the people contented, it might turn out tolerably well, but in the way it has been necessarily conducted in Florida, it will be a losing business—& this from no want of attention on my part, for solemnly, my time has been devoted entirely to his business since the first of february last—If Bacon succeeds I shall order Mr Roberts to come up here & attend to the thing entirely & the Negroes will be put on the plantation, the only difficulty is that money must be paid down Raft by Raft as the lumber comes to the Wharf, & during the Summer it will be difficult to raise Cash for Bills or in any other way—Pickitt is as a great a rascal as ever drew the breath of life & how John did not find him out before is to me surprising—He was employed before I went to the South^d^. & matters had progressed so far that there was no turning him away,

It is easier to sit in the "Whirlwind & direct the Storm" than to live in Sav^h^. & direct a Lumber establishment in Florida—

By M^r^. Pell I send you the last Newspaper & with best remembrance to all around you I remain ever My dear Eliza faithfully & affectionately yrs

R Mackay

Mrs Robert Mackay
N°. 5 Stanhope Street
p favour of Owen Pell Esq } Liverpool

43: ROBERT MACKAY TO ELIZA ANNE MACKAY

Savannah 26th May 1810—

My dear Eliza

There was an arrival last week from Liverpool at Amelia Isl[d]: with acco[ts] to the 7th April, everybody has Letters but Mein & I, which is very neglectful in Alex[r]. Mein, he has given over writing altogether I believe, for I have nothing later from him than the 5th Feb[y]: which is truly strange—You have been a most excellent correspondent, & I am sure I should have heard from you by this last opp[y]. if you had known of it—I still however promise myself the happiness of hearing from you once more before I leave this, which must now be soon, I know of no good opp[y]. from here, unless some more vessels arrive, the port is quite empty & I fear I shall be obliged to go Northwardly to get a passage —M[r] Simpson is on the wing for Charleston & talks of going to New York to take his passage in the packet, should he do this it is not unlikely I may accompany him, but I will endeavour to persuade him to go as far as Boston which shortens the passage a little, & will give me an opp[y] of visiting Newport which I wish very much to do—

I have made up my mind to return here in the Fall, by doing so I shall be able to have all our affairs here closed in some way or other & when that is done, we will decide finally on some place of permanent residence, for there is no pleasure in crossing the Atlantic twice a year & untill all my matters are settled here I must be going backward & forwards, & I really cannot again consent to be so long separated from you, therefore we will all return here together in the month of October or Novem[r]. & stay with each other untill matters are so plan'd as to allow us to fix on some place that is to be a home—The Georgia sailed on the 22nd & the Mary a few days before, Bob Scott & Mr Pell will tell you all the news, but in fact there is nothing going on—Dr Richardson has been staying with us for some days, his family are in Newport where they spent the winter, & he is just going on to join them, talks of selling off his plantation & Negroes & becoming Yanckie farmer

As soon as Mr Simpson is gone to Charleston I shall have but little to attend to but the arrangement for the Lumber contract, which I must see in a train of being completed before I go—in case I have not time to write him by this oppy. say that Bacon has returned from up the Country, but has not been quite successful in engaging as much lumber as we want, 200,000 feet we can get for the first ships that come, & if the demand for Timber does not increase we may get enough to supply all the vessels that come—I have wrote John by the Mary & Georgia & New Good Intent all which I hope he will receive that he may be convinced Williamson & I have done all that lies in our power for him, & had the St. Marys establishment been under an honest man, instead of Pickit all would have gone on well—I staid there, neglecting my own affairs as long as I could, & had I remained altogether perhaps might have succeeded—but if you can form an idea of what the Country up the St. Marys river is, you would not be surprised when I tell you, that I would not have staid there another Month for the fee simple of the whole province—Up the River is low swamp & betwixt St. Marys *town* & Pickits Camp, there is but one landing place—the rest of the Bank is always under water, & consequently uncleared—

I think if you would join the wedding folks when they return from London in a little expedition to the lakes of Cumberland, it would be a gratifying thing to all of you, you might manage to take Maryanne with you, & Hannah would take care of the other children while you were away, which would not exceed a few days—It may not be in your power for some time again to see the Lakes, & this will be the best opp^y.—you can finish the trip before I arrive, for it will not be in my power to accompany you, as it is likely I shall be obliged to go to London, & must necessarily have a good deal to attend to in Liverpool, preparatory to my return here—

By this ship the Benjamin, there are several passengers but I believe none that you know much of—the Widow Wilson, Mr Bridge, Mr Ross, Mr Manson, & Doct^r. [letter torn], (formerly Doct^r. Irvines partner) but now turned merchant—I wrote you by the New Good Intent & I believe there will be some other opp^s. besides this in the course of the week—Mrs James Johnston has another Son, but though a stout hearty child at first has been taken sick & now lies at deaths door[157]—

The Town is extremely healthy, I know of nobody at all unwell—Judge Jones is sailed in the Gossypium for [letter torn] from whence it is likely he will make you a visit, I have given him your address—Kollocks children[158] are gone to Dungeness with Mrs Miller to spend the Summer—

My best remembrance to all the good folks about you —kiss the Children & be assured that I always am My dear Eliza

Yours faithfully & affectionately

R M

44: ROBERT MACKAY TO ELIZA ANNE MACKAY

Savannah 27th May 1810—

I cannot let an oppy. escape without dropping a line to you My dear Eliza, my last were by the Mary, Georgia, New Good Intent & Benjamin, all within a short time, therefore I can have little new or interesting subject for a letter—However you will be pleased to hear I am well, the season is the most delightful I ever experienced in Georgia, not a degree warmer than you have it I am convinced—Mr Simpson is just leaving us for Charleston, & after a great deal of hard work for three weeks, I believe we have now got things in a train satisfactory to all parties so we remain friends & may either do business again together or not as we feel disposed—I shall now as soon as I see a prospect of getting Johns Lumber contract complied with, take my departure either direct for Liverpool or from the Northd. as opps. may offer, & it is not unlikely that Simpson & I may go together in the packet, I wish to be with you as soon as possible, my mind is now more at ease, & the earlier I am with you, the sooner our plans will be fixed for returning here which my mind is made up to, & I doubt not when we talk the thing over together, you will be satisfied is right—I think however it will be as well to say nothing of it for the present—We are still anxiously expecting the John Adams frigate with the arrangements said to have been made betwixt the English Govt. & Mr Pinckney—The report of the day is that our cabinet at Washington is at Loggerheads, the Smith party having nearly ruined the Country is going out, Mr Madison is at length convinced that they are very unfit men for their station—it is supposed Gallatin will run in as Secretary of State, who is certainly the cleverest man the party has, & seems to have studied & known the interests of the Country better than some of the Natives—This goes by the Ticonick a dull sailer & will probably be a long time reaching you—though the "race is not always to the swift"—Remembrance to all around you & am ever My dear Eliza

faithfully & affectionately

Robt: Mackay

Mr Ogilvie has sold out his whole possessions in Carolina for 8,000 £ & goes to England bag & baggage immediately —M^rs. Moodie is also going shortly—pray don't let her in at Stanhope St^t.

Mrs Mackay
Care of Mess^s. A: Mein & Co.
Merchants
p Ticonick) Liverpool

45: ROBERT MACKAY TO ELIZA ANNE MACKAY

Savannah 28th May 1810.

This mornings mail brought my dear Eliza's letter of 3rd April p packet, which I assure you I thank you for very sincerely, for I have no pleasure without hearing often from you—You have been really an attentive correspondent, & had you not been so I must have been unhappy, for Mr Mein has been for the last three months very neglectful, his last to me is of the 21st: March when other people have had letters for a week past of the 7th April—

I hope John has arranged with Sir James Wright for the payment of his debt to M M & Co. I depend upon that fund to settle all our matters in Liverpool before we leave it, which I have already informed you we shall probably do in the fall—

I have this moment parted from Mr Bacon, pray tell your Brother that he has engaged all the Timber he could for me on the River, deliverable here as fast as possible for 6½ Dols—, but the people being busy with their crops I can't expect more than one or two ship loads immediately —but he thinks we may calculate upon enough during the Fall to make up the contract, but I am afraid they will raise the price upon us—I have advised Mr Roberts to break up at St. Marys & send the negroes home, Picket steals everything—out of every hundred bushels corn sent to the camp, this rascal steals & sells about half, & from the small quantity of Timber cut, (which I have written Mr Roberts to explain to me) I suspect he must have employed the negroes to cut in some other spot for himself—I have just paid a Bill of Mr Roberts' for 400 Dols. which he was obliged to have to buy timber to fill up the George—Mr. Calder came up last eveng. from St. Mary's, he went up to the camp with Mr Roberts, he says Picket will do nothing—So much for employing this Villain—but he is a good democrat, & I suppose thinks it a crime to comply with any contract for the use of the British navy—Mr Simpson went yesterday morning to Charleston, he & I have agreed to ship ourselves on board the first good opp^{y}. from there or here that offers in the course of the month, if no vessel pleases us, we go on to New York for the packet—which on acco^{t}. of the expence I don't much like—Calder has brought me up a fine large Turtle—only a week from Providence—we intend cutting his throat the day after tomorrow & will drink all your healths after we have eat him—

We have nothing new, but some hope that Mr Madison is about to turn the Smith's out of Office—which will be doing a good thing—it is supposed that Mr Gallatin will then be Sec^{y}. of State, which will be doing another good thing, for though a foreigner he knows better what is good for us & I believe has it more at heart than some of the Natives—

God bless you, the dear Children & all around you prays My dear Eliza

Yr. ever faithful & affectionate

R M

Within a few days I have wrote you by the Mary
Georgia
New Good Intent
Benjamin
Ticonick &
now by the
Rebecca—

Mrs Robert Mackay
Care Mess^{s}. Alex^{r}. Mein & Co.
Merchants
p Rebecca) Liverpool

46: ROBERT MACKAY TO ELIZA ANNE MACKAY

Savannah 4th June 1810—

My dear Eliza

I have not yet got a good oppy. to go by, but am very anxious to be away—not from any fear of sickness, for no place can be more healthy, & the weather has scarcely been one day unpleasantly warm, but finding it necessary that we should return in the fall, the sooner I am off from here the better—Simpson writes me of a ship in Charleston that will soon be ready, but she goes to London & that is rather out of my way, the Mary Jane is here but sails on Sunday next, which I fear is rather soon, as Mein says he must go to Charleston tomorrow, & if he does I am doubtful of getting away on Sunday—

I am just going to dress for a dinner at Mr. Wallace's where all the old set will meet, the Turtle we had a few days ago was a very fine one, & Sophy did it great justice in the cooking—Mein begins to talk seriously of visiting England this Summer, & I hope he may do so, but I will not wait for him, if a good ship comes in the way, for you know he puts off setting out, always for the last moment—C: Simpson cannot get away from Charleston for five weeks to come—R: Mitchel really improves in health every day, indeed he seems to be very little affected now, but by a dizziness in the head occasionally—he sets out in about a fortnight for Ten[n]essee Springs, where he means to pass the Summer—We have had a most extraordinary report[159] here for a few days from St: Mary's of Mrs. Skipwiths making a runaway match with Ned Littlefield, her cousin, a lad of scarcely 22 years of age, I do not credit the thing myself—& really hope it is untrue—but there is no accounting for a woman's whims—Nat Greene[160] is here, & arrived from St. Mary's about the time the report did, but he knows nothing about it—however this is not extraordinary, as if there was any *secret* in the matter, they would scarcely let him know anything about it—The Mill has been tried & succeeds admirably, she is not yet in constant motion, but a very few days will now complete her—Mein feels not a little elated you may be assured—

Mossman Houstoun (now a Major)[161] is returned on leave of absence from New Orleans, he gives a most dreadful acco^t^. of things in that part of the Country—I have little to add everything is so dull—unless I repeat my anxiety to be with you as soon as possible—God bless you My dear Wife & Children prays your ever faithful &

affectionate *R M*

You may tell John that Williamson & I are going to the Island the day after tomorrow—I was at Caustons on Thursday last the Benny[162] looks well—

5*th* We had a most pleasant party yesterday at the Consuls & there are some head-achs this forenoon—M^r^. Tucker from Liverpool was with us—This is St. Mary's post day & there's no farther acco^t^. of M^rs^. S. so I am in hopes the report is false—

M*rs* Robert Mackay
N°. 5 Stanhope Street
p William) Liverpool

47: ROBERT MACKAY TO ELIZA ANNE MACKAY

Savannah 10th June 1810—

My dear Eliza

Since yours of 3rd April I have not heard from either you or Mr. Mein, & am afraid I shall have no more letters, as you would think I had left this, & I should now do so by the vessel which carries this, but she is loaded with Timber, & I do not think it a wholesome cargo at this season of the year, taken in wet, the heat of the vessel must create a great evaporation which can be neither agreable or healthy, I shall therefore go in the United States, a remarkably fine new Philadelphia copper'd ship, now loading here, just such another as the Georgia—I have engaged my passage, McCleran goes with me & Mein says he will also—I have written to C. Simpson & am hopeful he will be one of the party—Abner Woodruff[163] also goes, I am doubtful of Mein, but he is very anxious—We all dined at Coleraine yesterday & McCleran to oblige us set the Mill in motion—it is really a famous piece of mechanism & I have no doubt whatever will do well—Mr. Tucker (the cousin of Mr. McVicar) is here at present & stays with us, he was of course with us yesterday & was highly pleased with the Mill—Williamson & I passed last thursday with the Miss Hunters at the Island, we searched the whole forenoon for Lady W.'s marriage settlement which John wrote me to do, but could not find it, I am sorry for this as the sooner the matter is attended to the better—Whitehead is unwell, but not seriously so, we walked over all the fields & the Cotton looks better than any I have seen, it is remarkably fine, the day after I had occasion to go to five fathom hole,[164] & of course saw Turnbulls[165] crop which cannot at all be compared to that at Oatlands—The Benny however is not so well, the early drought injured it very much, & it is from frequent planting, very uneven & some of it sickly—Corn is placed where necessary so as to make the most of it—I have nothing new from the South^{d}. to inform John of, M^{r}. Roberts is breaking up the Camp, & I expect the people up soon, he will load one more ship there, by purchasing to assist in completing a cargo, Lumber is rising here very fast, & I am doubtful of getting much from Bacon Malone & Co. at 6½ Dols—We have had the most extraordinary Summer that ever was experienced in Georgia, the weather has been mild & pleasant, & I am sure not warmer than you have had it—I have scarcely slept without a Blanket yet, & only the night before last, Mein who had ordered his removed, was obliged to call up the servants after he had had his first nap to get it back again—Not a single muskitoe, but the Miss Hunters say they are very bad at the Island—July 11th You may tell John I have just rec^{d}. an answer to my letter to M^{r}. Gallatin, (which I wrote him about some time ago,) in reply to my question he says no British or French Ship whatever, with or without Commission can be admitted into our ports, if they are armed —Directed to your Brother I have sent by this opp^{y}. all the late papers, there is nothing whatever in them—but it is always a treat to look at them if only to see the names of one's acquaintances in the advertisements—If he is out of the way you will of course open the parcel—

I have a very affectionate letter from my Sister[166] thanking Mary Anne for her present (the Urn Rug), which she is very proud of & has shewn to the whole town of Augusta—

I don't know what I shall get here to carry to you—Petit is quite vexed that I should take my departure before his delicious cordials are made, his late stock being exhausted, but he says you may depend on a fine supply when you arrive, of a great many nice things—I have a few of Jones's hams which I believe are the only thing worth taking to you—Tom Young has at last done me the honour to invite me to his house—he called here a day or two ago at 12 O'Clock, & gave me a formal invitation to dine with him that day at 3—which invitation I thought proper to refuse, & I believe not very politely—

I have got by this mornings post a very friendly letter indeed from C. Simpson, he will not be able to come here in time for the United States which I am very sorry for, as I should have liked him for a fellow passenger—Remember me affectionately to all around you—kiss the children, & with the hope of soon seeing you I remain My dear Eliza

ever faithfully & affectionately
Your *Rob*[t]: *Mackay*

M[rs] Mackay
Care of Mess[rs] Alex.[r]. Mein & C[o].
p Mary Jane) Liverpool

48: ROBERT MACKAY TO ELIZA ANNE MACKAY

Savannah 23rd June 1810—

I shall so soon follow this letter that I have little to say to you My dear Eliza, indeed it is not unlikely I may be with you before it, the United States however is *long legged*, & is now detained with a head wind at 5 fathom hole, & can take no more cargo on board untill she gets below the Mud flats—Our stores are all ready, & wednesday next was the day appointed for sailing, but I fear we shall make out another week—my last to you was by the Mary Jane & I believe I then informed you that M^{r} McCleran & Abner Woodruff were my fellow passengers, since that a M^{r} & Mrs Laurence[167] & two squalling infants from Turtle river have joined the party—very much to our annoyance—

We had last Saturday a famous party at Coleraine, to witness the whole machinery of the Mill in motion at once, & for the first time complete, with a great deal of persuasion I got Williamson & Wife to go up—the Bourkes required less, M^{r} & Mrs Belcher were delighted, D^{r}. & M^{rs}. Cumming, M^{rs}. & Miss Oliver—all were pleased & happy —many other ladies were invited but it proved a very warm day & they declined going, the rest of the Gent^{n}. were, Harris, Col^{l}. Harden, [168] Petit, Nichols Carruthers, Small, Tucker, Owens &^{c}., Caig was in Charleston, the party would have been much larger but the heat of the wea^{r} prevented, it happen'd most unfortunately to be the only hot day we have had this Season, & it was I think without exception the hottest I ever experienced, however we enjoyed ourselves very much—the Negroes from all the places had holyday, three oxen were killed for them, & tables were spread under the Oaks where their dinner was served up to them, & a happier set never dined under Heavens Canopy—they did not mind the heat as much as us, for the Sun was scarcely down, before the Musick began & they danced the whole night,—we all got to Town before 10 O'Clock except Mein, who remained, but he came down in the morn^{g}. devoured by Muskitoes & sick enough of his lodgings—A squall the next day cooled the air again, & when I got up this morn^{g}. the thermometer was only 72°—We dined the day before yesterday with a large party at Williamson's, I think they give the best dinners in town, Sally ought to have a better house, a single room & so crouded does injustice to her good & neat management—The Hunters were not in Town or they would of course [have] been of the Mill party—this Fête Champêtre has been the whole subject of conversation for several days & made not a little noise I assure you—

Scarbrough's father[169] died a few days ago of an Apoplexy while the family was down here, an express was sent down when he was taken ill, Scarbrough, his Mother & Sister[170] set out immediately, but the scene was closed before they arrived—

Hannah's Mother is this instant come in to wish me a good passage, & with a great many messages—the old woman is quite well & anxious to see her daughter—M^{r} & M^{rs}. Belcher set out yesterday morning by land for Boston —a decent journey to begin at this season, they had better have gone there by way of Liverpool—Mr Thomas Savage was married on tuesday last to Miss Mary Wallace[171]—an excellent match in every way for the parties—these are the only changes here—

I don't know what to think of Mein & the Widow, he is now very anxious to go to England & will if he can possibly get away, but I don't think both M^c^Cleran & him can be spared this year—I have nothing from you later than the 3rd: April, nor from Mein since 21^t^. March, though there are accounts to 2nd. May—I have a letter from John of 6th April & I see by the post mark on one of his rec^d^. yesterday for Whitehead, that he was in London on the 16th. April—I wish some of you had wrote again, as I must now necessarily be a long time without knowing anything about you—that you are all well & that we may soon be together is the anxious & sincere wish of My dear Eliza yrs ever faithfully & affectionately

R M

Mrs Mackay
Care of Messrs Alex^r^. Mein & Co.
p Jenny— Liverpool

49: ROBERT MACKAY TO ELIZA ANNE MACKAY

Savannah 23rd June 1810.

I wrote you My dear Eliza just now, a long letter by the Jenny, which vessel sails with the present opp^y^. & as I was so near embarking in the United States, I thought it proper to drop another line to say that about the 1st. of the next month we shall be off, the Ship is at 5 fathom hole & draws so much water, that she must drop down below the mudflats before she can go on with her loading, & the wind being ahead I would not be at all surprised if we eat our 4th of July dinner here—however we shall not be much behind this letter as the United States looks as if she could sail—I am very anxious to be off, for we shall have little enough time to spare in England when I get there, I must go to London, which with other arrangements will soon run away with a few weeks—I am determined to be away some time in Septr., for my two last passages from England were about the middle of October & they were both bad—I am disappointed that none of you have written me after the beginning of april, we have accots. to 2nd. May & as I don't expect to see you much before the first week in August, it will be a long time—four months—without hearing a word of you—however I must submit, I only hope I may find you all well when I arrive—

Mrs Moodie is gone direct to London from Charleston, therefore I hope you will not be bother'd with her, Mr. Ogilvies family went in the same vessel with her—

I have no news to give you but the sudden death from apoplexy of old Mr Scarbrough, & the marriage of Mr. Thos: Savage with Mary Wallace—

The mail is just in & I find that Moffat is arrived a fortnight ago at New York, I have no letters, therefore am much afraid none of you have written by him, which will be a sad disappointment indeed, as I shall not see him before I sail, & there is not time for a return of post to hear anything of you from him—

A small Brig which began loading since I engaged my

passage in the United States, is now nearly ready, & I am sorry I did not know of her as she will be away first—however we shall be more comfortable in the Ship & she is a much finer vessel—I shall however write you by the Jane & by that time will be enabled to say pretty positively when we shall get away—

Whitehead still continues sick, but is getting better—The crop looks well, I was at Causton's last evening, the late rains have been useful but the Benny is certainly not equal to the Cotton—Say to John that Williamson & I have given Col^{l}. Johnston[172] a Bill for Sir G Houstouns[173] two Judgements, on A Mein & Co. which he must see paid, the Bill I have sent him on Logan Lenox & Co. for the George's cargo will nearly meet it, Bacon has just informed me he will have one cargo of Timber ready for me by the middle of next month—I have written Mr Roberts to send up a ship for it, & Williamson will attend to her, if he does not come up himself in time—I shall carry all Roberts' letters with me for John's satisfaction, they are breaking up on little St. Mary's & will only load one more ship there—Taylors & Favorita are sold for 5000 Dols. of which 3000$ is payable 1^{t}. Jan^{y}. & the balance 1^{t}. June following—

God Bless you all prays your ever faithful
& affectionate *R M*

Mrs Mackay
Care of Messrs Alex^{r}: Mein & Co.
Liverpool
p Euphemia)

50: ROBERT MACKAY TO ELIZA ANNE MACKAY

Savannah 28th June 1810—

My dear Eliza

Though I expect to be with you nearly as soon as this letter I could not let slip an oppy. of writing a line, the United States is nearly ready, but she is not yet past the Mudflats, & I fear very much she may be detained some days as she draws a great deal of water—Never was there a more pleasant Summer anywhere, cool & comfortable, at our end of Town no musquitoes, but Williamson & Scarbroughs families complain much of them—I wish you were here, we should certainly pass the Summer in Savannah & enjoy the fruit that is now coming abundantly to market—Enter old Phillis with a low curtsey, Two doz: Eggs & four Chickens as her contribution towards my stores—a message from old Bubah with four Poulets & Juno with three doz: Eggs & a Basket of Ginger Bread, a Jar of Sweetmeats from Kate McQueen,—very kind indeed—I think if the wind is fair on Sunday next we may get away—

Thank you for your letter by Moffat recd. since my last, & also one intended to come by Forbes which only appeared with that by Moffat—

By this oppy. I have sent A Mein a Bill of Five hundred pounds, which I have recd. as a paymt. at settlement of accots. with Geo: Scott, the Bill is on A. Mein & Co. & I hope will be honored, as it is intended to pay off the debts I owe in London to Grayhurst, Summers, Weston &c. &c. I am distressed to find John has been laid up in London, he ought to be very careful of exposing himself untill his constitution is strengthened—

I am pester'd to death with the memms. for half the Town—I wish I had told nobody that I was going away—

God bless you all prays your ever

faithful & affectionate *R M*

Mrs Mackay
Care of Messs. Alexr: Mein & Co.
Liverpool
p Jane)

51: ROBERT MACKAY TO ELIZA ANNE MACKAY

Savh. June 29th 1810

By this vessel to sail in ten days after me, I have already inclosed a Bill on A Mein & Co. for 500 £—since sealing that letter I have recd. the inclosed Bill for £92 . . Str which if I should fall into the hands of the French you will send to Mr Mein, it will be useful though a small Sum —If I am unlucky enough to go to France, you need not be uneasy, I will get away through Hottinguers influence or some other—Yrs ever

R M

Mrs Robert Mackay
at Messrs Alexr. Mein & Cos
Liverpool—
p Jane
Captn. Betts}

52: ROBERT MACKAY TO ELIZA ANNE MACKAY

Fort Jackson 8th July 1812

Your letter My dear Eliza is a most afflicting one indeed & what is to be done with the miserable object of distress I know not—it is most unhappy—

I assure you I was never on a more pleasant marooning party in my life[174]—it is a fact that we had not a Muskitoe all night, nor have I felt or seen one since we came down, although I was four hours on Centinel duty during the night, there was a fine breeze & it was really cool & pleasant—We have had our apartments scoured out, they are now clean & comfortable, the detachment consists of sober quiet men, the slightest breach of sobriety has not been committed since I have been here by anyone, which is more than can be said of the last detachment, who kept constantly drunk it appears & I daresay they will many get sick—I have no more night duty while we stay & I assure you everything is as comfortable as we could wish —Send to enquire how Mrs. Morris Miller is & let us know if you have an oppy., she was quite sick when Morris left Town & he has not heard since, consequently very uneasy—

It is likely Mr. Mein will be here tomorrow & I shall hope to hear from you, & shall be very happy if any better tidings of poor Miss Bourke—

Our pen Ink & Paper establishment is not very capital, & we have no Wafers—therefore receive this open with every affectionate wish for yourself & the Children of

My Dr. Eliza

Yours ever

Mrs Mackay— *R M*

IV. From England

IV. From England

England held many associations for Robert Mackay. From childhood he retained memories of holidays spent there; and in later life he was bound to that country by business ties. His ships plied on regular schedules between Savannah and Liverpool, and the imports of his firm were largely goods of British manufacture. As a natural consequence, Mackay's mental attitudes were shaped in an English pattern. This was true of most Savannah merchants of his day, for the colonial viewpoint, sustained by trade, prevailed in Savannah long after political independence had been won.

In 1804 the business of his firm took Robert Mackay to Liverpool. Disappointment in the town ("a most irregular dirty looking place," he called it) soon gave way to the enjoyment of English society. "The people appear so very hospitable free & easy," he wrote to his wife, "that I begin to feel myself very much at home. . . ." Mackay was dazzled by the wealth and importance of his new acquaintances. He boasted of meeting "all the Mercantile people of note," and of dining with a party of "African Merchants" whose traffic in slaves had raised Liverpool from a small port into one of the great commercial centers of the world.

From Liverpool, Mackay went on to London and then paid a visit to his wife's relatives, Sir James and Lady Wright, at Little Ealing in Middlesex. His hospitable reception by these exiled Loyalists confirmed his impressions of life in England. He met other persons of consequence, among them a former Lord Mayor of London, and wrote happily of the "pleasant society at Ealing, friendly & intimate as you can conceive." Under the spell of the English scene, his thoughts turned to the possibility of making his home in that "delightful Country." But this seemed impractical, as he found the cost of living prohibitive. Money "appears to be of no value whatever," he complained, "& for the mere necessary expenditures of the week I am astonished at the end of it, to see how many twenty shilling notes have been melted down."

All such obstacles, however, must have been overcome, for in 1806 the Mackay family moved to England. They lived first near London, at Kensington Gravel Pits, and later in Liverpool, where Robert Mackay had charge of the British interests of Mein, Mackay and Company. He returned to Savannah on several occasions; but for Eliza the pleasant English sojourn was not interrupted. The Wrights and Mrs. Hunter, her husband's aunt, introduced her to society; and in Liverpool she enjoyed the acquaintance of many American families brought to England by the cotton trade.

But looking after his affairs on both sides of the Atlantic proved a strain on Robert Mackay. After four years of "going backward & forwards," he decided to choose a permanent residence in either England or America. The merits of Liverpool and Savannah were weighed. In 1811 Mackay brought his family back to Georgia, early friendships having counted for more than the greater amenities of the English world.

53: ROBERT MACKAY TO ELIZA ANNE MACKAY

Liverpool 4th August 1804

I wrote my dear Eliza a long letter yesterday by way of Phil[a] which will inform her of my having arrived here on the 31[t]. July after a passage of only 22 days from Sav[h]., & having there given a journal of every transaction I shall add no more on the subject—On finding Miss Mein here I regretted exceedingly not having brought you all with me, or even Rob[t]. who would have been a most welcome visitor—Liverpool is a most irregular dirty looking place, but the air is cool & wholesome, & the situation a pleasant one—I sleep under a Blanket & Coverlid, & have such an appetite, that I cannot go to bed without a supper, which has hitherto been always composed of Lobsters & Beef Steaks, I have been introduced to all the Mercantile people of note & have got a fortnights dinners now on my mem[m], the day before yesterday we were at M[r]. Moss's,[1] brother to our friend in Nassau, where I met a party of Twenty to partake of a fine Bahama Turtle, these Gentlemen were African Merchants[2] & all of the first fortunes in the place, none of them having less than from One to Two hundred thousand pounds—Miss Moss is a pretty Girl & 30,000 £ which is hers, on her wedding' day, makes her very charming indeed—

The Theatre[3] is the handsomest I ever saw, I have been twice, & was highly amused with Fawcett[4] as Sir John Falstaff in the Merry Wives of Windsor, Lewis, Knight Emery & several of the best performers from London are of the present company & of course they meet with good encouragement—I went last night with Miss Mein to see "Laugh when you can", when Lewis[5] made us laugh whether we would or not, He is a most inimitable performer—The people appear so very hospitable free & easy, that I begin to feel myself very much at home & cannot consent to sail for two months to come, & if you were here I would not for twelve—This place has become quite of [*sic*: a?] fashionable resort, from the families of the Officers of the Militia & Army of Reserve, accompanying them to their stations—The Uniforms are rich & beautiful & no regulars in the world wear a more military appearance or do their exercise better, the Bands are excellent & add much to the gaiety of things—Prince William of Gloucester is Comm^r^. in Chief & resides about a mile from Town—This being the state of things, the West end of London does not shew a finer display of fashionables & I shall therefore compleat some of my memorandums here, which will be much less troublesome than in London & if the Eliza had been detained a few days longer, most of them should have gone by her, as it is, the Daphne must carry them—I have a kind invitation from M^r^. Davison to take a bed at his house in London, & for a change of air he has fitted up a room for me at his Retreat at Laytonstone, this is good of him, but I can be very little in London, Cheltenham is recommended so strongly I must be as much there as possible, I have therefore determined to set out for London the moment the Eliza has loosed her sails—This forenoon Anne was to have gone out with me to get you some neat Chip Hats, but it rains so hard we cannot leave the house, & tomorrow being Sunday I sadly fear you will be disappointed of receiving them as the Ship sails in the morning if the wind is fair—

Captn. Searle is here with M^rs^. Turnbulls family, he was yesterday married to Miss Deane, I wrote you of this match from Nassau last year if you recollect—I pay my respects to the Happy Couple tomorrow—Hero[6] is perfectly delighted with Liverpool & quite overjoyed to see Mein & his Sister, he stands in his English suit & cuts no small dash in his own eyes—

I have sent you a Milk pot which will be packed in a Box with some Chip hats &^c^. if the weather holds up to get them, & I see Miss Anne has already bought some little playthings for the Children—

I have a bridle also for your Brother & William has procured him an elegant Flageolet to charm the Nymphs at Peach Tree—I shall write him from London—Augt. 7th The Winds still ahead for the Eliza, enables me to say we go to London tomorrow—I have been living away at a fine rate & am absolutely getting so fat you would not know me—I dined yesterday out of Town with a M^r^. Leigh[7] who now occupies the superb seat of the late rich M^r^. Walker, I never saw so charming a Place in my Life—the house quite a palace & the Gardens, hot-houses, Green houses &^c^. &^c^. far surpassing description—The paintings of the best Class, & indeed everything of a piece, & to crown all, these fine things are owned by one of the most hospitable & agreable families I have known—I have a general invitation, to take a bed, eat fruit, use the horses &^c^., & I shall certainly avail myself of these kind offers when I return from Cheltenham—If I have time I shall say more to you, but at all events from London you will hear fully again—I hope soon for some of the many letters you promised to write me; to explain to you the anxiety I am under for all of you during the fall is impossible—

Remember me sincerely to the Cottage folks & with every kind & affectionate [wish] to yourself & the Children believe me ever My Dr Eliza

unchangeably yours
Robt: Mackay

Mrs Mackay
Care of Mess^{s}. Mein M & Co.
Savannah
Eliza) Georgia—

54: ROBERT MACKAY TO ELIZA ANNE MACKAY

Liverpool 8th. Augt. 1804

We are just about taking our departure for London & I sincerely hope the Eliza may go to Sea this morning—Miss Mein has packed a box for you & in it I have put a Bridle & a Whistle for your Brother which please deliver, & the Musick for Miss Bourke, except Rosina, which cannot be got here, I shall send it from London with the other things—In the mean time I hope our choice of hats will please you & the Children, & in the hope of soon hearing from you I remain My Dear Eliza

ever sincerely yours
R: Mackay

55: ROBERT MACKAY TO ELIZA ANNE MACKAY

Little Ealing 20th August 1804

My dear Eliza

I have been here these two days with Sir James & Lady W. who have been exceedingly kind, & anxious that I should make this entirely my home, I however return to Town tomorrow, as I have a good deal to do there & a great many friends to see—I arrived in London on the 12th accompanied by Miss Mein & Willm we had a most agreable trip indeed from Liverpool, staid a day at Woodstock & were highly gratified by a visit to Bleinheim which I think the finest sight in Gt. Britain, Miss Anne was quite enraptured—You would not know your Aunt W. she is amazingly fat & looks only half as old as when she left Georgia, Sir J. is however old & in ill health, but I have seen nothing in him but the greatest good humour & kind attention to everybody about him—There is to be a large party to dinner & among them some great folks, & as I hear the Clock strike 4 it is time I was going to dress, indeed I did not know it was so late when I sat down to fill up a page or two to you—Mr. Davison being in Devonshire with his family I have not yet seen him, but he writes me he will be in Town tomorrow, when I shall conclude upon my future plan & let you know when it will be convenient for me to pay you a visit in Georgia, for I really like this Country so much I have not yet given my departure from it a thought—I have been looking at a number of things for you, but prices are so high & funds so scarce, that I fear you will not see many of them—Lady W. is greatly disappointed at your Aunt Cowpers non-arrival in the Jamaica fleet, she fully expected her & has a charming house in view for their residence, next door, it is as neat a box as can be, with a snug little Garden to it &c. &c—

My Aunt Hunter & Eliza are well & make many enquiries after you & the Children, & have declared me a very unwelcome visitor without you & them, Mrs. De Cadignan is a widow at Paris, cannot come away in consequence of the War & Falconnet[8] & family are well in Naples—The weather has been very bad since I have been in the Island & in consequence have not been able yet to visit Vauxhall, but I have been at the Haymarket Astleys, Hughes's &c. &c.—Tom Young & I are fellow lodgers & sworn intimates & inseperable companions, Oliver is also in Town, a living spectacle of Gods mercy to Sinners—He is however to be married in November to a very pretty Girl at Berwick, & I am invited to his Wedding, but I hope to be nearer you at that time—Mein will be up as soon as the Daphne is gone & we then visit Cheltenham, where Sir J. & Lady W. talk of going at the same time—Anne has been out of Town at her Cousin Mrs. Millers, since we came up & the weather so bad that I have not since seen her—I am now in hourly & most anxious hopes of hearing from you, indeed I think so uninterruptedly of you that I must determine soon on some Ship to return by—My uneasiness about the Children during the excessive hot weather you are now obliged to experience makes me unhappy indeed, Heaven send you safe through it—Remem-

ber me most affectionately to John & all the Cottage family & with unalterable love believe me My d^{r} Eliza
Yrs ever *R. Mackay*

M^{rs}. R. Mackay
Care of Mess^{s}. Mein M & Co.
Savannah
Georgia—

56: ROBERT MACKAY TO ELIZA ANNE MACKAY

London 24th August 1804—

My dear Eliza

I am afraid the Daphne will leave Liverpool without a line from me, although I intended fully to have returned there in time to write a great deal by her, but here I have been since the 11th waiting impatiently to see Mr Davison who has been in Devonshire for M^{rs}. D's health, they arrived yesterday & I must of course be here some days longer to finish my conversations with him—In the mean time I have *amused* myself in completing the mem^{ms} of friends in Georgia & dining out with old acquaintances here, I have seen my Aunt Hunter & Cousin Eliza, who enjoy very good health & are as cheerful & charming as ever, I have staid three days at Little Ealing where I met with the most unbounded hospitality & politeness from Sir James & the greatest kindness & attention from Lady Wright—Their house is entirely new modelled & very neatly fitted up, on Sunday I accompanied your Aunt to

Church, a very handsome one with a good Organ, & a genteel Congregation & a tolerable sort of a Preacher—The day after, there was a party at Sir James's, among whom were Sir Charles & Lady Price (late Lord Mayor of London) with two of their Daughters, most charming Girls & I believe I should fairly have got possession of one of their Hearts if Lady W. had not most unfortunately let slip the secret of my having a Wife & three Children in Georgia—They have really a pleasant society at Ealing, friendly & intimate as you can conceive, I would make a great many sacrifices to live altogether (if we could possibly afford it) in this delightful Country—however that is out of the question at present, & all we can do is to visit it now & then, which we must certainly do as often as Our fortune will admit of, but you may rest assured it is not a moderate fortune, required to live with the comforts of Life, for money appears to be of no value whatever, & for the mere necessary expenditures of the week I am astonished at the end of it, to see how many twenty shilling notes have been melted down—I have dined with Mr Brandram who you may recollect was in Sav^h. with Lopes & Harrison, His father is a most respectable & worthy old man, it was quite a family party, which as occasion requires they can very much enlarge, as there are twelve Sons & daughters, & the youngest upwards of 12 years of age—We had however only the old folks & Six of the young ones, & I passed a most agreable day, I have promised to go next week to their Country Seat, & stay two or three days—Lopes is expected every day from Lisbon where he is arrived safe, it will give me a great deal of pleasure to see him, you know he is a great favorite—I wish you were here to see the Shakespeare Gallery before it is disposed of, however as all the Capital pictures with the building itself, form the grand prize, the Winner may be disposed to continue its exhibition—apropos—a plan just strikes me, I have bought some tickets, & should I prove the lucky man, which you know we must live in hopes of, we can live in London & shew the Gallery for a support, what kind of an attendant would you make in shewing the excellencies & beauties of the pictures to visitors?—Bob I think would point them out manfully, & Mary Anne & William would soon learn to lisp them from such good examples—

I find the prices of everything so extravagantly high that it will not be in my power to carry you half of what I intended, & as you must visit this Country before long, a favorable change may have taken place, & you will gratify your own taste in making choice of such articles as you may want, I went to order the Curtains for the Drawing room, & after pitching upon a tolerably neat pattern of Calico, & the mode of making them up, the price was Twenty pounds p Curtain, which I thought so exorbitant I immediately relinquished the idea of taking them—I shall however get the Calico & one Curtain, from which you must manage to make the others—The Chairs I shall also send you by the Tippoo Saib with Johns plate & some of the other matters, for I begin to think I cannot leave this before the 1^{t}. November—Oliver is here & very much improved indeed in both health & appearance—and I hope in temperance also—He has rented a house in Berwick, which he has furnished very neatly & in Novem^r^. he is to be married (he says) to the prettiest Girl in the Island—

27th I dined yesterday at Laytonstone with Mr Davison; Miss Mein, William, & A' Mein who arrived before dinner formed (with the family) our party—a sweet place as I ever saw—fine Gardens hothouses &^c^—I shall return to Liverpool the day after tomorrow with Mein & write you again from thence by the Daphne if I am in time for her—I send this by this eveng^s^. post to catch her & with a thousand good wishes & anxieties for the welfare of all of you, & a great many kisses to the Children, affectionate remembrance to all friends, & everything to yourself believe me My dear Eliza

ever Yours
R Mackay

57: ROBERT MACKAY TO ELIZA ANNE MACKAY

Liverpool 6th Septem^r^. 1804

Your very acceptable letter by the Hope my beloved Eliza, I rec^d^. the day before yesterday, the day after my return from London; M^r^. Miss Mein & myself came down together, & took little Ealing in our way, where we dined with Sir James & Lady W. on friday last, they were both well, & we in some measure prevailed upon Sir James to join us in our Cheltenham trip, he half promised to meet us there, & we are to write him as soon as a day is fixed to set out, Tom Young is also to be with us, so that we shall have quite a Georgia party—I wish you & the Children were with us, for your account of deaths & sickness has alarmed me much & increased if possible my anxiety to hear more frequently from you—Gracious God if any accident happens, I shall never forgive myself for leaving you behind, indeed it is the greatest folly I ever committed & I fear I shall ever lament it—I expected the Daphne would be gone before my arrival here, but she has been detained with a contrary wind, & I have consequently been busy writing to the house ever since I have been here—I have not yet decided when I can get away but I calculate on being with you in December at farthest, & shall be on the lookout soon for a good Charter & I then hope to meet with your Aunt & Cousins in Savannah—You astonish me at saying John had taken his passage for New-York, if he was determined to go to Sea, he had much better have come here, but I think his last visit to Carolina was so serviceable that he need not go farther than Sullivans Island[9] to regain his health—particularly with the attractions you mention to be there, I confess I like the idea of your going there better than to Florida & I sincerely hope you may accept your friend M[rs]. Hugers[10] kind offer—I shall take care of Doct[r]. Jones's mem[m]. & bring him the Glasses he wants—I am quite disappointed you had not rec[d]. yours from Charleston, I should like much to know if it pleases you, for there is an infinite variety here & I think I could make a good choice, I have chosen M[rs]. Williamsons plate, it is the most fashionable now made use of & from the same Man I have got M[r] Gibbons's Eperne, a new pattern just made for the Earl of Moira, on his marriage with the Countess of Loudoun, it is very neat & will cost about Ninety Guineas—These things all go out in the Tippoo Saib, Capt. Gribbin from London & I suppose she will sail in 8 or 10 days—Your Tea Urn & some other matters will go in the same Vessel, with your Brothers plate &^{c}., There is a parcel cont^{g}. a few Books I bought in London to read in the morn^{gs}., & among them some Woodstock Gloves for yourself, chosen by Miss Mein when we were at Blenheim, these I believe will go in a Box directed to Scott, who will deliver you the parcel, I have desired Grayhurst if I am not in London when the Tippoo S. is ready & my Letters are not in time by her to write you what he sends—I find I have delayed writing you to the last, & the Rufus sails also this morn^{g}. so that I fear she will go without a line from me—I was exceedingly gratified in receiving the Newspapers you sent me & shall expect another bundle by the James & W^{m}. which ship was to sail a week after The Hope, & one day later is of consequence to me now, I look out anxiously for her & hope for a continuance of good news from you, though I fear the worst—

I wish much to visit Scotland but shall not have time, Miss Jackson will never forgive me if I leave the Island without seeing her—

The Eliza must soon carry you the intelligence of my arrival she has been gone three weeks & she is a lucky ship, I trust she will have a good passage—Hero has behaved himself exceedingly well, he wants to be back in Savannah, though he does not dislike England, he has been at the Play, & highly amused of course—

Miss Mein writes you herself, therefore I say nothing of her, but that I believe the match I told you of will never take place—this is *entre nous*.

Hero has just come in, he says Daphne go to day tell *Misses* how d'ye & all the people—Accept from me everything affectionate for yourself & the Children & believe me my dear Eliza

unchangeably Yours

Rob: Mackay

I shall write John a line by the Rufus, which must serve you both—

58: ROBERT MACKAY TO ELIZA ANNE MACKAY

Liverpool 7th Septr. 1804

I wrote you yesterday My dear Eliza by the Daphne, she went to Sea with a fine breeze & I hope will have a good passage, the Rufus just sailing, I have only time to tell you that we have determined on going to Cheltenham on the 16th & I write Sir James this day to that effect, I hope he will be prevailed upon to put the plan in execution, it would be very serviceable to him, & I am sure very agreable to his Lady who must be tired of staying so much at home—You shall hear from me by the Tippoo Saib, in which Ship goes Mrs. Williamson's & your Brothers plate & some little matters for yourself, Grayhurst[11] will give you a particular accot. of the things sent if I am not in Town myself—The Pellisses I shall carry with me, none are worn by the fashionables but Black Cloth—I fear you wont like this, but better be out of the World than out of the fashion you know, I hope the Chairs will be ready to go by same Ship, I have not yet chose Curtains, but shall see about them by & bye—Miss Mein who has written you fully by Malcolm,[12] talks of going to Scotland in a day or two, so that we shall be deprived of the pleasure of her company in our trip to the Watering place—

It is unnecessary for me to bother you with my fears & alarms about the Children, I am all anxiety it is true & shall tremble at every letter I open from you after this—I shall never forgive myself for having left you behind, this is a lesson never to do so again—If John is gone to the North[d] I inclose a letter for him which please open in his absence—I flatter myself you are at Sullivans Island, & if you are I hope you will let Broadfoot know of it, that he may forward your Letters for you, he will be very attentive I am sure—

The capture of the Mary Guineaman is a great disappointment & a loss to us, I hope the Alexander may not share a similar fate—Remember me affectionately to all at the Cottage & believe me ever

My dear Eliza
Yr faithful
R Mackay

Mrs Mackay
Care Messs. Mein Mackay & Co.
Savannah
p Rufus—

59: ROBERT MACKAY TO ELIZA ANNE MACKAY

[*Liverpool, September 12, 1804.*]

Since writing the inclosed I have received My dear Eliza's most welcome Letter by the James & William dated 28th July, & a few lines from Mr. Scott of 31st. saying you were all well, the promised favors by the Neptune are now expected & as if my anxiety was to have no end, I am already wishing she was arrived, & that tomorrows post may bring me a weeks later news from my darling Wife & Children—Mr. Scotts letter is dated on the day I arrived here, how the time has slip'd away!, a passage across the Atlantic performed, & that a long one too, since I have been in England, it appears strange, but with all my anxious fears about you, with the variety & succession of new objects it seems like yesterday I came on shore—the trip to London is like a dream & altogether almost confirms it, that this delightful Island is in a state of enchantment—

I am distressed beyond measure at your account of Johns health, I wish he could have been prevailed upon to come here with me—a few weeks at Cheltenham would I am sure have restored him, the distance from England alarms us in Georgia, but it is only a Bugbear & shall never frighten me again, & as to expence you know people live here as they please, & on a trip of health there is no necessity for extravagance—

I am sorry the Glass is as you describe it, I shall send out some better with a few Dishes & other things that we are in want of—I have a long letter from Miss Jackson & a most friendly one indeed, quite disappointed at your not being with me, she insists positively on my going to Scotland, & has provided apartments in her own house for my reception, I shall certainly endeavour to go down if only for a day—

Mrs. Ws. plate is on board the Tippoo Saib & the Invoice forwarded to Mr. W. I hope it will please—Everything else for you & others yet procured I have directed Grayhurst to pack in one or two cases to your address, M[r] Scott will have it entered at the Customhouse & you will send the things to their different owners, whatever is omitted shall be forwarded or carried when I go myself—All Miss Bourkes mem[m]. is complete but the Coral & you will be surprized when I tell you that a string could not be got under three Gui[s]: & from that to Twelve G[s] but Lady Wright has sent (or will send) in lieu an imitation which is much more generally worn,—If the Chairs & Card Tables are ready, & I hope they are, they will also go—all these mem[a]. being compleated eases me of a monstrous burthen & Grayhursts assistance has as you may suppose been very thankfully accepted of—M[rs]. W[s]. Urn has plated mouldings as she directed, Yours has a Solid Silver Cock & is otherwise plain—If I can manage the Coffee pot shall bring it with me—Remember me very affectionately to all our friends & believe me as ever Yr faithful

R: Mackay

M[rs] R. Mackay—
Care of Mess[s]. Mein Mackay & C[o].
Savannah
Missis[s]ippi) Georgia—

60: ROBERT MACKAY TO ELIZA ANNE MACKAY

Liverpool 15[th] Sept[r]. 1804—

My letters from London inform me I am still in time to write My dear Eliza a line by The Tippoo Saib, I am without anything from you later than 28[th] July, though the

James & William did not sail untill 10th Aug^{t}, for which I think you deserve a little scolding, to have had 13 days later information from yourself, would have been so satisfactory at a time I feel so much anxiety for you & the Children—But I hope the Neptune will soon be in, & bring me the welcome intelligence, of your all being well on the 15th Aug^{t}., for I think she would not sail untill then —I have written you by the Missis[s]ippi but I believe she is still in the River, & if there is any conveyance on board a day or two hence I shall drop you another line—My friend Grayhurst will send you by this Vessel most of the things I had mem^{ms}. of, they will be all directed to you & you will deliver them, Your Tea Urn is plain & has a Solid Silver Cock, M^{rs} W^{s}. is plated with white mouldings, her plate is in a Box directed to M^{r}. W. & I hope will please her, it is the most fashionable now in use—her Cotton is not sold but the Sales I shall bring with me, Your Pelisse & hers I have not yet had made, but shall bring or send them before long—I yesterday made choice of some Glass for you to go by the Hope—7 Desert Dishes, 2 Butter Boats, Cream Jug, Jelly Glasses & some other little matters which I think will please you—I shall also have a Case of Crockery put up for Mein & you, & when the Curtains are procured I shall be done—Your Aunt Wright has not yet sent me Miss Margarets Letter, so I presume she intends giving it to me at Cheltenham, for which place I set out the day after tomorrow & hope to meet her there—The prices of Cotton here still continue low & the sale very dull, we shall lose a very considerable sum of money by our Shipments of last crop, of which there is yet unsold about 1000 Bales—however we can only hope another year will be better—Miss Mein having written to you several times since I have been here, I seldom mention her to you, she is quite as good & amiable as ever, as to disposition, but in person you would only know her from the features of her face, she is fully as thin as either of the Miss Hunters, but looks healthy & says she is well as ever she was, & quite glad she does not display so much of the Enbonpoint as formerly—Her brother[18] is as fat as when he left Georgia, but has a continued pain in his Breast which alarms him a great deal, but I think it only arises from his attention to the Counting house (which prevents his taking as much exercise as he ought to do,) & from leaning too much on the Desk when writing—he is very anxious however to change his Climate for a Winter & would have gone to Georgia this Fall if I would have agreed to remain in his place, & I am sure if you had been with me I should without a doubt have acceeded to his proposal—

The first good Vessel that sails in a month from this, if I can't procure a charter, I shall take my passage in, for enchanting as everything here is I long to be with you, & if anything can have added to this wish, it is the hope of finding your Aunt & Cousins from Jamaica with you—

I hope your Brother has gone to the Springs or somewhere, for the Summer in Georgia is too much, a fortnight at Cheltenham would have righted all his wrongs, & I insist upon it he might have come here at a less expence than he can go to the North[d]. for—to be sure a man may spend a vast deal more here, but he is not actually obliged to do so.

Remember me affectionately at the Cottage & to all

other friends—Kiss the Children over & over again for me & believe me ever My dear Eliza

Yr faithful
R M.

Mrs Mackay
Care of Messs. Mein Mackay & Co.
Savannah
Tippoo Saib) Georgia—

61: ROBERT MACKAY TO ELIZA ANNE MACKAY

Cheltenham[14] *28th Septr. 1804*

Another post in & no Neptune, never was a man so anxious as I am to hear from my darling Wife & Children, indeed I dream & think of nothing else, although surrounded by scenes of myrth & happiness in this gay delightful place, I arrived here on the 22nd & was very much pleased to find Sir J. & Lady W. before me, they lodge but a few doors from me, & I am of course almost constantly with them, He has improved amazingly by his trip already, & She looks as young & handsome as she was at one & twenty—Never was there so charming & so healthful a spot as this is, & the old Baronet is so well pleased with it, that he is about purchasing a house to make it in future his Summer residence, which is a very agreable thing to Lady W.—The place has not been so full of compy. since the King was here as at present—a vast deal of the Nobility, who mix indiscriminately & rub shoulders with the croud at the Well every morng.—We attend there about 7 in the morng. drink the Waters & parade the

Walks (which may be compared to the Elysian Fields) untill 9, go home to Breakfast, the forenoon is lounged away in the reading rooms, where Books & Newspapers from every where are furnished in abundance, or take an airing on horseback or go to a Concert, which was well worth attending while M^rs^. Billington[15] was here, but she went to Hereford two days ago; from 1 to 3 walk the Street or go to the Baths—then dress & dine at 4—On Monday & friday even^gs^. there are Balls, Tuesday, Thursday & Saturday Plays, & Cards at the Rooms—& Wednesday Dress Card Assembly—On Sunday Church—so you see every day & Night of the week is provided for, & it must be a stupid & dull animal indeed, who will not be plentifully amused in so amusing a place, indeed if you were here I think I should be quite happy—I have an excellent room & Breakfast & dine at a Publick Table at Russels, where none but very genteel people are admitted, so that in point of Society I am well off—I had a most agreable jaunt from Liverpool, passed through Chester, the antiquity of which & the beautiful walk all round the Town on the old Wall kept in good repair, & the extensive views from it beggar all description—staid a day at Shrewsbury & attended the Races, went to the Theatre at night & saw some of the most beautiful women in the world—The views about this place are I think the most romantic I have seen in England—but it is idle in me to attempt to convey to you a proper idea of them, you must come & see to be a judge of them, At Coalbrookdale I saw two Iron Bridges & the Iron works &^c^., & slept at Worcester where you were once at School, from this circumstance I felt a degree of pleasure at entering this Town, that its great antiquity nor its fame in History, nor anything else could inspire me with—here I saw the China manufactory, the first in this Country, several rich sets were completed for great folks, among them one for Lord Lauderdale at 800 £, a M^{r}. Nash 500 £, Lady Blandon 370 £, & a Tea & small Supper set for Lord Nelson 170 Guineas, they have [letter torn] here, which yr. Aunt & I visited yesterday, she was quite delighted with the beautiful specimens—The Cathedral at Worcester is well worth seeing & in it the Tombs of King John & Prince Alfred, quite perfect, are esteemed great curiosities—Whether it is the Air or the Waters of Cheltenham I don't know, but I never felt so well in my life & never had such an appetite, it is certainly of all others the spot for constitutions from Warm Climates, & every Georgian who visits England would be mad to leave it without bending his Knee at the [letter torn] Forty, the Old Lady who distributes the Tumblers of Water at the Well—Your Aunt went to the Play last even^{g}—I was her escort, the old Gent^{n}. could not be prevailed upon to venture out—The tragedy of Venice preserved was attempted but as the best players have all gone up to London where the Theatres are now open, we were rather disappointed in the performance, it was bespoke by Lord Hutchinson, the commander of the British troops in Egypt after the death of Sir Ralph Abercrombie—I put this in the post office in hopes it may be in time for the Tippoo Saib, by which Grayhurst writes me the chairs & three cases are ship'd to your address—I wish them safe—I have rec^{d} Miss Margarets Letter & shall attend to her mem^{m}. I would write her but am not sure of an opp^{y}. I hope they will be with you when you receive this—Assure them & all at the Cottage of my affectionate

Regard & believe me with love to yourself & the Children My Dear Eliza Yrs. ever

R M

I feel very uneasy about your Brothers health—and this increases my anxiety to hear from you, I hope he has changed his Climate, if no farther than Sullivans Island it may be of service to him, but the Virginia Springs or Ballston in New York would be much more proper—I wish he had come here, one week would have restored him entirely—The waters have proved so beneficial I shall remain ten days longer here & after that shall turn my thoughts to an opp^{y}. for Georgia, the first good Vessel that offers I shall take my passage in either from London or L:'pool, the latter I should however prefer—at all events depend upon my eating Xmas dinner with you, & engage Mein, Scott, Caig, Mitchel & Nichols to dine with us—I hope they will all be in the Land of the living—

62: ROBERT MACKAY TO ELIZA ANNE MACKAY

London 20th October 1804

The Neptune has at length arrived & I yesterday rec^{d}. my dear Eliza's letter of 4th Augt. which was the only line I had by this Vessel—so long & so anxiously expected —the Captn. tells me he did not sail untill the 18th so that you might have given me a fortnights later information, but this satisfaction is denied me & although I am now near three months in this Country, I have only accounts from you three weeks after I left you—indeed I thought you would have been a more attentive correspondent, & if you could only imagine how much I have suffered from hearing so little & so seldom from you, I am sure you would think so too—There are a few lines from M^{r}. Mein to his Brother of 29th Augt. from Charleston, in which he takes no notice of anybody or anything but the Alexanders Cargo—the Wilmot arrived at Liverpool a week ago from Savannah, & I had not a scrape of a pen from any soul, it is really cruel & unkind that no one would write a single line to say whether you were dead or alive—there is now nothing else expected & I must leave this Country in this most dreadful state of suspence, for I can hear no more of you before I embark, & this I shall do in the first tolerable vessel that offers for Sav^{h}. or Charleston, indeed I would go in McNeil but he has 38 passengers & consequently no room to squeeze another into—The want of your shoes must have been distressing to you, & how they have been mislaid I cannot find out, Grayhurst is gone to Scotland & Harvey says he knows nothing about them—The Tippo [o] Saib now some time on her passage will however supply your wants—I wish her safe as all the mem^{ms} are completed by her, & I hope will give satisfaction to the persons they are for, I have had trouble enough about them God knows —I think John is fairly trifling with his constitution, why in Gods name stay in Georgia so late as 4th. Aug^{t}. & still with the intention of going away, the heat is so debilitating that every moment lost makes the cure the more difficult, I am very uneasy on his account, & should like to know where he determines to go, but I must be kept in the dark about him & you & everything else untill I see you, which will at least be five months without knowing whether you are dead or alive—if I had neglected to write you by every conveyance that I have known of from hence or from Liverpool, I wonder what you would have thought of me —I can only say that my health is most perfectly reestablished & that I should have enjoyed myself for a week or two in this place with some satisfaction, but when Vessels arrive some without any information of you whatever, though sailing from our very door & others with old news, I cannot have much pleasure anywhere & I am therefore only anxious to be at Sea on my return & this I hope will be the case in a very short time—M^{r}. Small was kind enough to send me these Sav^{h}: papers by the Neptune to 10th Aug^{t}. & if he had only wrote one line at that date how satisfactory it would have been, but even this little favor has unfortunately been denied me—I am sorry the horses are of no use to you, I should have thought a frequent airing would have been very serviceable, as well as pleasant to you & the Children, & how you can do without them is to me incomprehensible—at all events they will never do you any more good, for I never yet knew a horse go to Coleraine to be taken care of, that was not worked to death in a Waggon or rode to death at night by the Negroes—they will just be the fags of the plantation, & I consider them as totally lost—

I should write to John but suppose my letters would not find him, as he is gone from Sav^{h}., I wish he would sometimes drop a line to Sir James W. it would make his Aunt much more contented—They came from Cheltenham ten days ago, & I left it last Sunday, I have a letter from them this morning, with an invitation to accompany Lady W. & the Miss Knoxes to a famous Ball at High Wycomb, but I am not in dancing spirits & have of course written an apology, I fear my not going will prevent your Aunt which I am very sorry for, as it is not often she can be spared to go to Publick places—A. Mein was to give me information of the Hopes sailing as I wished to write by her & forward you a case of Glass, but he has neglected to do so & I hear this instant she is gone, which I am sorry for; although she was upwards of 200 miles from me I regret that she should have sailed without a letter from me, it is the only Vessel since I have been in the Country that has gone without one—I cannot write in good humour for my disappointment gets the better of every other feeling at this moment, & I shall therefore conclude with wishing you much more happiness than at present enjoyed by

Your ever affectionate

R M

Yr. letter by the Neptune
I only rec[d]. yesterday & is only
the third from you at all,
Vessels every day from Charleston with late intelligence, how easily the mail would have carried a letter round there to be forwarded—

63: ROBERT MACKAY TO ELIZA ANNE MACKAY

London 23rd. Oct[r]. 1804—

The detention of the Two Friends enables me to drop another line to my dear Eliza, who I am now more than ever anxious about, as the papers here are filled with paragraphs of the destructive ravages of the Fever at Charleston & Savannah, Heaven protect you, our darling little Children & our other friends, in safety through this dreadful scourge—I have a letter from John at N: York dated 10th Septr. he has had a narrow escape indeed, but I am truly relieved on his acco^{t}. to find he is at last in a land of health—I wrote you a day or two ago by this opp^{y}. I believe a very ill natured Letter, true it is I was much out of temper, arrivals & no acco^{ts}. of or from any of you in Georgia, except your own Letter of 4th Augst. when there are actually letters from others dated in Sept^{r}.—I fear I shall find dreadful blanks among our acquaintances on my return, I wish I was on my way, but several matters have come in the way to prevent me, but the St Andrew now daily expected will not be detained long, & in her I have determined to embark, I shall remain here untill she arrives at L:'pool, & then hurry down to hasten as quick as possible her departure—I hope therefore to be in Charleston before Xmas, & as news from you on my arrival will be the first thing I shall look for, I shall expect a long letter in waiting for me at Broadfoots, my stay there will not be long as the first Stage will carry me round—I have not yet bespoke the Pelisses, waiting for the latest fashion, but I shall bring them with me, I intended to have carried you a great many pretty things, but really such is the extravagance of this place & such the difficulty of getting money, that I really shall be disappointed, another year our situation will be different, we shall be out of debt & I hope a little more independent—I continue as partial as ever to this Country, & still have it in view some day or other to make it the place of our permanent abode, but there is a great deal to be done before this arrangement can take place, & much must depend upon the punctuality of the people of Georgia—Oliver is down at Berwick where he lives in stile, he is now on the brink of matrimony having wrote up for his Wedding suit & ordered it down immediately—I have given up all thoughts of a trip to Scotland untill you are here to accompany me, & then I shall really enjoy such a tour, for however much I have been pleased with the enchanting scenes I have beheld, there has always been an alloy, that you were not here to praise them with me—I find Mr. Scott has been very ill, I hope he has quite recovered, indeed I am miserable from the fear of losing some of our friends—It is probable the Neptune will return from hence to Savh: but she is a dull sailing Vessel & I shall not go in her—John seems to be quite charmed with N: York, the fact is we are all pleased beyond expression with the first place we see after leaving Georgia, the lofty Welch Mountains appeared like a spot in Paradise to me as we approached this Coast & they are not more fertile than our Pine Barren, but certain it is with all its local advantages Georgia sinks in the comparison with most other places I have seen, & a Summer retreat from the fever, or a residence in some other Country for good & all must be our resort in future—however these things we will talk over when we meet & form our decision before the 1t. July next—God preserve & protect you, our sweet Children & our friends around you prays My darling Girl

Yr. ever affectionate

R: Mackay

Mrs Robt: Mackay

Care Messrs. Mein Mackay & Co.

Savannah

Georgia—

64: ROBERT MACKAY TO ELIZA ANNE MACKAY

Liverpool 15th October 1806
Wednesday

I should have written you My dear Eliza by last evengs. mail, but to tell you the truth I arrived here exactly at 5 O'Clock in the afternoon, & walked as fast as I could from the Stage to Mr. Meins to save my dinner, at his house I found a message waiting for me from Mr Gibson to dine with him, where I would find a number of my friends, I went accordingly, they were half done dinner, I was very hungry, & in making up for lost time & enjoying the conversation of some old acquaintances I staid untill the mail was closed—I had quite a pleasant trip down & got into Manchester about 7 O'Clock on Monday eveng. there I slept & took the Stage next morng. here—At Manchester I met Harrison in the Street as I was going to the Coach, he was very civil, he is going to live in London has a Sister lives near you & has taken Your address that she may call & see you, he says you must be very intimate—Mr. Roberts & his Son arrived here the day before me, he is a very good looking boy, but well grown for he is as tall as I am, Meins Countinghouse is full therefore he goes with me in the Georgia—I have just been on board to chuse my berth, & have had a meeting with the passengers, I like them all very well & I have no doubt but we shall be very comfortable, & I shall be as happy as I can be separated from you & the Children, The ship will positively sail on Sunday if the wind permits, but I wish you to write me on Saturday as she may be detained & a line from you on the last day will be gratifying, indeed a line on monday & even tuesday untill you hear we are sailed I shall be obliged to you for,

& if I am gone there are other Vessels sailing which will bring them after me—I hope you continue to feel pleasant in your situation, you must see your friends as often as you can, go to Town frequently it will amuse you, your money supplies you will write to Mr. Davison for once a Month, & I beg that you will by no manner of means live too frugally, always have plenty of what's good & dress well & neatly, as you may receive forenoon calls you ought to be prepared for them, your expences you may calculate about 40 £ or 50 £ p month, & you will draw for your first months supply as soon as your present stock is exhausted, indeed when you are in want, it would be as well to go Wamford Court & receive the money yourself, but "take care of your pockets" after you have got it—I shall look for a letter from you tomorrow, for I begin to be impatient & anxious already to hear, you must write me after I am gone at all events once every week & just direct your Letter to me as if I was here, to save the postage of a cover, & Mein will forward it—Pray remember me affectionately to our friends at Little Ealing, & Millenium House, I shall write Catherine before I sail—Dont forget me to the Bishop, you must ask him to dine with you before Catherine goes—pray don't neglect this, & you can ask your Aunt Hunter & Eliza with them—Mein desires to be remember'd—take care of yourself & our sweet little ones & believe me

ever yr. affectionate *R M*—

Mrs Mackay
at Mrs Opie's
No. 7 High Row
Kensington Gravel Pits
Middlesex—

65: ROBERT MACKAY TO ELIZA ANNE MACKAY

Liverpool 18th October 1806
Saturday

My dear Eliza's Letter of the 14th I received yesterday & the Letter for Georgia Mr D. writes me is in the hands of a friend who will deliver it free of postage—I have a letter from Miss Cowper with two for Savh. to Miss Hunter & John but none for Mein, she says to me she intended writing more but circumstances prevented—They are determined not to go to Kensington, but leave Cheltenham this day for where she does not inform me, therefore I cannot answer her Letter—Everything is ready for our departure & if the wind is fair we shall tomorrow morng. go to Sea, therefore as I shall be hurried this is probably the last letter I shall write you from hence—You would receive mine yesterday informing you of my arrival here —I flatter myself with the hope of a line from you tomorrow, John having commenced his ordeal I am of course truly anxious to know how the sweet little fellow stands it, no doubt bad enough the second night & I could not help thinking I heard him cry in the night, indeed My dear Eliza it goes hard with me to part with you & those little darlings for so great a length of time, but it cannot be helped we must reconcile ourselves to it with resignation & I hope my going to Georgia may bring matters & things into such a train as to prevent the necessity of our parting again—I am truly glad you have Mary & sooner than lose her you had better make any reasonable addition to her wages—I left a packet of papers marked Resources papers or Acco[ts] I want them in Savannah as the transaction is not settled, therefore I wish you to inclose them in a cover & direct it to me, & when you visit M[rs]. Davison take it with you & request M[r] D. to send it me by the first conveyance direct to Sav[h]. to avoid the postage—It is likely M[r]. Roberts may call & see you as he talks of going to London, if he does ask him to be with you as much as possible, for poor man I believe to save the expence of a dinner is of consequence to him—

I am glad to find Lady W. went with you to my Aunts, pray remember me very affectionately to them all & tell Catherine I am so hurried I have not time to write her, but shall do so from America—You can at all times rely on the friendship of Alex[r]. Mein & should you want anything write him—I have so many things to do & to talk about with Mein, that I scarcely have time to sit down to write & am so confused I dont know what to say, therefore I must conclude with wishing you good bye—May God Almighty bless & protect you my dear Wife & Children & bring us all happily together before long prays Yours ever affectionately

& faithfully
Rob[t]: Mackay

M[rs] Mackay
at M[rs]. Opie's
N[o]. 7 High Row
Kensington Gravel Pits
Middlesex—

66: ROBERT MACKAY TO ELIZA ANNE MACKAY

Liverpool 19th Octr. 1806—

I have just time to acknowledge My Dear Eliza's letter this instant recd.—I am truly happy you are well & that John bears his seperation from you so well—The wind is fair & we are to go on board in half an hour, if it continues I shall dine at Sea, & Mr Mein will drop you a line as soon as the pilot returns to say we are fairly off—everything bids fair for a prosperous passage, a finer ship never floated, a pleasant set of passengers & we have taken good care of the Stores, so that I hope you will be informed of my arrival in three months from this day—

I have a letter this morng. from Mrs. Turnbull at Hammersmith, she has been sick or would have called on you, Mrs. Serrell her daughter & a Mrs. Haven from Nassau will also call—they are all pleasant & respectable people & you must be sociable with them—I think if Hannah & the Children could some day stroll into Berner Street Oxford road & see Mr Mackay it could not be improper & I should like it—

I am happy to say that Rutledge was not drowned with the many who perished in the N York packet—

You will open all the Letters that arrive after my departure & if any of consequence you can send them to me or communicate the contents—

Mein is pestering me about accots so that I don't know what I write, I will not bid you farewell in case the wind should come round to prevent our getting out, in which case you will receive another Letter—Kiss the darling little ones a thousand times for me, remember me affectionately to all friends & believe me to be My dear Eliza ever sincerely & faithfully

Your *R: Mackay*

M[rs]. Mackay
at M[rs]. Opie's
7 High Row
Kensington Gravel pits
Middlesex—

67: ROBERT MACKAY TO ELIZA ANNE MACKAY

Liverpool 10th Sept[r]. 1807—

My dear Eliza

I arrived here at 4 O'Clock this afternoon after a disagreable passage with respect to accommodations, but of the most pleasant nature as far regards myself, I am thank God now as well as when I parted from you, & am astonished beyond measure at the change I have experienced for the better, when I left Savannah I believe none of my friends thought I could possibly reach Liverpool, but I myself thought otherways & it has turned out so—in fact I concealed my situation from you, I was worse than you saw me in 1802, but you will not believe this when you see me, & I will say no more on the subject than that when Alex[r]. Mein saw the signal up for the Georgia, he was prepared to hear I was buried on the passage, but on seeing me he declared I was in better health than when I left him—

Well, now you have had enough of myself, let me thank Heaven that you & our darling little Children are all well, I have read your last letter to Miss Mein, together with two to myself & I am so elated that I can scarcely write—William is with me & well, but the wildest yankie I ever met with—I hope an English School will tame him a little—Your Mother & John (I wrote you) sailed a fortnight before me for Boston, of course I have no later information of them, all the other folks are well, Sally & Elizth. Bourke *honored* me with a call a day or two before I came away, & they are the only female part of the family I have seen since the month of May, for I was confined to my bed & could not go to see them—I have several letters for you & Miss Cowper but they are old dates, & to save postage have thought it best to deliver them myself—when I shall do this I don't know, Mein tells me he thinks of going out soon to America, & if so I shall be kept here a few days, otherwise I intended setting out tomorrow to see you, but at all events be assured I shall be with you as soon as possible—

I have just seen Scarbrough & the *Countess,* she *says* & *swears* she goes to London with me—God help us, she is just ready to lay in—I shall write you of course of my movements on Saturday, (tomorrow there is no Mail), my present intention & wish is to return in the Georgia, but if Mein goes this may alter my views, but I can say nothing certain to night—

I beg you to remember me particularly to all the good

folks about you kiss the Children & believe me My dear Eliza

faithfully & affectionately yours

Robt: Mackay

Tell Hannah her children are well (& husband)—Hero is with me—

Mrs Mackay
7 High Row
Kensington Gravel Pits
London—

68: ROBERT MACKAY TO ELIZA ANNE MACKAY

Liverpool 12th Sept. 1807
Saturday—

I wrote you my dear Eliza on thursday informing you of my safe arrival here, & I now just sit down to say that some time tomorrow I shall set out with William for London, & as we are to post it up I suppose some time on tuesday next we shall meet—I have had a great deal to do with M^r. Mein & shall be obliged to return here in ten days, as he must go out by the Georgia, or some other Ship to sail in three weeks—It is likely if we return this Winter, that we shall go in a Ship Mr Davison has chartered for Charleston from London, which will deprive you of a jaunt to Liverpool, but will save a great deal of money, which is rather a scarce article this year—I would write you a long letter, but really my head is so full of figures

& accounts, & my fingers tired of holding the pen, that you must accept of this as mere information of my leaving Liverpool tomorrow—Mein & I went from Change[16] took a Mouthful of Cold mutton, & have been busy here at the Countinghouse untill now almost 9 O'Clock—Ann dined out with a large party—we were of course to be with her, but business was most urgent & we were obliged to give way to it—

Good night, God bless you all, & in the hope of soon seeing you believe me as usual your ever faithful & affectionate

R: *Mackay*

N. B. I wrote you by the Charles from Savannah a letter just before I sailed, containing memorandums for you in case anything should happen to me on my passage, which should you receive by post I beg you not to open—it was only to point out your mode of support in case of such an event & I now hope there is no use for them—Adieu

By hurrying off tomorrow, I escape a vast deal of trouble, as the Countess wanted to travel with me, but I shall go too quick for her present shape—She dined with us yesterday—as great a——as ever—

Mrs Mackay
7 High Row
Kensington G. Pits
London

69: ROBERT MACKAY TO ELIZA ANNE MACKAY

Liverpool Tuesday Even^{g}. 29th Septr. 1807

My dear Eliza

I arrived here at 4 O'Clock this afternoon, & just got to M^{r}. Meins house in time for dinner, my trip to Manchester was a very pleasant one, the Coach was just such another as that to Oxford with quicker driving, two of my fellow passengers were pleasant agreable people, young men, the other an elderly Lady who did not trouble us with a single word during the passage, though we were of course exceedingly polite to her—I had a very comfortable supper last night & an excellent bed after it at Manchester, & could have been here at 12 O'Clock, but missed the first Coach in the morning, not from Laziness, but misinformation as to the hour of departure, there is so little fatigue in travelling in this Country that I feel as if I had not gone farther than Denmark-Hill—Miss Mein is delighted to hear you are all well, & received me with her usual affection & kindness, do write her, she loves you dearly & feels the disappointment of not hearing from you —I was very lucky in getting a seat in the Defiance, three were engaged when I got to the Inn & there were several applications immediately after me, & the Mail on Sunday from London is not a pleasant conveyance—I stupidly came away without my trunk keys, & must break a lock in the morning to get out some of the things I shall want—Hero appeared as glad to see me as anybody, & enquired with a strong appearance of affection after you—The day appointed for the Georgia's sailing is tomorrow, but Mein tells me Peirce will detain her for him untill Saturday, so that M[r] Davison has no time to loose—I shall not write you again untill I see what our plans are to be as every shilling even in postage tells—This is not to prevent your writing me for if I don't know very often all about you I shall be miserable—But if Mein sails on Saturday I shall very soon be with you—I am writing from the Counting-room & Mein is pestering me with so many questions that I scarcely know what I write, therefore you must just remember me with much affection to all about you & believe me My dear Eliza

ever faithfully your

R M—

M[rs] Mackay
7 High Row
Kensington G: Pitts
near
London—

70: ROBERT MACKAY TO ELIZA ANNE MACKAY

[*Liverpool, December—, 1807.*]

My dear Eliza

The Eliza is really arrived but not Capt. Stookes as he continues in his old Ship the Mary—There are no private letters from Mein or Scott but what relate entirely to business—Scott in a postscript to one of his Letters to W. & A. Mein says "tell Mackay M[rs]. Williamson has presented her Husband with a fine Child,[17] but of what sex have not yet learnt—Jn°. M^c^Queen & Williamson are setting out for Florida to see old M^r^ M^c^Queen who they have acco^ts^. is dangerously ill & not expected to Live[18]—M^rs^. M^c^Queen is ailing a little, & upon the whole most wonderfully recovered—Everybody else quite well"—This is all I have on private concerns—the news of your Fathers illness is afflicting, but you must reconcile it to yourself, his constitution is so good that I have hopes he will get over it—at all events it is as well to be prepared to meet whatever acco^ts^. the America brings—She was to sail a few days after the Eliza—My Letters are dated 5th. Dec^r^.—& they all promise to write very fully by her—

Poor Tubman is dead[19]—but nobody else that we know, except W^m^. Brailsfords daughter[20] who married Jacob Wood (& indeed we did not know her)—

Yrs *R M*

M^rs^. Mackay
13 Rodney St^t^

71: ROBERT MACKAY TO ELIZA ANNE MACKAY

[*Liverpool, January—, 1808.*]

The America[21] My dear Eliza is totally lost on the Coast of Ireland on the morn^g^. of the 7th Inst^t^. but all hands saved —The inclosed is the only letter for you or me from any of the family, not even a line from John, I thought it directed to me & opened it before I discovered the error—the melancholy intelligence it contains I anticipated, you must bear it with fortitude & resignation—The America is well insured—

Yrs. faithfully
R M

Mrs. Mackay
13 Rodney Street—

72: ROBERT MACKAY TO ELIZA ANNE MACKAY

My dear Eliza

The pilot is leaving us I have only time to say, the Ship is as stiff as a Church & everything as comfortable as I could wish—I have no doubt of a good passage, at all events we have commenced it with the fairest prospects—Write me by every possible conveyance—

God Bless you My dearest love—kiss the Children & believe unalterably

Yours ever
R: Mackay

Ship Georgia—
2 O'Clock—12th. Octr 1809

Mrs Mackay
Stanhope Street
Liverpool

73: ELIZA ANNE MACKAY TO ROBERT MACKAY

[*Liverpool,*] *March 21st 1810*

I have written to you my Dear friend since the receipt of yours by the Packet since which I have had the pleasure of hearing thro' Mr Mein of your being in Savannah tho' there is as yet no letter from yourself but I am in great hopes that some will arrive in a day or two I long to hear all about our friends there & to know something about my Brothers affairs which I am very much afraid will not go well in his absence besides giving you a great deal of trouble—I tremble for the contract since hearing that there are much fewer hands at work on the lumber than he expected but I dont know what he last heard from Mr Roberts as I have no letter from him since—they enjoyed last week extremely for Sir James was so kind as permit Aunt Wright to spend a few days with them & you may be sure they made the most of the time by going to as many public places as possible—they have been to see Aunt Hunter who they think very much altered in appearance for the worse she has had late letters from Mrs Falconet then in Paris but not a line from Catherine tho' she could not be ignorant of the opportunity as twas her who told Mrs F— of it—I am quite angry with her for being so unfeeling—the good Bishop often visits them in hart Street—I had written this intending to send it by Mr Moffat to New York—but William is just come in & [tells] me that there is a Vessel about sailing to Amelia I shall therefore prefer sending this in that way as tis so much nearer & if I can get my letters back again that are on Board the rose will send them also but in case I am not able to do that I must repeat to you the disappointment I felt at finding what I had written to you before the sailing of the last packet (requesting that if there was no previous opportunity it might go by that) was still here by which means I am almost sure you will have heard of my Brothers marriage[22] from other people first which is a most mortifying circumstance to us as I am sure you will have great reason to feel hurt at its never having been mentioned to you—but this I have explained in my others so will say no more about it now as it cant be altered—I have never written to M^rs^. Smith in answer to the letter she wrote me about Archys coming here to school—it is certainly a very heavy & I may say unpleasant charge that of young people but at the same time I could not refuse her if her heart is set on sending him here & if you do not object to it—but I shall tell her that in my opinion children are always happiest brought up in the country they are to live in except they have a fortune and can do as they please—if you return here with an intention of staying I will thank you to bring with you the large writing desk that contains some letters I value I dont know if it is full or packed in such a way as to bear the Voyage & there is no key to it but that to Mr Scotts book case fits it if you choose or rather will take the trouble to see—please also to ask Miss Hunter for my large Bible this you must not forget as I have not written to any one else about it n[e]ither have I told Sally to send the childs chair but I wish to have it & perhaps I may not have time to write to her again before you leave Savannah you will not I hope be obliged to remain there long I expect you here in three months from this time Margaret who is always chattering about you says you will be back then—Elizabeth has taken her weaning remarkably well & she is now getting two other teeth without its making her very sick—Mary Anne has had a sore throat for a few days which has obliged her to keep the house but now she is away at school again which the boys are much pleased at for they expect her to take care of them & consider her a great protection on their way to & from school

You have certainly been writing some very satisfactory letters to M[r] Gray that has reminded them of us for since the arrival of the Packet I have had both a call from Miss Gray & M[r] James Gray & an invitation to dinner which I did not choose to accept but they do not know that I was not really engaged & the compliment is all the same— M[r]. & M[rs] Harvey are here from London, at Present only in Lodgings but looking for a house which they find it difficult to meet with I went to call on M[rs] H with Anne as M[r] Mein requested it—I am very happy to tell you that Aunt Cowper is much better D[r] Brandrith was here this morning & says there is considerable alteration in her favor which has relieved Miss Anderson & me from great anxiety—thank you again for your letters by the Packet I am delighted with the account of the hospitality you have received in Norfolk, I have not heard yet how you left it but I am very thankful twas not in the Georgia for she had been out twenty days without being heard of I hope no harm has happened to her but at any rate rejoice that you escaped such a tedious time—My Aunt desires to be affectionately remembered to you William begs his respects the children send their love & I can only say that I pray always for your safety & return & am most truely Your Affectionate

Eliza

be so good as forward the enclosed as directed—I have written to M[rs] S that if she is determined to send her son I will do the best I can with him but that I do not advise his coming & am not desirous of the trouble—at least to that effect if she sends him she will I suppose wish him to come with you but I have said not a word of that & you will do as you think best for my part I would willingly avoid the trouble without being unkind

Robert Mackay Esqr
Savannah
Georgia

74: ELIZA ANNE MACKAY TO ROBERT MACKAY

[*Liverpool,*] *May 3rd 1810*

I have had the pleasure to receive many kind letters from you my excellent correspondent my Dearest friend since I wrote last indeed I began to fear I should not have another opportunity of writing to you before you should leave Savannah not that I have any thing particular to say but that I am anxious to make every return in my power for your attention in letting me hear from you so frequently which is a great happiness to me—both of yours of 5th March have come to hand, that by M^r^ OReilly was forwarded me from Glasgo I have not heard of his being in Liverpool yet but I shall be very happy to see him when he comes—I have one of a later date 11th March & hope soon to hear of you being in Savannah for I am very uneasy as the summer advances for fear you should be detained there too long—& how you are to get away I dont know for I can hear of no prospect of the Non intercource being removed for it seems Macons bill did not pass & all talk of it has subsided—May God direct & prosper you—Human reason is not a sufficient guide—I am sure you must have had a tedious time of it in Florida but you rejoice me by saying that you think the contract can be complied with—I am sorry to find that I raised your curiosity with respect to my Brothers marriage it was unintentional for I considered what would take it as a mear joke & so I am persuaded you would if my Brother had said nothing of the affair himself—at any rate I am angry that I did not act differently, it was contrary to my inclination at the time and as it has really taken place the reserve appears now to have been unnecessary—I am surprised to hear of Mr Gibbons's marriage to the admired Miss Dayton who I find has been as great a bell in Savanna as she could have been any where—I think she could have had but one inducement or else she has a strange taste & is pleased with society that no one ever thought more than *tolerable*—I am sorry to hear that Andrew M^c^Lean[23] is not more prosperous I hope he is happy in his family & then better times may come I [am] sure he was glad to see you for I think he has an affectionate temper—We were much shocked to hear of the death of poor George Baillie his race was soon run, we are every day hearing of some thing to remind us of the uncertainty of our existance or the continuance of our present happiness—I have heard to day of a shocking accident that happened to M^rs^ M^c^Gregors son who is at school a few miles from town—he with some [others] had been climbing and in his haste to be soonest down again staked himself thro' the bowels with a broken branch of the tree that stuck out from the trunk of it—his friends immediately went to him accompanied by Brandrith & Macartney & some others who thought his recovery almost impossible indeed Brandrith said it w[d] be a mirricle but as this happened 4 or 5 days ago & he is not worse they now begin to hope—M[rs] M is in a family way & they had but the day before moved up to Everton glad to leave Rodney Street where she had been so unfortunate as to witness the death of her Brother by his own hand—I dread the time when our Boys will be getting from under our own immediate care—but indeed no care can ward off an accident for they some times happen to the most careful—our Dear John is a bold little spirit but at the same time a very sweet temper William is very gentle but extremely eager after whatever his fancy is fixed on which may lead him into much mischief—but we will hope the best for them all & not take trouble on trust—William is obliged to stay at home all this week as he has a very painful bile on his neck which he bears with great patience—the rest are all well—Elizabeth cannot walk alone yet but is otherwise not backward & continues to be as great a pet with Aunt Cowper as ever—Marg[ts] ancles are still very large but we pour water over them & I shall soon begin to take her to the bath

Our friends are at Little Ealing but we shall expect them home next week—I have heard nothing of Aunt Hunter lately but they will tell us all about her when they come—Miss Mein is to go to day to Northamptonshire on a Visit to M[rs] Pell her heart does not appear much in the jaunt but her Brother will have it so tho' he cannot go himself & M[r] Gray who is to escort a friend of Miss Maxwells to London is to see her safe there—We have neither received or paid Visits lately so I can tell you nothing of gaiety my Aunts sickness has been a very good excuse for that & I keep good friends with all my acquaintance by a call now & then—Mrs Smith has another son & I hear that Mrs Duglas is out again I saw her child at the window the other day tis a sweet little thing—Our garden has suffered much lately for want of rain but we have found a great amusement in watering it & I hope it will be in nice order when you come on that that may be soon for pities sake hurry away as soon as possible—my Aunt desires her best regards the children their love & I am as always my Beloveds

most affectionate *Eliza*

Robert Mackay Esqr
William Mein Esqr
Savannah
Georgia

75: ROBERT MACKAY TO ELIZA ANNE MACKAY

London 4th Septr. 1810.

My dear Eliza

Yours without date came to hand yesterday, just as I was setting out on a visit to Kensington, with the intention of taking my cousin Eliza to introduce me to the Middleton's,[24] however on arriving there I found M^{rs}. M. with her Grandmother, & surely one of the sweetest creatures that Nature ever formed, she is so pretty & so elegant that I cannot attempt to describe her, she shewed me a letter just rec^{d}. from her Mother, full of affliction at parting from her, & I do not wonder at it, so lovely & so accomplished, barely 16 years old, to be entrusted entirely with strangers—but the family is amiable & I hope will never abuse the confidence that Falconnet has given them —They have taken their passages in the Hunter, to sail the first week in October—I forward you a letter from my Aunt, in which she tells me she has given you very good reasons why she cannot keep a Servant at Miss Davis's—I cannot get a plated Coffee pot here that appears to match your Tea pot, they have them of different shapes, but none that please me exactly, therefore I think you had better get one where you got the Tea pot—The silver one, on reflection we had better let alone for another year, they ask from 58/a £3-10/. for the plated ones here —I have got you a very handsome Bread Basket—Pray tell me what kind of a Shawl to get for you, for I really am no judge of these matters, & all is choice—I forgot all about the Musquito Netting—write a note to Mr Dixon requesting him to forward your mem^m. to M^r. Isaac,[25] & he will procure what you think requisite—The Manchester mem^ms. I shall attend to, & let me know what else is wanted here—Harvey has finished all the Jewelery as you directed, now do let me know what you want to complete your establishment in that way, I don't know what to chuse, for I can't tell what would match—I should carry Miss Mein a present of some kind say what it is to be— I think you ought to have a Ring to keep yours on, give me the proper size of the finger & say what kind you would like best—Campbell has called & been very civil, & I had a note to dine to day with Sir Alex^r. Johnston his Brother in law, but I was obliged to decline the invitation as this was the morning of attendance on Mr Brodie, I have been with him, but not yet finished, I must see him again on friday—on Saturday M^r^. Horne is to be in Town—We are both of opinion there will be no further use for the caustic, which I shall be very glad of, for its application is not very pleasant—However this cannot be decided positively untill friday—Covent Garden is to open on monday, I see clearly I cannot get away before then, so that I shall have an opp^y^. of seeing this fine Theatre—

I hope John will be here tomorrow, this Rainy weather will be very unpleasant for his trip, it is a pity he put it off so long—Love to all around you—Yours faithfully

R M

Ought you not to have a pair of Gilt or plated Clasps for the waist—say what pattern—

Mrs Mackay
N°. 5 Stanhope Street
Liverpool

76: ROBERT MACKAY TO ELIZA ANNE MACKAY

[*London, September 11, 1810.**]

[The first page of this letter is missing.]
I suppose from M^rs^ M^c^Q.—Indeed I regret my love that I should see so little of our darling daughter Maryanne & of all of you, but what can I do, It frets me when I think of it, & I must only submit as well as I can—I have neither seen or heard of the Burnleys—I have not been in the City since Thursday, John & I dined together on Saturday at

the Rainbow after visiting old M[r] Tatnall[26] & M[r] Penman —The day before that I was with the Surgeon, & Sunday & yesterday at Windsor—Remember me to all around you & believe me ever

My dearest Love

Yrs faithfully & affectionately

R Mackay

Say what combs you want & send a pattern of the size & shape which you can draw over one page of your letter—

M[rs] Mackay
5 Stanhope Street
Liverpool

* The date is in the handwriting of Eliza Anne Mackay.

77: ROBERT MACKAY TO ELIZA ANNE MACKAY

London 24th Sept 1810.

My dear Eliza

Yours of the 20th I rec[d]. on Saturday, but could not answer as I was writing to Georgia, & had a long walk to take with John, who I suppose left town yesterday for L'pool, by way of Oxford & Birmingham & I presume may be with you about wednesday night—I parted with him at the Theatre on Saturday even[g]., & he was not then sure at what hour he would set out, as he had the choice of several coaches, & I have heard no more of him, as Harvey & I went yesterday to Finchley & spent a very pleasant day—I am sure we are very much obliged by M[rs]. & Miss Cowpers kindness, I know the charge they have undertaken is a most troublesome one, & with conditions attached to it must be more so, but the only one asked, is imposed upon me by a necessity that cannot be surmounted—I therefore leave the matter entirely with yourself, to do whatever you please in it—Now John is gone, I shall feel my detention here more irksome than ever, but must still muster up patience, for I am not done with Sackville Street yet, & so much is this complaint of mine situated in the dark, that we cannot tell exactly when it will be overcome, however I think it cannot be much longer now—John & I, calling the other day at Mr Ogilvies met M^{r} & M^{rs}. Middleton coming out of the door, I like him very much, he seems quite a pleasant fellow, & easy manners—as to John he swears my Cousin is an Angel—On going up stairs we found old M^{rs}. Middleton there & had some chat with her—for all which I refer you to your Brother—as well as for an account of a dinner he invited the good old Bishop to at the Bedford, where we made the old man quite chearful & happy—I shall keep your Queen's stuff for a day or two untill a shawl is fixed upon, & send them together by the heavy coach—

I am now obliged to hurry down to the City to send my letters to Georgia & remain always My Dear Wife & Children Yours most truly

R M

N. B. I have ret^{d} from the City in time to open my letter, merely to add that there is nothing new—Davison is gone to the Country again—Tell John I have bought the Lottery ticket at Hazards as directed—the N^{o}. is 3413 & cost 30/6—with 6^{d} more for registring—I had it entered in Miss Cowpers name & gave her address 5 Quebeck Street

Oxford Road—So that she will know its future—I stop'd at the Old Bailley & heard a number of trials for petty offences—none however very interesting—I think it likely Grayhurst will take Liverpool in his way, expecting to find me there—I do not know how you can manage a Bed for him, but of course every other Civility I know you will shew him—

M[rs] Mackay
5 Stanhope Street
Liverpool

V. From Southern Ports

V. From Southern Ports

Although the transatlantic trade was the first concern of Mein, Mackay and Company, this firm did much business also with the ports of the South Atlantic. Robert Mackay's correspondence shows that he made frequent trips to Charleston and that he went once to Norfolk and to Amelia Island in East Florida.

In the spring of 1805 Mackay was in Charleston awaiting the arrival of a vessel that his firm and some Carolina associates had sent to Africa for a cargo of slaves. Always susceptible to the charm of an Old World way of life, he confided to Eliza: "I am as much pleased with Charleston as ever & sincerely wish we were fixed here." His letters written during this brief stay tell of the attentions of friends (it is interesting to note that he observed the King's birthday at the home of the British Consul); but he does not describe a place with which they were both familiar.

This was not true of his letters from Norfolk. Going from England to that bustling Virginia port in 1809 and remaining six weeks to obtain "a cargo of very fine Tobacco," Robert Mackay had leisure and opportunity to pass judgment on the town. His first impressions were unfavorable ("This is without exception the dirtiest hole that ever was built," he wrote to his wife); but as courtesies continued to be extended to him, he informed Eliza: "I assure you I am quite delighted with Norfolk. . . ." The "people are civil," he added, "& I think the Society a pleasant one." Mackay had every reason to feel at home, for Norfolk, like Savannah, was a merchants' town, its leading citizens grown rich in the West India trade reopened to Americans since the beginning of the Napoleonic wars. His later observations of Norfolk reflect a fresh attitude to a new and congenial place, and provide source material for the social historian.

From Norfolk, Robert Mackay went to Charleston, and after stopping over in Savannah, proceeded down the coast to Amelia Island to settle some family affairs. His wife's father had died a few years before, and the estate that he had accumulated under a benign Spanish officialdom was now in litigation. To Mackay fell the task of salvaging as much as he could from Don Juan McQueen's always numerous creditors. Smuggling the McQueen Negroes into Georgia, in the dead of night, in violation of the Federal law that prohibited the importation of slaves into the United States after January 1, 1808, provided Mackay with a new experience in a career of unquestioned probity. Notwithstanding the success of his mission and the pleasure of seeing once more the family of General Nathanael Greene, Mackay begrudged the eight weeks that he spent in East Florida.

On returning to Savannah, he wrote to his wife, then in England: "I assure you Sav^{h}: has the appearance of something very superior compared with Amelia Island." This was a conclusion he would reach thereafter when comparing Savannah with places far more attractive than Amelia, "that Country of Robbers, Sandflies & Musquitoes."

78: ROBERT MACKAY TO ELIZA ANNE MACKAY

Charleston 30th May 1805

A fair wind, & the most pleasant weather I ever experienced, brought me here to dinner yesterday—an excellent passage, but I did not escape my fever, I had an attack in the night while at Sea, in the old way, a severe Ague & a smart fever after it, which only left me about One O'Clock, but whether the Sea air was more bracing or from what other cause I know not, I did not feel that weakness & debility after it that always accompanied it in Savannah—this day I am very well, but to be prepared against another attack I have sent to Dr. Barron[1] who is to call on me presently & I hope some plan or other may be devised to prevent a return—Both of the Broadfoots[2] had prepared Beds at their houses for me, & from our old friend Lee I found on my arrival a note saying that I could stay nowhere else but with him—this was at last determined upon & I last night slept in his house on a very comfortable bed—He says he will return to Savannah with me, & feeling interested in Meins success in all his lawful undertakings, he makes this trip in order to aid & assist him in his *Courtship*, for even at this distance it is known that Mr. Mein is over head & Ears in love with Miss C.—I have heard nothing in the way of news worth communicating to you yet, tell John I understand Mr Bowman[3] is pretty well, that is, he was riding about Town yesterday—I shall call & see him tomorrow, as also Major Butler[4]—The Brig Lovely Lass arrived the day I sailed from Sav[h]. I shall expect to hear on Sunday morn[g]. what sort of a thing Meins Jersey Waggon is & whether it will serve to carry us to the Springs—if not I can easily get one here that will answer. On tuesday I shall hope to know that you are all well—Remember me affectionately to your Cousins &[c]. &[c]. Kiss the Children & believe me My dear Eliza ever yours

R: Mackay

M[rs] R. Mackay
Mess[s]. Mein M & C[o].
Savannah—

79: ROBERT MACKAY TO ELIZA ANNE MACKAY

Charleston 1[t]. June 1805

I have had no return of fever since my arrival & D[r]. Barron tells me that I need not expect it again, my friends have all been very careful of me, I dine out every day but from great caution & prudence have not in any one instance exceeded—I went last even[g]. to see the last play for the Season & though young Roscius was on the Stage I was so compleately tired of the performance that the third act sent me home[5]—I saw M[r]. Bowman yesterday, his family is in the Country, he goes tomorrow to bring them to Town, after which he is coming round to Savannah in one of the packets—you must have a room prepared for him—he is very infirm—so much so indeed that he is lifted about like a child, & cannot of himself stir from

ROBERT MACKAY
(1772–1816)

From the drawing by Edward Greene Malbone

his chair—I am quite disappointed at not seeing the Ladies but hope they may come to Town yet, before I leave it—My stay here is uncertain, the Resource[6] must be loaded, & I find I must be on the spot when the Montezuma's sales are going on—She has not yet arrived but we look out for her hourly, at present I am fearful it will be a tedious thing getting off her cargo, as many other Vessels are expected, & there will consequently be a vast deal of competition in the sales—Major Butler I have not seen though we have called upon each other, I wish to hear from John how his Carriage is to be sent round, I believe I will have it ship'd, for I cannot go in it myself—pray let me have a description of Meins Jersey Waggon—I am as much pleased with Charleston as ever & sincerely wish we were fixed here—I shall look out for a comfortable house that may be engaged for the beginning of the Winter, I am convinced you will be as much pleased with it as any of us—I am in full hopes my next may inform you of the Montezuma's arrival—when I can determine as to my stay here & arrange to a certainty the time of our departure for the Springs[7]—You must let this Letter serve for John as I have not time to write him—Remember me affectionately to all our friends, Kiss the Children & believe me

ever My D Eliza Your

R M

Not a piece of Longhaven to be had in Charleston—

Mrs Mackay
Mess^s^. Mein M & C^os^
Savannah—

80: ROBERT MACKAY TO ELIZA ANNE MACKAY

Charleston 4th June 1805

This mornings Mail brought My Dear Eliza's welcome intelligence of the welfare of herself & the Children, though I was sorry to observe Mrs McQueen was again indisposed—The Springs alone will restore her & I wish to God she was gone—I have Johns Carriage & bought yesterday a pair of Horses for 250$. the finest little knots you ever saw, I wish Stephen sent to me by return of Stage to carry them round & perhaps I may accompany him—I shall make some arrangement with my friend Broadfoot to attend to the Montezuma without me, & I shall of course soon see you, be assured I never felt more anxious about you all, in my life, it already appears an age since I left you—No return of Ague, I believe it is gone, the change has been serviceable for I am already picking up—Except Sunday, when we had a large party at Lee's, I have dined out every day—this being the Kings birthday I am at Mr Moodies[8]— I have not yet returned his call but I see him every day—I am glad you have seen Mrs. Scarbrough, she is admired here very much—I am sorry I can say nothing of the Bowmans as they are not in Town, the old Gentleman has asked me three times to dine with him—but I was always engaged—He hopes we shall all take Charleston in our way to the Springs—I wish to pass a few days on Sullivans Island, I think the air would do me much good, but I have made so many engagements in Town cannot get away—I hope Forbes will not neglect sending on the Jersey waggon—The horses I have bought & our own pair will take us to the Springs very comfortably indeed—

I shall continue to write while I remain here & I hope you will let me know [by] every stage, how you all are—

Remember me affectionately to all around you, Kiss our darling Mary Anne & William for me & believe me ever

My dear Eliza
Your
R. Mackay

Mrs Mackay
Mess^s^. Mein Mackay & Co.
Savannah
Georgia—
Mail—

81: ROBERT MACKAY TO ELIZA ANNE MACKAY

Norfolk 5th Decem^r^. 1809—

I am here about an hour, it is now late in the even^g^. & I have only time to inform My dear Eliza that I am safe here, & never better in my life, though we have had a most infamous passage in point of weather, by far the worst I ever experienced, but the Georgia has performed as I expected of her—to admiration—I anchor'd at 11 O'Clock last night in Hampton roads about 14 miles from here, & got a passage boat (such as our Savannah pilot-Boats) early this morn^g. to bring the Captn. & myself here, but as if head winds were to persecute me to the end of the chapter, we had no sooner left the ship, than the wind which was fair came right ahead & blew so fresh that I have been all day beating up to this place—

There are a great many of our Men of war in the roads & really as fine ships as ever were—the situation of this place is pretty, & so is the approach to it, though rather low—but of all the dirty holes I ever saw, it think it beats[9] —I have just returned from the extremity of the Town where I have been to wait on Mr Maitland,[10] Brother of M^r. Lenox's partner in New-York—he was prepared to expect both you & I (by his brother,) & really rec^d. me very kindly, It is impossible for me to say what I am to do with the ship as yet, but think I shall load her immediately for Amelia—The talk here is another embargo & probably a war with England—this I understood from a Motley group who were in the passage boat, but Mr Maitland thinks matters will remain as they are for the present—I have no letters from Savannah nor have I been able to gain any information of our friends there, I expect a few Sav^h: papers from the printing office, which may possibly give me some acco^ts, but it is said the Continent has been generally exceedingly healthy—

The vessel by which this goes sails early in the morn^g. & you must therefore put up with this hurried scroll—by the next opp^y. I shall write you more fully—Remember me to all around you—God bless you & our darling Children prays My dear Eliza, ever your affectionate

R: Mackay

82: ROBERT MACKAY TO ELIZA ANNE MACKAY

Norfolk 7th Decem^r. 1809—

I wrote a few hurried lines on the even^g. of my arrival to My dear Eliza, & another scroll yesterday morning merely to say I was safe here, indeed I had not time to say more, & anything would do to convey the information, some vessels that sailed after me having shorter passages I fear you would feel uneasy, I cannot account for it but we certainly have been more unfortunate than others, however we have arrived without any accident, & all's for the best, for had we made the coast ten days sooner than we did, we should have shared a very severe gale of wind, which happened at that time in this Latitude & dismasted a number of vessels, one of which got in here the day we did, & two were towed in by the men of war the day before—We anchor'd in Hampton roads on the night of the 4th I left the ship next morning with Captn. Peirce to come here, & were all day on the water in one of the passage-boats, so that we only reached Norfolk the evening before last, I immediately called upon Mr Maitland, Brother to Mr Lenoxs partner in New York, who received me very civilly, he expected that you were to be with me, & Mrs Maitland regrets that she has been disappointed of the pleasure of seeing you—Peirce & I slept at the Eagle Tavern, & sup'd in the company of a Chaplain & some of the petty Officers of the men of war at present here, but I found their society so noisy that I was very glad next morning to change my lodgings, & I am now fixed at a

Mrs Streets, as far as I have yet seen as good a lodging house as I ever was in, I called yesterday on Col^{l} Hamilton & was politely rec^{d}. by him & Mrs H. & am to dine there tomorrow, yesterday I was with a small party at Mr Maitlands—At breakfast this morning I was pleased to observe Miss Cowpers *friend* Mr Morgan sitting opposite to me, he stays in the house, & was very glad to see me, his own & his horse's services are placed entirely at my disposal, he has quite recover'd his health & looks very differently from what we saw him, I find him a very pleasant, clever fellow—We have here also the Collector a staunch old Democrat, & a very sensible well-informed man, together with some of the Naval Officers who wear epaulets, they dress with a remarkable degree of neatness & appear to be Gentlemen but I have yet made no acquaintance with them—Mrs Decatur[11] is in town but I have not seen her, her husband commands the United States frigate, at present stationed in this River—I was recognised in the Street this morning by a Sweet Spring acquaintance—a M^{r}. Brown, who perhaps you have forgot, & have met with Captn Steed who commanded the Intrepid when I came from England in her, & now I believe you know all the people in Norfolk that I do—I fear I shall be disappointed in the object of my voyage to this place, the Season is too far advanced to obtain a choice cargo of Tobacco, but I have written to Richmond & shall have answers the day after tomorrow, if they are such as I expect them to be, I shall instantly dispatch the Georgia for Sav^{h}: & probably go with her, where I hope to find our friends well, for as yet I have not heard a word of any of them—With respect to politicks everything in the way of negotiation seems to be at a stand with both England & France, M^r^. Jackson is dismissed & God knows what the result is to be, Congress as yet has done nothing, they are deliberating over the Presidents message, & the correspondence betwixt our Secretary of State & Mr Erskine & Mr Jackson,[12] & people were at one time fearful of another embargo, but at present the opinions here appear to be otherwise—I don't write John presuming before this reaches you that he will have left England, & I hope he will have a pleasant passage home, but I expect to hear of his motions when I get to Sav^h^:—I give this a chance of going by the Packet though I am doubtful of its being in time, but if too late for this, it will reach you by the next & only be a month older when you get it—My other scrolls will I hope be quicker with you, to make you easy as to my arrival God bless you My dear Eliza & our darling little ones—Say all thats kind to those around you & believe me ever your

R M

Mrs Mackay
Care of Mess^s^. Alexander Mein & Co.
Merchants
p British Packet from New York } Liverpool

83: ROBERT MACKAY TO ELIZA ANNE MACKAY

Norfolk 8th Decem^r^. 1809—

I have this instant heard of another opp^y^. by which I may drop a line, having written you already two scrolls from hence, & sent one to N: York to go by the packet, I am glad of another chance of conveying information to My dear Eliza that I am safe here, & have been here since the even^g^. of the 5th I am sorry to say my voyage here will not be attended with any good, we are too late in the Season for a choice of Tobacco which was what we wanted, & it is very probable that I shall proceed in a day or two with the Georgia for Savannah—I have heard nothing of or from any of our friends in the South, but I hope soon to be with them & to find them all well—I have been very kindly rec^d^. here by Mr Maitland & I think the people appear to be very hospitable, but it is the dirtiest hole I ever saw, the streets have no pavement & are knee deep in mud—All negotiation is at an end with England, & there seems to be nothing doing with France, God knows what is to be the result, but I think the opinion here is that there will be no new commercial restrictions for the present—By this conveyance I send Mr Mein the whole of the correspondence betwixt Mr Smith[18] & Mr Jackson, which is very interesting,—I have not time to add more than affectionate remembrance to all around you—God Bless you & our sweet Children prays your ever faithful & affectionate

R M

Mrs Mackay
Care of Messrs Alex^r^. Mein & Co
Merchants
Liverpool

84: ROBERT MACKAY TO ELIZA ANNE MACKAY

Norfolk 12th Decr. 1809—

My dear Eliza

I have forwarded a letter for the packet, but fear it will be too late, I have also wrote you several scrolls from hence, I have this inst^{t}. heard of the present opp^{y}. & have but a few minutes to write both you & Mr Mein—I was made very happy by the rec^{t}. of yours of 16th & 18th, I never knew the Coffee Apparatus was forgot, for our Steward a frenchman made it so good I never had occasion to enquire for it—therefore I am sorry you made yourself uneasy about it, however having told Hero not to forget it, I have just asked him for it, & his answer is, that "it is on board"—I am delighted to find the Children are at School & are pleased with it, I think of you & them from morning to night—I hope we shall have large gains from the Lottery speculations—I am glad you have seen Mr Laughton, but you must know I don't give full credit to the acco^{t}. of his frequent calls in Arundel Street—Why not in one instance leave a Card?—why did he not tell me that he had call'd, when I so often met him in the Street & asked him to come—?—I have a letter from W. Mein dated 24th Novem^{r}. but he does not mention a soul in Georgia, or anything else but business—Mr Scott arrived in Charleston I see by the papers on the 3rd. Inst^{t}—I have just been looking over the deaths & marriages in some New York papers of last month, & am sorry to observe among the former M^{rs}. Stites[14] of Sav^{h} in the same paper is Mrs Farley[15] & old Mother Eustace, who are of less consequence, among the marriages nobody that I know but Miss Mary Clay[16] to a Mr Gray of Boston—

I have some hopes of getting a great part if not the whole of a cargo here, after all, & which I think will turn out well, as I see no prospect whatever of an accomodation of differences with England—though I do not think there will be a war either, but while things remain as they are, American produce must be high in Europe—

I hope soon to hear from you by the Packet of a late date, she is expected in a few days—Don't forget to pay Mr Hay for the things from Birmingham—I think of going up to Richmond tomorrow—

Remember me affectionately to all around you & believe me My dear Wife & Children ever faithfully & affectionately Your

R Mackay

Mrs Mackay
Stanhope Street
p Protectress) Liverpool

85: ROBERT MACKAY TO ELIZA ANNE MACKAY

[*Norfolk, December 24, 1809.*]

I sit down once more to write My dear Eliza from this place, which I have been expecting for some days to leave, but the prospect of procuring a cargo of Tobacco for the Georgia, though not very flattering, is such as to induce me to try it, & I hope I may prove successful, as under the present situation of affairs, if it arrives in England I think it must do very well—I have only rec^{d}. the first letter you wrote me, & am now looking out for later acco^{ts} from you & hope I shall not be long without them, as I begin to feel a little anxious—From Sav^{h}: I have only had one letter from W. Mein, in which he mentions nothing but business, I have looked over a great many files of papers, but have seen no deaths of any consequence but M^{rs}. Stites & this must be a very afflicting one to her friends leaving a young family behind—I observe that Col^{l}. John Chester of Connecticut is dead, who is I presume the Gent^{n}. you knew there—Of marriages I see nothing but Mary Clay to a Mr Gray of Boston, I expect letters next week in answer to those I wrote on my arrival to Sav^{h}. & then I suppose I shall hear all the news—

This is without exception the dirtiest hole that ever was built, a most beautiful situation, one of the finest & safest harbours that can be, the most plentiful, best & cheapest market in the world, but the Town itself, notwithstanding there are many excellent houses in it, appears to be going fast to ruin, it is built on a bank of mud & no pavement on the streets, so you may easily imagine what kind of walking they have in wet weather, of which there has been a good deal since I arrived—The poultry is brought ready cleaned to market in the great quantities, & I am convinced there is more fat than lean upon its bones, a Turkey of this description is sold from half a dollar to ¾—The ducks which are so fine I cannot attempt to describe are bought for 75 Cents a pair—the first day I dined at M^{r}. Maitlands we had a pair on table, which I really mistook for two Geese & remarked to myself that it was the first time I had seen two of those gentry make their appearance together, you may judge of my surprize when I was told they were ducks, & were so tender that they almost melted in my mouth—The Beef is as good & there is a most excellent fish market, the Oysters I am convinced cannot be matched in any part of the world, either in size or flavour—At our lodgings kept by an old widow lady, we have the most abundant table, everything of the best, (& no cooking can be superior to hers,) I have an excellent room to myself, our breakfast is like an English dinner, with the addition of tea & coffee, which are both as good as they can be,—at dinner we are furnished with brandy & water, Cyder & Phil^{a} beer—Tea in the even^{g}., (& supper when we chuse it), & all for 5/3 Sterling p day—Wine is the only extra charge—If any living can be better or cheaper than in Norfolk—I have never yet heard of it—I have been at a Ball here but the Ladies did not answer my expectations, they are not pretty & dress most abominably—Since writing to the last paragraph Mr Drayton has arrived here & handed me your last letter of the 8th. Novr. which I assure you was most acceptable, & I cannot tell you how gratifying it was to see one who had seen you lately—He only staid one night & went away next morning to Charleston—I am now loading the Georgia & going on with all the expedition that is possible, but after all our exertions to make something by this adventure, I fear it will turn out a loosing one—By last nights mail we have acco^{ts}. of a Bill before Congress, which there is little doubt will pass, & which opens the intercourse with both England & France, in *American Ships*—& prohibiting all their vessels from entering our ports, untill their obnoxious Edicts are recalled—This of course will make

American produce very low in England—however there is no help for these things, we must take them as they come—

It is probable I shall go on to Sav^{h}. by land, but I shall not get there before the 1^{t}. Feby. by which time I hope to meet John, who Mr Drayton tells me will certainly embark some time this month—

You say nothing of the fate of our Lottery tickets, from which I judge they are all Blanks—I have yet no letters from Sav^{h}. but the one I have mentioned from Mein, which is truly astonishing—I hope you will have a pleasant Xmas of it, I eat my dinner with Mr Maitland, who with his family have been particularly kind & attentive, they are very worthy & most respectable people—They have 4 daughters & a Son, (have lost 3) The little boy is about Margarets age & absolutely little more than half her size, but a fine merry little fellow, & astonishes one to hear such an atom speak so plain—The eldest daughter is about Eleven, a very pretty Girl & remarkably well behaved, the Second & third are also fine Children 9 & 7 years old, & you may assure Mary Anne, hold up their heads & behave like Ladies, the 4th. Girl is about 4, been very sickly & of course a little spoil'd—M^{rs}. M. is of a very religious turn, has been brought up a Presbiterian but inclines to Methodism, & I doubt not she will ere long join that sect, though she yet consents to her children learning to dance & play the Piano—I have been to Church to hear an English Clergyman who has the Episcopal living here—he is rather a Creole of Jamaica—M^{r}. Sims—& without exception the most impressive & elegant reader I ever heard from a Pulpit, the Church is very large—very cold & was very thinly attended, I meant going today (being Sunday) but the day is one of the coldest I ever felt, so I thought I would pass the forenoon in writing for the Packet—I wrote you yesterday by a vessel to Falmouth, but I am fearful letters by these chance opp^{s}. seldom go safe—

I assure you I am quite delighted with Norfolk though the streets are so dirty—the people are civil & I think the Society a pleasant one—I am to dine on wednesday with a Mr Myers[17] a rich Jew & considered one of the most respectable Merch^{ts}. here—Perhaps I shall have time enough to write again by this packet, though from here my letters can tell you little else than that I am well & as much yours ever—Remember me affectionately to all around you, & believe me My beloved Wife & Children ever

faithfully & affectionately yours

R M

Norfolk 24th December 1809—

Mrs Mackay
Stanhope Street
p British Packet }
Via New-York } Liverpool

86: ROBERT MACKAY TO ELIZA ANNE MACKAY

Norfolk 15th Jany 1810—

I yet address you My dear Eliza from this place though some time ago I had no thoughts of remaining so long in it, but it has been a great convenience to me to load the

Georgia without the trouble of going up the Country, & I have completed it, having dispatched her three days ago for Amelia Island, with a cargo of very fine Tobacco —I have still however some thoughts of going through Richmond on my way to Washington, which being so nigh I should like to visit, as it may not probably come within my chapter of accidents to have another opp[y]. soon—but I have by no means decided & may when I have settled everything here, jump into the stage & go directly on to Sav[h]:—I don't know what to write about from this place to amuse you, the Society is after all nothing very fascinating & the place is very dirty, but the people are kind & hospitable, & live better than any place I ever was in, & for less money—I wish you could see some of the tables here, loaded with the very best of everything, & at a smaller expence than a single dish of roast beef costs in Liverpool—In M[r]. Maitlands family I am very intimate, & have rec[d]. from him the most unbounded kindness & attention, I dine there almost every other day & generally call every even[g]., M[rs]. M. with all her religion is a fine cheerful body, I am sure I don't know how I shall ever repay a tenth part of the civility I have rec[d]. from these good people—I have also a standing invitation to dine every day at Col[l]. Hamiltons, which is very often renewed with much hospitality, but I have not availed myself very often of it—the fact is I have been anxious & uneasy untill I got the ship away, & now she is off, I feel the same anxiety & uneasiness to get to Savannah, where I am sure I shall find many letters from you waiting my arrival, for they have stop'd sending them here, supposing I would be gone—My friends there have been very uncommunicative, Scott barely says they are all well, R. Mitchel at N York quite sick—Doct^r^. Brickel & Saul Simons dead—I have met M^rs^. Decatur twice in the street, but she did not appear to recollect me, she has none or very little acquaintance among the Ladies, I understand from no other reason than her not cultivating it, therefore it is her own fault—he is a decent sort of a man, but not the one I should have thought Miss Wheeler would have selected, he has a pleasant time of it—his ship the United States[18] one of the finest in the world, lays in all her glory almost within hail of his windows, & being Commodore of the fleet here, is no small character—Our ships however I suspect will be of little use but to look at, there is no prospect of a war with France, which would be the only chance for our young Officers to signalize themselves, & should there be a war with England, the superiority of force is so great the ships could not go to Sea, however I hope there will be war with neither, Congress is at present engaged with a Bill to open the Intercourse with both of these Countries, which appears to be the best thing they can do, though the world will no doubt laugh at us for pursing a system of Embargo & Non-Intercourse for upwards of two years, which after doing ourselves a great deal of injury, we abandon without gaining a single point we contended for, & in fact are just where we were two years ago, with the losses sustained by pursuing a ruinous & imbecile system—I am glad to find you have got the things from Birmingham & are pleased with them, I hope you have not forgot to pay Mr Hay for them—I cannot imagine the reason that my old friend M^r^. Stavely has been so dilatory, he promised me to send them immediately—I suspect our Lottery tickets are all blanks, or we should have heard more of them, Capt. Grandison, of *whisker reputation*, & who M^r^ & M^rs^. Gardner came from Liverpool to N. York with in the Montezuma, has I see by the papers drawn a 20 thousand pound prize in the British Lottery—Where was all our luck, when such good things were going?—I am glad to see you are pleased with the neighbours about you & that they seem attentive,—I was delighted that the children saw the procession, I am sure they must have enjoyed it much, poor things I am anxious enough to see them—they will grow out of my knowledge in a very few months at their present ages—As to Eliza, I suppose by this she is stepping & begining to use her little tongue—I presume there is by this an addition to M^r^. Tayleurs family—I hope they are all well—I have really not had time to write to Crump as I promised to do, pray tell him so, & say that I shall certainly do it when I get to Savannah, which will now be ere long—I hope Miss Mein will stay the winter in L'pool. I shall be much disappointed if she is gone when I return, for I see no hope of my paying her a visit in Scotland—Don't give up Miss Gray's acquaintance, she lives at a great distance to be sure, but you must make out a visit sometimes—they have been very attentive to us & we must not forget them—I don't know what order you will receive my letters in, for we don't know here when the packets are to sail, I send them by chance & it is not improbable but they may sometimes be too late—By this day I hope you have heard of my arrival here—Remember me affectionately to all around you & believe me my beloved wife & children ever faithfully & affectionately

Your *R M*

M[rs] Mackay
Care of Mess[s]. Alex[r]. Mein & C[o].
Merch[ts]
p British Packet from New York— } Liverpool

87: ROBERT MACKAY TO ELIZA ANNE MACKAY

Charleston 27th Jan[y]. 1810—

My dear Eliza

I had a *delightful* passage of four days from Norfolk—it rained, hailed & snowed almost the whole way—but we had an excellent packet, a Capt[n]. who knew the way by his Soundings, & found us in everything good & comfortable—I wrote you from Norfolk that I should go up to Richmond, Washington & Baltimore, but I afterwards got uneasy about the Georgia & hurried on by the Ploughboy—I arrived here last monday & expected to sail the next morn[g]. in Coopers packet for Sav[h]: but the wind has been Southerly ever since & here I am still, the Miss Gadsdens are to be my fellow passengers round—I was to have dined yesterday at M[r] Draytons, but expecting the wind round I sent my things on board the packet, & hearing there was a large party of Ladies I thought it would not do to go in Boots, so I joined James Broadfoot & Ancrum[19] in a family dinner with Boyd[20]—I was the day before at A. Tunno's,[21] & the day before that at Boyds, who had a large party collected to meet me, he has been very attentive & wished me much to take a bed at his house, but this I declined, I am at Mrs Calders[22] as Broadfoot is full, to day I go to my friend Mr Rutledges who has been as kind as usual, I intended to go to the Concert the even^g^. before last, but Hary Grant[23] lugged me to the Club from Tunno's against my consent, where I played cards & won twenty dollars—Both Ancrum & Grant have offer'd me a sulkey & horses to take me on, but the roads are so bad, Rutledge advises me against it, he goes himself next week by water—I have been fortunate in meeting Barnwell here, he is exactly what he was at the Springs, wants me to go with him this morn^g^. in his boat to Beaufort, from whence he will send me home, but I think we shall have a fair wind tomorrow, which will be better than an inland passage—The night before I left Norfolk I got a letter from Williamson saying John had declined coming home this winter, & thinks he was crazy for making the lumber contract, which can never be complied with, says the Governor will not extend permission for his negroes to remain in Florida & urges me to come to Sav^h^. immediately, that I may go down to Florida & see after things—says Sally's situation[24] prevents his leaving her at present, when I get to Georgia we will talk over the matter, but I think Capt. Roberts will be as useful as any of us, but if I can do any good, I shall instantly set off—I shall write John from Sav^h^. & should have done so before, but expected to find him at home—Judge Stephens[25] & M^rs^. Levett are actually married—cursed fools—I have no other Georgia news but what I have already written you—

I don't write Mein untill I get to Sav^h^. having nothing to say from here, I have not heard of the Georgia's arrival at Amelia, but have no doubt she is in, you can tell him this & that the Leo (I hear,) sailed about a fortnight ago for Liverpool—

William Heyward (Miss Pontoux's husband) is dead[26] —God bless you all prays My dear Eliza yours ever faithfully & affectionately

R M

Mrs Mackay
care Mess^s^. Alex^r^. Mein & Co.
p British Packet from New-York— } Liverpool England

88: ROBERT MACKAY TO ELIZA ANNE MACKAY

Ship Georgia, Amelia Island
13th Feby. 1810

I began a letter to you a little while ago, & by the time I had reached the third page, I found I had got among Lumber & plantation matters, so I have turned it over as an Epistle to John & sit down to tell you that I arrived here in the boat Eliza on Saturday morn^g^.—Left Sav^h^. on wednesday, embarked at Beaulieu[27] where I was very kindly rec^d^. by M^rs^. Neyle,[28] her husband was from home, slep't that night at Owens's,[29] who accompanied me that far, the next night I lay in the Boat near to Maj^r^. Butler's, I could not go ashore as the poor old Man is in a state of derangement from the death of his Grandson,[30] in whom all his hopes & expectations were wrapt up, the next night

I got to Cumberland where the good folks at Dungeness rec^{d}. me with the usual hospitality, Cornelia was at her own plantation, but came home the next morning to breakfast, she looks charming & interesting in her weeds,[81] but is very thin—accompanied by *Brother Ray*[82] & Mr Whitney I came here after breakfast & found the Georgia half discharged, in the even^{g}. I went up to St. Marys with Mr Pell & there saw Mr Roberts & Delany—with the two last I went the day after being Sunday to see how the Lumber cutters were going on & returned that even^{g}. having been 27 miles up the St. Mary's, they have made a beginning but have not got things quite in order yet, & Picket is exorbitant in his demands of wages which he will not diminish from his last contract, & we can't better ourselves just now, as no other person can be had—I wrote you twice from Sav^{h}. where I passed a very pleasant week & there mentioned Sally's having added a Son[83] to the family on the 3rd Inst^{t}. & was doing very well—I have promised to make Dungeness my home, while in this part of the world, but having sent Sam off with the Eliza to take 26 of the people to Oatlands I am at present without a boat, but when it is necessary shall get the Rambler from Delany—Mr Pell & myself with Capt. P. *keep house* on board the Georgia, Hector Mitchel, Ja^{s} Carruthers & M^{r}. Calder are astern of us in a Schooner, where I am told they have frequent Turtle dinners—we are in a plainer stile, accomodating ourselves with a slice of ham & a Beef steak from the Amelia market, which I assure you is far from bad—at present however we are going upon a fine round of Beef I bro^{t}: from Sav^{h}, there are many other messes on board the different ships in the harbour but few of the members are known to you, the weather since I came down has been most delightful indeed, but I had heavy rain the whole way from Savannah—We have abundance of Oranges, & Capt. P. has just brought to a boat with fish, so that we make out very well—

In a day or two I shall go to St. John's & see there what's doing, I will of course do all I can to forward things but they are as yet strange to me, & such a pack of Scoundrels to deal with is beyond conception, a Cock-pit produces far more honour & fair dealing—

I saw Mrs Gordon & Seagrove at St. Mary's & young Ker[84]—the whole of the Ker's are removing to Sav^h^. to live, a Son of Littlefields,[85] his eldest, is come on to St. Mary's to establish as a Lawyer, he seems a genteel young Man, & I hope may do well, he does not like the place much, & I am sure I am not surprised at it—I hope you continue Margarets cold bath, it is the only remedy we have to cure her of the Rickets, & pray remember the request I have made yourself of consulting D^r^. Brandreth on your own case, & of attending to his advice strictly—recollect how much depends upon you, & besides you will look old when you are only a very young woman if you don't mind—

Remember me affectionately to all around you & believe me always My dear Eliza

Yours faithfully
Robt: Mackay

Mrs Robt: Mackay
Care of Mess^s^. Alex. Mein & Co.
p Hibernia }
Finlay— } Liverpool

89: ROBERT MACKAY TO ELIZA ANNE MACKAY

Ship Georgia, Amelia Isl[d].
18th *Feb*[y]. *1810*—

The day before yesterday being post day, I went up to St. Mary's & there rec[d]. My dear Eliza's two letters of 28th Nov[r]. & 6th Dec[r]. forwarded from Sav[h]: by M[r] Simpson, you may suppose how anxious I was to get these, & what my disappointment was at waiting a whole week for them—However I am at last gratified to hear you were all well at so late a date & very thankful to you for your punctuality in writing—From your letter & Johns together, I observe with much pleasure that he is at last about to take to himself a wife—I cannot help however observing your air of mystery in concealing the name of the happy object of his choice, or of leaving any channel open through which I might have made a tolerable lucky guess—however I suppose a few weeks will unroll this concealment, as he says he will write fully on the subject in his next—I can only assure you it is not from vacant curiosity that I should have felt gratified at knowing who the Lady was, but from that real warmth of friendship & affection, which creates in me the same interest that I think I experienced when choosing for myself—I am however perfectly satisfied that his selection will be a good one, & I shall add that it will be her own fault if she is not one of the happiest wive's in the world—Your manner of expressing the subject has precluded the possibility of its being a renewal of an old attachment—therefore I am left in a wide field of conjecture, yet who else could it be, when to the very date of your letter he was shut up in the house?—

I have written you by the Hibernia of my arrival here on the 10th & that I had been up the St: Mary's to see after the lumber cutters, since that I have been here except post day when I went up to get my letters & left Mr Roberts at St. Mary's—Mr Pell & I keep bachelors hall on board, & what with ships provisions, (for all the finer stores have been long since exhausted) a little fish which we get now & then, Amelia beef & other matters, we make out very well, today being sunday I have luckily a fine haunch of Venison for dinner, which we bought yesterday for half a dollar—This kind of marooning agrees most wonderfully with me, I can assure you, you never saw me with as much beef on my bones as I now have & I only want you with me to be very contented & very happy—The time draws on, & I hope we shall not be much longer seperate, as soon as I have loaded the Georgia here, which it is probable I may now do for Liverpool, I shall get on to Sav^{h}. & finish as fast as I can what I have to do there & take my passage in the first good ship to join you—By that time I hope some plan will be matured so that I may form an opinion of what we are to do, whether return to live in Sav^{h}. or continue in Liverpool—I have some how or other a notion that I like Georgia best, but I dread it on the children's account—Smokey chimneys are horrible to be sure & I hope you have got clear of them —I am glad you have got the house in other respects habitable, & I quite long to see the Garden & our little happy souls frolicking & enjoying themselves in it—I hope Margaret improves upon her bathing, for I am quite distressed to think of Rickets, pray attend to its being kept up regularly, & do my darling Soul recollect yourself—let me beg of you as you love me to apply to D^r^. Brandreth & be governed by his advice—I have mentioned this so often that I shall not repeat it—I know you will now agree & conform to my urgent request—As to Hannah you had better keep her quiet untill I return, as if we all come to Georgia in the Fall, it is better that she should be with us, if not—she will come with John or some other person who will take care of her—Her husband is very well & anxious to see her, he told me he would send her a letter—& sure enough old Phillis presented me with one from him to forward—but it happens to be the very identical letter she wrote to him—directed back to her, without a single word in addition—I suppose he thought a letter was a letter, & whether this one or one brought from the Post-Office, it was all the same, however it is either very great neglect of her, or very great stupidity in him, & I think you had better not mention it to her—I observe that your list of acquaintances is increased by M^rs^. Smith & M^rs^. Lake's having called upon you, this is particularly civil of Mrs Smith, & really shews a kindness on her part that we could not calculate upon—M^rs^. Lake I have always understood lives in such a gay way, that I suspect such plain folks as we are will scarcely form an intimacy with her, but we must be civil in turn—I am sorry to find my friend Miss Gray's name has not once found a place in any of your letters—we are indebted to that family for many attentions & civilities, & I cannot reconcile it to myself in any shape, that you should cut her acquaintance, or even be on distant terms with her—I should have been pleased to hear something of M^rs^. Douglas, through M^rs^. Tayleur or some other way you may hear of her—I never in my life saw such delightful weather as we have here, & the quantity of fine ships in this harbour gives a busy & interesting appearance to the situation which is in itself pretty—John will tell you of our visit from Don Bartolo's[86] family, I was pleased to see them so much gratified—Your account of the children is delightful & I really long to see them & you—but I must put up with all the patience I can, a few months longer absence, in the mean time I hope you will continue your punctuality in writing, I never knew you so good a correspondent before, & I am very gratified for it—for what pleasure can equal that of hearing from those we love above everything—Kiss the Children for me & remember me affectionately to all around you—I shall write soon again & always am my beloved Eliza most affectionately & faithfully your

R M

Mrs Mackay
Care of Mess^{s}. Alex^{r}. Mein & Co.
Liverpool—

90: ROBERT MACKAY TO ELIZA ANNE MACKAY

Amelia Island 20th Feb^{y}: 1810—

My dear Eliza—

Some of the Ships I have written to you by from this place, have been detained for a long time with contrary winds, but a fine Northwester this morning took them out, & has in some measure thin'd the harbour, however there are still a great many here, & yet a vast deal of property to be removed—

Mr Roberts came down from St. Mary's this morning, brings us nothing new, intends passing a few days with Mr Pell & I are at Bachelors hall, (for such we stile the Georgia,) the Cabin is completely a Counting-room & we are both much engaged in writing all day, but the old gentleman amuses himself, in reading, walking the deck & some times goes on shore—We have not had besides him a single visitor on board, let me however except Don Bartolo & his family who came to see the ship a day or two ago & went away highly pleased, we all seem to be here for the purpose of attending to business, & though Carruthers, Hector Mitchel & Calder mess on board of a vessel at a small distance from us, we have never exchanged a call—we some times meet on the beach or before the Commandants door for a few minutes & there ends our intercourse—I have sent Capt. Peirce to Savannah to lay in provisions for the Ship, as there is now every prospect of the Intercourse being renewed, in which event I shall load her directly from hence to Liverpool, having written you often all my subject is exhausted, & living on board Ship in Amelia harbour, I am of course not much in the way of replenishing—the post comes but once a week, the last brought My dear Eliza's very acceptable letters of 28th Nov^r. & 6th Decr. by M^r. Simpson, by the next I have little to look for that can afford me much gratification, I however turn my eyes very often across the Bar, in the hope of discovering some Liverpool vessel, & I am not without expectation of seeing Moffat & his Wife very soon, as Gibson told me he was to come out this month, & this is most probably the place he must embark for, by him I shall surely get letters from you, for you have been so good &

punctual a correspondent, I know you will not allow such an opp^{y}. to escape you—Your acco^{t}. of the Children is pleasing beyond description, & yet it makes me melancholy when I think how far we are apart, but I am reconciled when I remember that a few months more will bring us together again—I am not at all dissatisfied at being here on any other score than your absence, were you with me I should be happy even under the despotism of a Florida Governor & his petty minions ashore here—I promised & intended to make Dungeness my head quarters, but I find my time & attention so entirely occupied here, that I have not been there since I called in passing, I saw Sands in St. Mary's on post day, he said he would come to Amelia & spend tomorrow on board the Georgia, I beg'd of him to bring Cornelia & the Girls with him, but he "would not be troubled with such baggage" was the only reply I got—I confess I shall be as well satisfied if he brings us a boat load of vegetables—for though we have abundance of plain fare & make out very well, we have no delicacies to display to the ladies—We have had the most delightful weather since I came here that was ever seen, if anything rather warm, but generally a pleasant breeze, & the moon shines so bright, that we can almost read by it—I have just bought for half a dollar one of the finest strings of Sheep-head you ever saw, so that tomorrows dinner is provided, our Steward dresses them in a very superior way, something like the Tautog of Rhode-Island—

I put some letters for you & John the day before yesterday on board the Thornton & Fisher both for Liverpool, & besides wrote him fully of his matters here by the Hibernia, all which letters are now at sea with a fair wind, this goes by the Thetis the vessel which brought Mr Roberts here, she takes away about half of our cargo of Tobacco, I forward a letter from Delany for your Brother to which I need add nothing for the present, having a good deal of other writing to attend to—Mr Roberts also writes so that a letter from me is not necessary—As soon as the Georgia has commenced loading I shall go to St. John's for a few days—As yet tell John I have collected nothing but the Bonds due this month by G. & A. Atkinson[87] (together 1698^{85}/100 $) & am to get 20 or 25 Bags Cotton from Don Bartolo, which shall be ship'd by the first opp^{y}. together with what Delany may have ready—Kiss the Children for me, & tell them how much I love them—Remember me to all around you & believe me ever My darling wife your faithful & affectionate

R M

Mrs Mackay
Care of Messrs Alex^{r}. Mein & Co.
Merchants
p Thetis }
Capt. Davis } Liverpool

91: ROBERT MACKAY TO ELIZA ANNE MACKAY

Amelia Island 24th Feby. 1810—

My dear Eliza

I went yesterday morning to St. Mary's being post day & got a few lines from both Mein & Scott, but not a word of news or anything interesting to communicate to you,

I was in hopes we should have heard of the Intercourse Bill being passed, but it is hung up for the present in the Senate, & there is no saying how long they may keep it there,[88] this is to me a very great disappointment, as I wish to load the Georgia immediately off from here for Liverpool, however I can't help it, & I see no other prospect at present but to send her to Sav^h^. & wait the event of things, for it is impossible to send her to an English port from this, without infringing the Laws & making myself subject to unpleasant consequences, which however hard the restrictions may be I am determined never to do—I had written Williamson very particularly about some of the Florida matters, & was much disappointed at receiving no letter from him by return of post yesterday, but Mein mentions that Sam was to set off, as yesterday, in the Eliza & I suppose he will bring some of the things wanted by Pickett, & I daresay I shall then hear from Williamson—Capt Peirce who I mentioned to you I had sent to Sav^h^., is to return in the Eliza—When she arrives I shall go down to St. John's, then to Picketts & afterwards make the best of my way to Sav^h^ Mr Pell went up by the mail boat this morning, therefore I am alone at Bachelors hall, the harbour is thinning & I shall see fewer faces on shore daily, Carruthers, Gray & several others went with Pell, I shall endeavour not to be long after them—I have really nothing to make a letter about, but cannot let a good opp^y^. escape, & I know that a single line will be pleasing to you—Tell John (who I hope is by this time a happier man than he ever was) that Atkinson has paid his last Bond due next Feby. from which I deducted the Interest at 5 p C^t^. for the time anticipated, the proceeds I have remitted to Williamson, I see little hope of collecting anything else at present, I wish most sincerely he had all his concerns out of this Province—

There is nothing in the Sav^{h}. papers but the death of M^{rs}. Gunn,[39] who will really be a loss, for she has long been valuable as the best Tavern keeper in the place—I don't know whether I have mentioned that Genl. Mitchell is Governor of the State, that Milledge has resigned all his publick honours & assumed the station of a private Citizen, Judge Tait is elected to the Senate in his room—Spalding[40] has bought Sutherlands Bluff for 50,000 Dol^{s} & *tells me* he is now the most popular character in the State of Georgia —Kiss the Children for me, remember me to all around you & believe me ever My dear Eliza Yours faithfully

R M

Mrs Mackay
Care of Mess^{s}. Alex^{r}. Mein & Co.
Liverpool

92: ROBERT MACKAY TO ELIZA ANNE MACKAY

Amelia Island 26th Feby. 1810

My dear Eliza

The inclosed I received by Capt. Peirce last even^{g}. from Sav^{h}. he came down with Sam in the Eliza with some supplies for Picketts & I am just going up there with him, I shall be back tomorrow night & then visit St John's, after which I shall make as fast as possible for Sav^{h}. for I am completely sick of this place—I have not a word of news from Sav^{h}., Miss Hunters letter will give you all that's going on I suppose—The Non-intercourse is not yet removed & I fear it will be kept longer than I had an idea of —which is perplexing—Mr Dehon[41] of Newport is appointed to the new Church in Charleston (St Michaels) which is an agreable change for him I should think—

I am beginning to be impatient to hear from you again, remember me affectionately to all around you—Kiss the Children & believe me ever faithfully My dear Eliza Your

R M

Mrs Mackay
Care of Mess^s^. Alex^r^. Mein & Co.
Liverpool—

93: ROBERT MACKAY TO ELIZA ANNE MACKAY

Amelia Island 5th March 1810.

My dear Eliza

I begin to be very anxious for some arrival to hear how you My darling wife & children are—I have had nothing since Mr Simpson, indeed there has been but one ship from Liverpool after him & as she had very few letters, I imagine it was not known she was coming—this out of the way place would be more pleasant than it is, if one could hear more frequently from you—There was a ship from London yesterday, she left Portsmouth the 10th. Jany. which is three weeks later than anything we have had from England, but the Capt. says there is not a word of news & has not a paper, which is truly provoking—By the Maryanne

I wrote John of my visit to Pickets, & informed him things were going on very well, about 300,000 feet of Lumber nearly ready & I have now, no doubt but the contract will be very easily complied with—I think of going to St. Johns tomorrow, I am about to lose my *house* here, as the Georgia is preparing to go to Sav^{h}. & will sail the first wind, so that I shall soon follow her, finding I can do little good to John's affairs by remaining here—

By a letter from Mr Scott last mail, I find that on the 27th Ult^{o}. Miss Gibbons was married to Mr Trumbull, the knot was tied at 11 O'Clock in the forenoon, nobody present but Mr Holcomb & the family—My trip last post day to St. Marys was more pleasant than hitherto, as I found several of the Lawyers from Sav^{h}: who had arrived to attend the Court, Berrien,[42] Lawson &^{c}., I was invited to meet them on Saturday at Mr Seagroves, but was obliged to come down here in the forenoon—I have been so constantly engaged here that I have not yet made a second visit to Dungeness, though so short a distance from me, I shall however see them on my return from St. John's & stay there a night en passant—

Scott mentions to me that George Baillie was at the point of death at Philadelphia, he has been there since last summer, M^{rs}. & Miss B. are with him—I have only a short letter from Mr Williamson by post, & suppose they are all well, as he says nothing to the contrary—his time he tells me is so occupied on the *Bench* of the Inferior Court, that he has no leisure for anything else—By the Adventure I sent a bundle of Newspapers to Mr Mein, which you may have a look at by sending for, but there was little in them—

Pray remember me to all around you, & believe me ever my darling Wife & Children Yours faithfully

R M

I met And^{w}. McLean on my last visit to St Marys, he lives above McGirths bluff on St Johns, & had brought his whole crop, 9 Bags of Cotton to market, he plants with five negroes & has four children poor fellow—I had a great deal of conversation with him & he enquired very affectionately after you & the children, he came down last even^{g}. & slept on board, but went off with the Tide at 4 this morn^{g}—

Mrs Mackay
Care of Alexander Mein Esqr.
Liverpool
p Mary—)

94: ROBERT MACKAY TO ELIZA ANNE MACKAY

Amelia Island 5th March 1810.

My dear Eliza

To see anybody that has lately seen me I know will give you pleasure, I have therefore Mr John OReilly[43] (the Fathers brother) to introduce to you, & have requested him to call as soon as he arrives in Liverpool, he sails tomorrow morning early, in the Spanish Ship Visconde Wellington, for Greenock, but goes from thence to Liverpool, he will describe Amelia Island to you & no doubt tell you that he would just as soon live in England—however let me not abuse our living here, we have bought a fine Turtle only three days from New Providence at the price of Beef, & a small supply of things have just arrived from Savannah so that we are very well off—I go to St. Johns tomorrow & shall be back here in a few days, & after that push for Savannah, for which place the Georgia sails the first fair wind, Hector Mitchel has invited me to shift my flag to his vessel, when my own has left me, which I shall very willingly do, for the few days I remain after her—

I am getting impatient for arrivals, it is a long time since your last, which Charles Simpson brought, came to hand, & I long to hear & know all about you & the Children—Mr Roberts has a slight touch of the Gout, which has vexed the old Gentleman sadly, as he thought he had got clear of it altogether—He is not so bad as to be confined to bed, but it is with difficulty that he can hobble about the room, he stays at Mr Sharps, who is married & lives in St. Mary's —My last letter from Scott mentions that George Baillie was in Philadelphia at the point of death—he & his family have been there since last summer—

You will of course be attentive to M^r^ O'Reilly—Kiss the children remember me to all around you & believe me ever My dear Eliza

Yours faithfully
Robt: Mackay

Mrs Mackay
N°. 5 Stanhope Street
p favour of
Mr John O'Reilly— } Liverpool

95: ROBERT MACKAY TO ELIZA ANNE MACKAY

Amelia Island 11th March 1810—

My dear Eliza

I have been kept here longer than I wished by several days of hard rain, which is unpleasant at any time but terrible in a Canoe, however the prospects brighten this morn^g. & I expect the Georgia will be at sea on her passage to Sav^h in an hour from this & I on my way in the Eliza for St-John's—I can't tell you how I was gratified to hear from you by Mr Tucker in the ship Savannah a few days ago, it was your letter of 20th Jany. by which I am happy to find you were all well & pretty comfortably fixed—The Bill to open the Intercourse, amended by removing all restrictions whatever, (except the admission of Publick ships of War) has passed the Senate & in a few days will become a law—so that we are once more at liberty to go where we please—The Georgia will be loaded from Sav^h for Liverpool & if she was a month later I would go in her—Poor George Baillie is dead, he has been for some time at Philadelphia & was supposed to be recovering, but a relapse has taken him off suddenly—M^rs. Baillie had a Son not long before his death—

Young Tom Gibbons is married to Miss Dayton of New Jersey—the most extraordinary match I ever heard of—She is apparently a Lady of refined & most accomplished manners, & the most elegant figure I ever saw—has hitherto been a first rate toast in the Northern States & came to Sav^h to spend the winter with the Gibbons family—His description I need not give you—how such a couple can promise themselves happiness is odd—This marriage gave rise to the report of Miss G. being married, which is premature, for the 15th is the day fixed for making Mr Trumbull & her happy—

A propos of marriages—you say not a word nor give a hint of John's progress—you have really started one's curiosity & given it time to cool—There are other vessels expected & I hope by the time I return from St. Johns to have more letters from you—Mr Roberts has had a touch of the Gout, but is better & now able to go about again—Pray remember me affectionately to all around you, God bless you My darling Wife & Children prays

Yr. ever affectionate

R M

Mrs Mackay
care Messs. Alexander Mein & Co.
p Mary) Liverpool

96: ROBERT MACKAY TO ELIZA ANNE MACKAY

Amelia Island 20th. March 1810

I have just wrote you My dearest Eliza by the Paragon (which I think a safer oppy. than this) a long letter, but altogether on the affairs of your Fathers Estate & intended for John, but will also serve to let you know what I am about—tired enough you may be assured of this province & I would give the world to be away—I am removing the Negroes as fast as possible into Georgia, Don Bartolo having given security against Atkinsons attachment & I hope soon to be done & to get back to Sav^{h} I came from St. Johns on the 15th. & took up my abode with Hector Mitchel who has a most comfortable cabin on board the Report—Ja^{s}: Carruthers, & Mr Calder are with us & having at present a good supply of Turtle from the Bahama's, & some poultry from Sav^{h}. we make out better than any mess in the harbour—I went to St. Mary's on the 16th. & met M^{rs}. Miller & Louisa there, they had been detained several days for want of a Boat to carry them home, & I was very happy of having the Eliza to send them down in—They have been very civil & useful, in receiving & taking care of the Negroes sent over to Dungeness—By Sam's return they sent me a very acceptable supply of fine Cabbage, Carrots, Turnips, Beets &^{c}., so that they are very popular at present on board the Report—I can't say when I shall get away from here but I hope in a week or two, The Timber contract goes on very well, & Mr Roberts has one of Logan & C^{os}. ships to load which will begin in a few days to take in—I have remitted to Mr Mein for John's acco^{t}. a Bill from Waterman[44] for 225 £ St^{g}. being for the Lumber on Nassau River which Picket sold him—also 18 Bags cotton p the Gute Frau, which I wish safe the crop is not all ginned yet, but I shall ship it as fast as I can get freight for it—I staid three days at Delany's & Slept at Fort George on my return, there I was rec^{d}. with much kindness & attention & many enquiries after you—I have no news at all, the Intercourse Bill has not passed yet, but we expect every day to hear of it—The Georgia arrived at Sav^{h}. safe, the day after she left this, & I hope will soon be loaded for Liverpool, I shall not be able to go in her, but will follow soon after her—Doct^{r}. Proctor[45] is married to Harriet Houstoun—& I see that M[rs]. John Turnbull[46] is dead—you remember she was a short time in Sav[h]. a pleasant little woman—The Negroes seem all glad to go to Georgia, but I have been dreadfully pester'd by many of those that were sold, begging to be taken back, saying they were enticed away by wicked people—in one instance I have given way to keep peace with a large family—Old Minah who was sold with her daughter to Richard,[47] says it was all a plan of his to get her, & her other Children making such an uproar about seperation I have taken her back—she is of little value & it makes not much odds, but makes it pleasant to preserve peace & quiet—& I am sure it is very agreable to me to make them comfortable & as happy as they can be—I am now looking anxiously for other arrivals for late letters from you, your last was by the Savannah—In it you refer to one I have not rec[d]—God bless you My dear Wife & Children—believe me ever yours

R. M

M[rs] Mackay
Care of Mess[s]. Alex[r]. Mein & C[o].
Liverpool
p Mexicana)

97: ROBERT MACKAY TO ELIZA ANNE MACKAY

Amelia 21st March 1810—

My dear Eliza

Several vessels being ready to sail together, intending to take the benefit of convoy under the Pert, british Sloop of war at present here,—it is necessary to write by the different opp[s]:, consequently there can be little variety in the letters written within a day of each other—I am afraid John will complain of my not writing him, but as I have so little to say from hence, but what relates immediately to his affairs, you can give him a knowledge of matters—By this opp[y]. I send for him a Bill of Exchange from Waterman for 225 £. under cover to M[r] Mein, so that it may be accepted in case John should not be in Liverpool, this was rec[d]. in paym[t]. of the Lumber on Nassau which it was thought most prudent to sell, Picket fixed the bargain but I have not seen him since to ascertain the particulars—

I am busy removing the Negroes into Georgia as fast as possible & hope soon to finish, as I am really tired of being here & wish much to be in Savannah, Picket goes on well with the Timber & I have no doubt will complete the quantity very easily, M[r] Roberts has one ship now on her way up the River to take in—I have sent up Wheels, Chairs &[c]. to begin hawling & John may rest perfectly content that things will go on well—I however hope that it may be so arranged as to complete this contract in Georgia, as dividing one's force betwixt two Countries & under such peculiar circumstances is very unpleasant—I have not succeeded in selling any of the Lands, I was in hopes that I might have done something with M[c]Intosh[48] & went to Fort George for the purpose, but I could only obtain from him an offer to exchange new Rice lands on the Alatamaha,[49] which in the present situation is doing nothing—The Escrivano has offer'd for Taylor's 5,500$. provided he also has a family of negroes sold with it, & a long credit for both—& Arredondo[50] has offer'd 5,000$. for Hendrick's & the Ship-yard,[51] one third down & the rest in one & two years—Neither of which offers have I accepted—In the dispute with Capt. Atkinson we have obtained an order for another Arbitration, but unluckily the papers on both sides, coming from St. Augustine in the Mail, the boat was upset & the whole lost together—I have therefore little doubt but the first award must be paid, as Atkinson has already told me, that Arredondo, Cashen & Arambide who were the Arbitrators, are ready to swear to the justice of the demand which is 1400$—Delany has upwards of 20 Bags of Cotton packed, which I should have ship'd before now but for want of freight, it shall go the first opp^{y}. his own letter to John which I forwarded some time ago, gives him a knowledge of all that has been doing—We are still in suspence about the opening of the Intercourse, it has been expected for some time, & in consequence we are kept in a most unpleasant state of perplexity—they ought after going so far—either complete the thing at once—or say that it is to be continued—then we should know what to calculate upon—The Georgia has arrived at Sav^{h}. in one day from here, & I hope will soon be loaded for Liverpool, I should like much to be ready to go with her, but I fear that is impossible—however I don't intend being longer than a month after her, if I can help it—

It is extraordinary that Mr Hamilton has no acco^{t}. from any of his friends in England of the death of his wife, & at this hour he does not believe it—I had a message from him the day before yesterday, to know upon whose authority I had circulated the report, & informing me at the same time, that he had a letter saying both M^{rs}. H. & the child were quite well—there is something odd in this—Charles Simpson brought the information here as well as your letter to me—I really am sorry that I can write nothing interesting enough for you to read, but from this sad place of Musquitoes & Sand-flies what is to be expected—I have not been at Cumberland since I came down, but met M^{rs}. Miller & Louisa the other even^{g}—at St. Mary's where they were in distress for a boat to carry them home—this furnished me with an opp^{y}. of returning some of their civility & I sent them down in the Eliza,—by her return to Amelia they furnished me a very acceptable supply of fresh vegetables—The next even^{g}. the boat John arrived from the Mills with a cargo of negroes, which in the middle of the next night were landed at Dungeness—the Eliza, I then sent off for the remainder of the negroes, & the John went up to Pickets with the Wheels from the Garrison & some Corn from St- Mary's—It is reported that Ray Sands & M^{rs}. Skipwith are about to make a match of it, but when I called there as I came down I saw nothing like it—Louisa is certainly improved by her northern tour, I shall pass a day with them on my way home, which I hope will now be before long—Since the Georgia went away I have been with Hector Mitchel in the Report a vessel of his—Ja^{s}: Carruthers, Calder, him & myself keep bachelors hall together & make out very well—We have had several visits from Capt: Hall of the Pert, who is a very genteel young man, & we have been twice on board of him—I have been applied to by Billy Saunders for your address, he is going master of a spanish ship to Liverpool & sails in a few days —he will of course call upon you—I have seen no more of him than barely meeting him at dinner at Holzendorfs tavern in St. Mary's, when I go up there on post-days—I begin to feel anxious for another letter from you—though recollect I am not complaining, for you have been very good—but you know how much it would add to my happiness could I hear from you every day—your last was the 20th Jany. by the Savannah—

I have had many enquiries after Hannah among the people—her Brother Niger & all of them are quite well—Inclosed is a letter from her Nephew, written by me after his own diction—In hourly hopes of an arrival that I may again hear from you & with affectionate remembrance to all around you I remain My dear Eliza

ever faithfully yours
Robt: Mackay

Mrs Mackay
Care of Messrs. Alexr. Mein & Co.
Merchants
p Wm Heathcote } Liverpool
Capt. Campbell }

98: ROBERT MACKAY TO ELIZA ANNE MACKAY

St. Mary's 27th March 1810—

My dear Eliza

I left Amelia yesterday morning I hope for the last time, & went over to Mrs. Millers where I passed a very pleasant day, in the afternoon I came up here to pay off the little Bills that were due & to get a ham & some bread for my passage home in the Eliza,—For the last fortnight I have lived on board of H. Mitchel & we have been well off, from a good supply of Turtle & some other matters—

Delany sent me on friday night last, the remainder of the negroes & I have engaged a Drogger, (Capt. Timmons) to take the whole from Dungeness to Caustons, except those I can stow away in the Eliza—There is no possibility of shipping the Cotton for want of vessels, nor has there been since I came here, except the 18 Bags by the Frow—We have not a word of news—the Non-intercourse Bill still suspended & quite uncertain how it will end—

Capt. Billy Saunders informs me he sails for Liverpool in a few days, & I have just time to drop you a line to say what I am about, I shall stop one day at Spaldings & make as much haste home as I can—the Sand-flies beat everything I have met with—

God Bless you all—yesterday was our dear little Williams Birth day—I hope he is well & enjoyed it—Kiss them for me & believe me ever faithfully yours

R M

VI. From the North

VI. From the North

In the summer of 1816, Robert Mackay took his family to the North. He could have had little doubt that he was now established in business and respected as a citizen. The War of 1812 over, his vessels had resumed their schedules between Savannah and Liverpool; while the positions of honor bestowed upon him by the city of his choice were many and varied: "Capt. Artillery, Alderman, Church Warden, J[ustice of the] I[nferior] Court, Bank Director"—so runs the list in a contemporary document. He had reason to believe that any office of civic trust was his for the asking: no Savannahian more popular than he walked the sandy streets or attended concerts and balls.*

But it is doubtful whether Robert Mackay gave thought to such matters as he made his progress Northward. His mind was on family affairs: the selection of schools for his older children, and his wish to be present at the division of the silver that had belonged to his grandfather, Godfrey Malbone, who had died a half century before. The Mackays rented a furnished house in Newport; servants were brought from Savannah; and in this "delightful climate," according to his daughter's memoirs, "there was every prospect of peace and happiness." But this was not to be. Troubled by bad health, Mackay left Newport to take the cure at the Northern spas. From New York he wrote in his usual humorous vein to Eliza: "it was impossible to walk two steps without falling foul of a Georgian." A thought of mature reflection crept into his description of

* "Family Compact" of Judge William Stephens (1818), manuscript in the Library of the Georgia Historical Society, Savannah.

the Hudson River steamboat on which he traveled to Albany: "What will this immense Country come to in the End, when at this early day, all the Luxuries of the World appear to have become necessary to the people for their common comforts?" But his impressions of Ballston Spa and Saratoga Springs were recorded with his customary verve. Satisfied that he had recovered both "flesh & health," Mackay announced after six weeks that he was eager for "a draft of the Good Porter in Newport in place of this Salt Water," and departed in high spirits to rejoin his family.

In September he again left Eliza in Newport and went to Morristown, New Jersey, to place his sons in school. On his way back to her, he wrote from Philadelphia, on October 1, 1816, what was to be his last letter. It gives further proof of his enthusiasm for new places ("This is a most charming City I think the handsomest I have ever been in"). He died suddenly in New York four days later.

99: ROBERT MACKAY TO ELIZA ANNE MACKAY

New York tuesday morn^{g}.
16th. July 1816—

My dearest Eliza

We arrived here at 6 O'Clock last even^{g}. after one of the sweetest passages I ever saw, only five passengers besides ourselves, & every thing good to eat & drink & famous beds, I wish you had been of the party, the views surpass every thing I have met with, & the beauty of the Country is delightful—This is more of a summer Climate than

Newport—I have seen nobody yet but Mr Bolton who I met just now & Mr Gairdners son who is a smart young British Officer—He informed me that Simpson was married to Miss Harvey, but I have no letters—Poor Mr Harvey has failed in Liverpool—an unlucky event to happen so immediately after his daughters marriage—We have been recommended to go to Miss Rogers's[1] house N°. 8 State Street where Williamson &^c. &^c. lodged but as we go to Albany at 8 OClock tomorrow morn^g. I think we shall remain at the Tontine Coffee house[2] where we took beds last night—It is now only 8 in the morn^g. & I can't call on Forbes[3] or Lenox & Maitland[4] before 9 or 10, If I am not too late for the Mail, I will inclose you some money, if I had had time to see them on our arrival, we would have embarked in a steam boat this morn^g., but this day must be lost & you will not hear again untill we are at Albany or Saratoga—We had very cold wea^r. on the passage & I have caught a Cold in my head but I hope not a durable one—

Williamson & C°. have left Town I learned from M^r McKinne last even^g., so I shall not see them untill my return from the Springs—

I can add nothing, having seen nobody but my best affection to all the Children, Miss Hunter &^c. &^c., & that I ever am yours

most affectionately

Robt: Mackay

By the Packet Express I have sent back a basket that bro^t. down our Porter, under the care of the Steward, a Black man named Cambridge—who promises to deliver it himself—

Your letters for Jam[a] are gone this morn[g]. in the Brig Jane—

Remembrance to M[r] Brinley[5] &[c]. &[c].

M[rs]. Mackay
Care of Tho[s]. Brinley Esq
Newport
Mail— R. I.—

100: ROBERT MACKAY TO ELIZA ANNE MACKAY

Saratoga Springs 20th July 1816
Saturday

My dear Eliza

Long before this day I hope you have rec[d]. my letter from New York, since which I must now, (being the first moment I have had leisure or opportunity,) inform you of my progress & transactions—I told you I arrived on monday Even[g]. at N York, where in consequence of Mitchels lameness & Gairdners Gout, we agreed to sleep at the Tontine Coffee house being just by the Vessel, we went there & lay but did not sleep, for I'll swear never were beds so well inhabited before, Cervantes describes some of the Beds that Sancho occupied, but he never slept or attempted to sleep at the Tontine in N York, or he would have told his story more feelingly I am certain—

The next morn[g]. after breakfasting, our first step was to provide a place, where we might find a little sleep at night, & we pitched upon Mechanic Hall, kept by your former Landlady M[rs]. Marcellin,[6] there we went & secured a footing & I certainly never felt more satisfied with bed, provisions, attendance & everything else that we wanted in my life—In the forenoon I saw Lenox Maitland & Co. Mr Robert Lenox[7] & Coll. Forbes, with all the inhabitants of Savannah I believe, who seemed to have been transported to N York to meet us, it was impossible to walk two steps without falling foul of a Georgian, & as I was lugging Mitchel along by the arm to dinner, who the devil did I fall in with but Mrs. Pinder & Miss Bellinger, who seized us instantly & put us in requisition to assist them in hunting lodgings, they had come on under the care of Mr Pelot, who in consequence of some mistake had got largely into debt, & was closely pursued by the Sheriff, whose instances were so pressing that Mr Pelot decamped in the night for Georgia or else where, & left his fair charges to shift for themselves;—but it was past 2 O'Clock & the Steam boat went at 5, & we had Mrs. Marcellins dinner to eat, therefore though their request was very cogent & their situation making it very reasonable, we were obliged to decline complying & left them, after promising Mrs. Pinder, which she would not let me off, from doing, to endeavour to procure a lodging for Majr. McCall[8] & herself at Newport, & to write them when I succeed, In vain I told her I was then on my way to Quebeck & would not see Newport for Six weeks, but promise I was obliged to —After Dinner we called at Forbes's being in our way to the Steam boat & took a Glass of Wine, & at 5 went on board, where I found Lenox & Maitland waiting to see us off; certainly there never was on earth or ocean in this World before such establishments as these Steam Boats are—Cleopatra's Barge was quite a Cockle shell to them,

& in point of elegance not at all to be compared, it would take a months conversation to give you any thing like an idea of them, we had 160 Passengers in the Richmond, & nothing like croud—plenty of room & never in each others way, three courses of dinner, all hot & not one thing at a second or third that had been at a first table the choicest fish, meats, pastry &c. &c. imaginable, & in a stile, without seeing, I am sure you would not believe or think possible, & all this to travel to Albany 160 miles for 7 dols., where in 24 hours we arrived & slept in a comfortable Inn, with good beds & every thing very neat & after Breakfasting set out in the Stage for this place, We stopt at Ballston for dinner & arrived here at about 5 OClock yesterday afternoon & where as well as at Ballston, we have found every thing on the establishment of the Steam-boat, nothing but all the Luxury, that can be thought of—What will this immense Country come to in the End, when at this early day, all the Luxuries of the World appear to have become necessary to the people for their common comforts?—From Forbes Lenox, Maitland, & Geo: Johnston we recd every attention but could not dine with them—I have now to tell you of some things not of so pleasant or agreable a nature—I sent on about Six weeks before we came, 5,000 Dols. worth of Wine to Lenox & Maitland to remit me Cash for, to pay the Custom house & about 3000 Dols. of other Goods to Forbes for our expences &c, but such is the stagnant state of all sorts of business, that not a Cent can be got for anything, in fact I feel miserable on the subject, the Custom house will wait for nothing & God knows what I can do, I have directed Lenox & Forbes both, to sell for what they can get & send the money on to Sav[h]: to pay as far as it will go—but I assure you I don't feel very comfortable on the subject just now—I requested of Forbes to inclose you a draft for 2 or 3 Hundred dollars which you will request T. Brinley to get discounted for you, & that will I hope keep you clear, untill I get back to you—

These are notions of course for your own ear, but they are facts & I am sorry that I am obliged to record them to you—

Since writing the above I have dined at the large Table, which consists of three long Tables spread as long as an immense room will admit of, by accident I got the head of the middle one, & who by me but M[rs]. Haig[9] the only Georgia female at Table or in the house, she was as communicative as usual, & did at length venture to say that Capt[n]. Haig was in very bad health & hoped I intended to drink nothing but the Saratoga Water while I remained at the Springs for fear of her husband joining me—

Miss Heyward & her Mother also were at one of the Tables, but the Son & Brother is here also, & I have not met him yet, if I do I will find out their destination & act accordingly.

It is quite impossible to say yet what effect the Water is like to have on me, or what length of time I shall be obliged to stay, but having come this distance I am determined to give them a fair chance, I however do not find the Water so strong or so powerful as I expected, but they tell me a few days are required before their effects are known,—I find the post comes but once a week to this place, but daily to Ballston, Mitchel & I mean to ride over there tomorrow after breakfast & look for Letters, where you will please direct for me, the distance is only Eight miles & where we shall remain a week after we have finished here, the next time I write I shall have seen more of things here & shall be better able to tell how I like them, but from what I have seen, I should be very glad if we had not such a regiment of young ones to havoc you here, though I certainly see nothing very fascinating among the Ladies as yet—

I hope you all continue well & that our poor little Sarah[10] has got well over her weaning, I am satisfied that the air of Newport will be of as much service to all of you as the air here, particularly as you are not in want of the Waters—M^{r}. Thos. Tunno[11] is here & came on very bilious & debilitated, much in my way with incessant head-achs, but he is getting rid of all his complaints, he goes with Gardner his Son & Mitchel, next week to Niagara & a Tour to Quebec & other parts of Canada, from which he expects great relief—I should like to accompany them—though I believe we shall be as well off at Newport & gain as much health there as anywhere else—

You must be tired of this long epistle, I will therefore give you a respite by stopping & will write again to you by next post, unless I stop long enough at Ballston to-morrow—Affectionate remembrance to all around & believe me My Dear Eliza ever & sincerely Yours

Robt. Mackay

Ballston 22nd. July 1816

M^{r}. Tunno, Mitchel & myself—have just come over here for a ride & a charming one we have had, no letters in the Office for me, I hope the next post will bring me Acco^{ts}

that you are all well—No Georgians but Haig & Wife & ourselves at Saratoga & no company *her*

Yrs *R M*

M[rs] Mackay
Care of Thomas Brinley Esq
Newport
Mail) Rhode-Island—

101: ROBERT MACKAY TO ELIZA ANNE MACKAY

Saratoga 23rd. July 1816

My dear Eliza

I wrote you a line yesterday at the end of my last letter, when I went up to Ballston to forward it by post, we dined there & returned here in the Afternoon—I this morning saw a letter written by Doct. Hosack, on the subject of the Ballston Water, I think Mary Annes Case is described in it & the waters particularly recommended, if she does not improve in her health, I would like to have her sent to New-York, where I would go down & meet her & return with her to Ballston, let me know what you think of this & if you like it, it might be tried at once, direct for me all letters that you write for the ensuing week at Ballston Spa, New York, & they will reach me, I have been here since friday, & have found a most enormous appetite—but you will say I had enough of that before, & I am really recovering flesh & health, but untill this day, strong as this Congress spring is, the water has had no other effect on me than increasing appetite & a general feeling of being better than I was, but now the Water has begun with me I cannot leave it untill it has given me a good clearing out, & then I must take a week at Ballston to finish off & brace up, so that it will be two or three weeks yet before I can turn my face towards Newport, where I assure you I am very anxious to be, for I can think of nothing on Earth but you & the Children—Col[l]. Johnston came here last Even[g]. & Rob[t]. Watts, M[rs]. Johnston is in Philadelphia, M[r] Mein & family are arrived at N. York & I think it probable he will be here in a day or two, as I have written him to come up, & after I see him it will be determined whether he goes to Newport or not. M[r] Forbes told me of a capital School for our Boys near to N. York which he is to write me fully about, & if he is right in his description, it would suit us better than any other, of which I hope a day or two more will give me information—M[rs]. & Miss Heyward still are here & stick to the waters, but their Gentleman Relation has not yet returned & there is so much reserve on the part of the Ladies at this place that we have yet not made acquaintance of any kind & I suppose shall not while we stay here—M[rs]. Haig sits by my side at every meal & her Husband also, she is a poor creature as I ever met with & has not made one acquaintance among the croud male or female, Capt Haig is I think in a bad state of health & the waters appear to do him no good M[r]. M[rs] & the Miss Telfairs are expected this Even[g]. from New York—I hope my time will soon be expent here that I may join you at Newport, which except the mere Mineral qualities of the

Springs, is far finer air & a much healthier place than this, my stay will therefore not exceed a moment longer than will be considered absolutely necessary for the effect of the waters, I ought to hear from Mein tomorrow or the day after so that I may fix at once when I shall go to Newport, I mean to stop part of a day at Pomfret in Connecticut to see M^{rs}. Fog[12] on my way back to you—

My remembrance to Miss Hunter, her brother was well when the Georgians here left him—

God bless you all my dear E. & grant you plenty of health & happiness, tell Mary A. I will write her when I get back to B: Ton

Yours ever & sincerely

R. Mackay

I long to get a draft of the Good Porter in Newport in place of this Salt Water

M^{rs}. Mackay
Care of Thomas Brinley Esq
Newport
Rhode Island—

102: ROBERT MACKAY TO ELIZA ANNE MACKAY

New York 11th. Augt. 1816

My dear Eliza

You must by this time think I am neglecting you, but you must forgive me, for really with Mr Mein, Mr Gibbons & Mr Jackson & others, my time has been so occupied

I have not had time—I arrived here yesterday morning from Bal[l]ston & after calling on Mess^{s} Lenox & Co. I went over to Elizabethtown where I was heartily welcomed by M^{r} & M^{rs}. W^{mson}. & Children, Ja^{s}. Oliver & M^{rs}. Gibbons, M^{r} & M^{rs}. Turnbull &^{c}., I was obliged to stay & dine there, which being 17 miles from this employed me all day, I am now going with Col^{l}. & M^{rs}. Forbes to Church to hear Mr Bowen & my intention was to set out tomorrow morn^{g}. for New Haven, but I have promised to stay a day or two longer so that friday must take me into Connecticut, & thence as fast as possible to Newport, where Mein & family are to follow me in a few days, & where we must look out for Lodgings for them—I wrote Mary Anne on the 3rd. from Bal[l]ston & hope to hear from her before I leave this. I have determined on nothing about the Boys as yet, your Sister recommends Mr Rudds School at E: Town & Mr Forbes M^{r} McCulloch at Morristown, both said to be excellent, but the former too Crouded, I will fix on one or other in a day or two—My wine will not sell, & I am quite at a loss to raise 4900$. for Custom house purposes, but hope things are in some kind of train, to get along—Your Sister is quite well & very comfortably fixed at E: Town, but her Children do not look hearty, Mary has constant fever & looks not a bit better than in Sav^{h}.—but they are satisfied with the health of the place & think they are better, & are all delighted with the Schools, I don't like either, but this they won't hear, therefore I let them enjoy their opinions—

I shall see you so soon I don't know what to write you but affectionate remembrances I shall tell you a great deal of nonsense when we meet—God Bless you all & believe me ever My dear Eliza Yours sincerely & affectionately

R M

Mrs. Mackay
Care of Thomas Brinley Esq
Newport
Rhode-Island

103: ROBERT MACKAY TO ELIZA ANNE MACKAY

New York 14th Augt. 1816

I spent yesterday with Wmson at E: Town where I was glad to find Mrs. W's troubles ended for the present in having produced another fine Girl[18] who with herself are very well indeed—My intention was to have left N York this day for N Haven per Steam boat but I am sorry to say that I have not yet been able to fix with Mr McCulloch about the Boys, but Forbes is to hear from him by post finally on Saturday, when his Letter will be sent to us at Newport, & I sincerely hope the affair may be fixed—He is the very man I wish the Boys to be with, & Mrs McCulloch all that we can wish for, he has only 15 Scholars & will not exceed that number, they are kept to themselves & the master is their principal play-mate, French the Language commonly spoken & when a little advanced Italian —Mr Forbes has entered the names of his own 3 boys for admission, & has promised for us also, so that I hope we shall have them placed as a certainty in a short time—I don't like E.town at all, though W: & Wife are delighted with it,—

On board the Sloop George & Mary I have ship'd my two trunks she sails this morning & on friday I go in the Steam boat for New haven—Capt Walden promises to deliver the trunks to Mr Brinley, who knows him very well, please tell him to receive them & send them all on a dray & beg him to excuse the trouble I give him—I saw your letter to Sally—

I shall delay my time in Connecticut as little as possible, but not being allowed to travel on Sunday in that State, shall lose that day & try to see you on Monday if possible—

affectionate remembrance to all of you

Yours ever *R M*

Mrs Mackay
Care of Thomas Brinley Esq
p Capt: Walden with two Trunks } Newport Rhode Island

104: ROBERT MACKAY TO ELIZA ANNE MACKAY

New York 27 Septr 1816

My dear Eliza

I[t] wanted 20 minutes of 12 yesterday when I left the wharf in Newport & I landed here this day at 6 in the morning having Day Light at Hellgate 2½ hours—this will about beat Miss Hunter—The Boys are well & happy —tomorrow we go to Morristown Mein is with me Mitchel &^c^. &^c^. I hope this will find you all well & happy

I hope to be back to see the Plate divided,[14] but fear shall be too late—I hope they will give us fairplay—I have not time to say more but write a line & say which Musick is for Mary Anne, I dont know what to bring—

Yrs ever *R M*

Mrs. Robert Mackay
Care T: Brinley Esqr.
Newport
Rhode-Island

105: ROBERT MACKAY TO ELIZA ANNE MACKAY

Philadelphia 1st. Octr. 1816

My dear Eliza

I arrived here this morning after leaving the Boys with Mr McCulloch on Sunday, with whom I am particularly pleased, as well as with Mrs. McC. who is a sensible clever little woman, I wish you could have come on with me to see them, I think you would have been delighted, but I will tell you all about them when I get back which I shall make as soon as possible—Mrs Williamson has put it in her husbands head to send Jane & Nancy to Newport to stay all next year & they are as anxious about it as you can imagine, & it is determined that I call at E: town on Saturday & take them on with me so you must try to get them boarded with Miss Smith & you may expect us together the beginning or middle of the next week—

I have met Nicholas who is as kind as can be supposed, & we dine with him tomorrow, though Majr Butler[15] has sent us the most pressing invitation, which we have declined, but have given him a promise for the day after tomorrow after which we set off for home, where I hope I shall get in time to see the Plate divided after all, to which I hope there will be no objection now,—

I found M^rs^. Wmson & all hands well she writes you herself & I hope her Letter will reach you in time to drop her a line before Saturday as on that day I calculate to set out for Newport with her Girls—And I should like to hear from you first, but I have never been asked a word about it, they have just said—You must take them & fix them as you think proper—I din'd to day at the Washington Hotel & after dinner went to visit the U. S. Ship Franklin 74. one of the finest Ships I ever beheld—I hope to hear from you at N York to see what musick Mary Anne wants—Look after Stores & see to secure enough for us all—Lizette is very well & says How d'ye to all of you—

I am afraid I shall be obliged to go to Newport in the Stage, which will be very fatiguing—I don't know whether you you can write [*sic*: read] this I am writing very late at Night for tomorrow mornings Mail & I am so sleepy I can hardly keep my eyes open—This is a most charming City I think the handsomest I have ever been in, Remember me to all around you & kiss the little ones—

God bless you My dear Eliza prays

Yours ever & sincerely

R. M.

M^rs^. Mackay
Care Thos. Brinley Esqr.
Newport
Rhode Island—

Notes

I. "ROBERT MACKAY'S COMPT[s]. TO MISS M[c]QUEEN"

[1] In April, 1795, when Robert Mackay wrote this note to Eliza McQueen, her brother, John (1773–1822), was about to leave for East Florida to consult their father about his future. Born in Charles Town, the eldest of the family, he had been brought up in Europe. ". . . he was so long . . . [in France]," his niece, Margaret Mackay Elliott, wrote in a memoir, "that when he returned to England [at the age of nineteen,] he had entirely forgotten his natural language and only reached . . . [the house of a friend] by showing the direction written on a card."

This visit to Florida provided a dramatic incident in John's life. He lost no time in telling his father of rumors he had heard in Savannah of a French plot to seize East Florida from Spain. Don Juan McQueen, in turn, notified the Military Commander of the frontier, with the result that John was summoned before the acting Governor to make an official "declaration." This document, drawn up with all the formality of the day, was forwarded at once to the highest colonial authorities in Spain. The French invasion never took place, possibly because of the younger McQueen's timely warning.

John remained in Florida five years. He entered the firm of Panton, Leslie and Company, and at their office in Pensacola received a thorough mercantile education. About 1800 he gave up this position, returned to Georgia, and devoted the rest of his life to planting. He is credited with the introduction into the United States of the ribbon type of sugar cane. "This cane," Thomas Spalding, a pioneer in the sugar industry, wrote in 1848, "was brought from Tahiti in the Pacific to Jamaica by Lieutenant Bligh. It was brought from Jamaica to Georgia by a friend of mine, John McQueen Esq." (Quotation from a letter in "Sapelo Island," edited by Margaret Davis Cate; manuscript owned by the Sea Island Company of Sea Island, Georgia.)

[McQueen's "declaration" is in the Archivo General de Indias, Seville (Papeles de Cuba, Legajo 1438); a translation is in the Library of the Florida Historical Society, St. Augustine. Several letters from John McQueen, Junior, to his sister, Eliza, are published in *The Letters of Don Juan McQueen to his Family*, edited by Walter Charlton Hartridge (Columbia, South Carolina, 1943).]

[2] This reference to "the Spanish Grammars" shows that Eliza McQueen was improving her knowledge of that language in preparation for a visit to Florida. From other sources it is known that she reached her father's plantation on the St. John's River two months later, in the company of her mother and other members of the family. John

McQueen's impressions of his daughter at that time are given in a letter to his wife's sister, Lady Wright. "Miss Eliza has grown," he wrote, "but not so much as I was given to understand she had—but she is a good Girl of whom I am very fond" (*The Letters of Don Juan McQueen to his Family*, 27).

[3] The Cottage was a forty-five-acre plantation at Thunderbolt Bluff on the Wilmington River, five miles from Savannah. About 1788 John McQueen acquired this property, which had historic associations, for it had been the home of a prominent colonist, Captain Roger Lacy, the friend of John Wesley; and here, beneath an oak on the edge of the bluff, the founder of Methodism had conducted some of his earliest outdoor services. When John McQueen was forced to leave Georgia because of his debts, the Cottage was bought at public auction by Anne McQueen's brothers, Archibald and John Smith. It was maintained as a joint home by Mrs. McQueen and the Smiths, and in the parlor of "this little dwelling" (see above, page 34) Eliza McQueen was married to Robert Mackay.

[Materials for a monograph on the Cottage, assembled by the Savannah Writers' Project, are in the Library of the Georgia Historical Society, Savannah.]

[4] By "my present establishment in business," Robert Mackay was referring to his association with the brothers Alexander and William Mein begun on January 1, 1798. The firm of Meins and Mackay enjoyed immediate success in "the Shipping and Factorage line," maintaining a wharf at the river's edge and a store on the bluff above, at No. 1 Commerce Row; but it was dissolved in 1801 because of Alexander Mein's decision to return to Great Britain. William Mein and Robert Mackay then formed a partnership that lasted until Mackay's death in 1816.

[For notices and advertisements of these firms, see the *Columbian Museum & Savannah Advertiser*, February 9, 1798, and the *Georgia Gazette*, June 6, 1799, April 17, 1800, and January 22, 1801.]

[5] "Miss C." was Margaret Cowper (1777–?), first-cousin of Eliza McQueen and the younger daughter of Basil and Mary (Smith) Cowper. At the turn of the century, she was a reigning belle, her popularity extending beyond Savannah, which she often visited, and the Island of Jamaica, where her parents lived, to the larger circles of London and Liverpool. Her gay love affairs provided Robert Mackay with anecdotes over many years. In 1810 she married her first-cousin, John McQueen, Junior. The story of their protracted courtship is told in the phraseology of the period by Margaret Mackay Elliott. She writes that McQueen, on arriving in England in 1792, aged nineteen, "renewed a fancy he had always entertained

for his lovely cousin Margaret. After some time he addressed her, she refused him, but years after, when neither party was young, she rewarded his long attachment by the gift of her hand. . . ." For Eliza Mackay's account of the wedding, see above, page 173.

[6] "S." was William Scarbrough (1776–1838), a young man of fashion and business ability, now on the threshold of a spectacular career. The son of a wealthy planter of Beaufort District, South Carolina (see below, page 296), he was sent abroad for his education. After attending one of the English public schools and the University of Edinburgh, he served a commercial apprenticeship on the Continent. About 1798 Scarbrough established himself as a merchant in Savannah, and soon became a leading citizen. Allusions to a romance with Margaret Cowper are made in several of Robert Mackay's letters, but in 1805 Scarbrough married Julia Bernard of Wilmington, North Carolina (see below, page 272).

Scarbrough's interests were not confined to commerce and society: he had an aptitude of no mean order for mechanics. It is said that he discovered a new method of making long bridges, and that he also constructed a model of an aerial ship.

But what has given Scarbrough a national reputation was his support of the first transatlantic steamship venture. In 1818 he became one of the incorporators and a director of the Savannah Steamship Company, which the next year sent the *Savannah* to Liverpool. President Monroe visited Savannah while this vessel was in port and was the guest of Scarbrough in his newly completed Regency mansion.

Scarbrough's prosperity, however, was soon to end. Land speculation had already involved him in financial difficulties; the nation-wide depression of 1819 completed his ruin. He died in New York in the summer of 1838, only a few weeks after the *Sirius* and the *Great Western* had shown the practicability of steam transportation on the Atlantic.

[*Dictionary of American Biography*, XVI (New York, 1935), 410; *The National Cyclopaedia of American Biography*, II (New York, 1899), 237, 238.]

[7] Sarah, Lady Wright (1763–1816), Eliza McQueen's aunt, was the wife of Sir James Wright, second baronet (see below, page 274). She and her husband, a major in the Regiment of Georgia Loyalists, shared the fate of the dispossessed Tories. After the Treaty of Paris they went to England and settled near London at Little Ealing, County Middlesex. In this semi-rural retreat Sir James led the life of a country squire, and Lady Wright, known for her social graces, was hostess to many persons of note. From their home Robert Mac-

kay wrote several letters (see above, pages 128 and 133) that give intimate glimpses of a group of exiles, these American Loyalists, singularly neglected by historians.

[8] William Mein (*c.* 1768–1835), a Scotsman, came to Savannah about 1796 and went into business with his brother, Robert. In 1798 William Mein, his other brother, Alexander, and Robert Mackay established the firm of Meins, Mackay and Company. When Alexander Mein left for Liverpool in 1801, William Mein and Robert Mackay formed a partnership. This business house, according to a contemporary estimate, "conducted commercial operations upon an extensive scale, and with great intelligence and liberality" (*The Georgian*, August 4, 1835). To supplement the revenues from his counting-house, Mein acquired in 1804 an interest in a Savannah River plantation, Coleraine, together with Onslow and Argyle Islands, valuable for their rice fields. It is apparent that Mein enjoyed his role of landed proprietor, for mention is often made in Robert Mackay's letters of barbecues and "fêtes champêtres" at Coleraine. After Mackay's death, William Mein settled their joint affairs, sold his plantation and the rice islands, and returned to Scotland. He bought an estate at Ormeston in Roxburghshire, the management of which gave purpose to his declining years.

[Mein's obituary in *The Georgian* (Savannah) of August 4, 1835, contains biographical particulars. For an account of his agricultural interests, see *Savannah River Plantations* (Savannah, 1947), 199–201; this exhaustive study of land ownership and utilization was prepared by the Savannah Writers' Project under the editorial direction of Mary Granger.]

[9] Sarah Williamson McQueen (1784–1819), the "Sally" of subsequent letters, was Eliza McQueen's only sister. In 1795 her father described her thus: "Miss Sally has much improved since I saw her last . . . . I do not think she is quite so prim and formal as formerly but her Chin has grown longer and she carrys my Mark wherever she goes" (*The Letters of Don Juan McQueen to his Family*, 27). Nine years later, in 1804, Sarah McQueen became the wife of her second-cousin, John Postell Williamson (see below, page 271).

[10] Mary Cowper (1751–1821), aunt of Eliza McQueen, was the eldest of the eleven children of John and Elizabeth (Williamson) Smith. She was married in 1769 to Basil Cowper, a Savannah merchant conspicuous toward the end of the Revolution for his loyalty to the Crown (see below, page 255). After the war, the Cowpers lived in London and on the Island of Jamaica. Their two daughters were Mary Anne (1776–1856), and Margaret (1777–?), who married her first-cousin, John McQueen, Junior.

[11] James and Bennett Forbes were merchants of New York.

[New York Directories.]

[12] ". . . my Sister M^{rs}. Chilcott" was the wife of Robert Mackay's half-brother, Richard Chilcott. In family records her baptismal name is given as Elizabeth, but these sources do not indicate her surname and contain no further information about her except that she died without issue.

[13] "Died this morning, universally lamented, Dr. Goodwin Wilson, copartner of Dr. James B. Young."—*Georgia Gazette*, August 29, 1799.

Doctor Wilson was a prominent citizen of Savannah, an officer of the Society of the Cincinnati in the State of Georgia. In his will he made a number of interesting bequests: his "Electrical Apparatus & Surgical Instruments" were left to his partner, Doctor Young.

[Doctor Wilson's will is filed in the Court of Ordinary, Chatham County Court House, Savannah.]

[14] Esther (Morel) Neyle (1772–1799) was related to Eliza McQueen through the Williamson line. She was the daughter of John Morel, a planter of Ossabaw Island, Georgia, and the wife of Sampson Neyle, also a planter, who had moved from South Carolina to Georgia.

[15] Basil Cowper, uncle by marriage of Eliza McQueen, was in his later years a merchant of Jamaica. His career had been led in many parts of the British Empire. A native of Scotland, Cowper had started business in London. About 1760 he removed to Savannah and with the Telfair brothers, Edward and William, founded the firm of Cowper and Telfairs. This soon ranked among the leading commercial houses of the Southern colonies. From their profits, Cowper and Edward Telfair acquired one of the most productive plantations on the Savannah River, the Grange. Although he was a Patriot at the beginning of the Revolution, Cowper joined the British when the cause of freedom seemed lost. For this sudden change of allegiance, the Royal Governor and the Council rewarded him with the office of Justice of the Peace, and he served also in the Loyalist Commons House of Assembly. After the Revolution Cowper was banished from Georgia. He went with his family to London, but, unsuited to a life of idleness, emigrated to Jamaica and resumed his mercantile pursuits. He died on that island, at Barron Hill, in 1802.

[William Harden, "Basil Cowper's Remarkable Career in Georgia," *The Georgia Historical Quarterly*, I, 1 (March, 1917), 24–35; *Savannah River Plantations*, 193–195.]

[16] George Baillie belonged to a well-known family of coastal Geor-

gia. He is mentioned in several of Robert Mackay's letters, one of which gives the news of his death in Philadelphia in 1810 (see above, page 222).

[17] St. Simon's Island, Georgia, notable in history as the site of a decisive battle fought in 1742 between the British and the Spaniards, was developed toward the end of the century into a number of great plantations. The Baillies were among the large landholders of the island.

[Margaret Davis Cate, "Fort Frederica and the Battle of Bloody Marsh," *The Georgia Historical Quarterly*, XXVII, 2 (June, 1943), 111–174; for the general history of St. Simon's, see Caroline Couper Lovell, *The Golden Isles of Georgia* (Boston, 1932).]

[18] At Montgomery, a small tidewater settlement on the Vernon River, twelve miles south of Savannah, Eliza's uncle, Alexander McQueen, owned a cotton plantation. This served as a delightful meeting place during the hot summer months for a wide family connection.

[19] Phineas Miller had come from his native Massachusetts to Georgia as agent for the executors of Nathanael Greene. It was not long before he courted and married the General's widow. As the husband of the sprightly and accomplished "Katy" (Littlefield) Greene, friend of Washington, he took over the management of Mulberry Grove, near Savannah, and the Greene holdings on Cumberland Island. Miller died in 1806.

[20] Amelia Island lies at the mouth of the St. Mary's River. With the rest of East Florida, it passed from England to Spain in 1783 and in 1819 was ceded by Spain to the United States. Robert Mackay spent eight weeks on Amelia Island in the winter of 1810; for his letters written at that time, see above, pages 206–229.

[21] New Providence, one of the Bahama Islands, was the home port for many adventurous privateers who, under the protection of the British flag, preyed on the commerce of the South Atlantic.

[22] Tybee is an island at the mouth of the Savannah River. Long known for its lighthouse, which dates from the colonial period, Tybee Island is now a popular summer resort.

[J. H. Estill, *Tales of Tybee* (Savannah, 1906).]

[23] Robert Mackay's sister was Catherine Chilcott, daughter of Mary Malbone by her first husband, Richard Chilcott. Of this marriage and its issue, Margaret Mackay Elliott wrote:

Mary Malbone had married in very early life a man called Richard Chilcott contrary to the wishes of her family. This man stayed little at home and his wife continued to reside with her parents. She had two children, a son Richard, who entered into the Merchant service and died young, and a daughter Catherine Chilcott, who married at 15 a person named Williams who soon after moved to the South. Mrs. Chilcott being then a widow accompanied her daughter to Augusta—and soon after married Robert Mackay.

Catherine (Chilcott) Williams married three times. Her second husband was Andrew McLean, a merchant of Augusta. He died in 1784 (*The Gazette of the State of Georgia*, August 26, 1784), and in 1789 his widow took as her third husband John Course (*The Georgia Gazette*, January 15, 1789).

[24] "[Died.] Yesterday afternoon, Mrs. Neyle, wife of Sampson Neyle, Esq."—*Georgia Gazette*, September 19, 1799.

In 1803 Sampson Neyle married Maria McQueen, daughter of Alexander and Elizabeth (Fuller) McQueen and first-cousin of Eliza Mackay.

[25] Harriet (Villepontoux) Neyle was the wife of William Neyle (*c.* 1768–1802), a native Englishman, who, after living some years in South Carolina, removed to Georgia and became a planter. The Neyle lands on Hutchinson's Island in the Savannah River had an unusual name for a rice plantation, "Poplar Forest."

[26] James Johnston, Junior (1769–1822), nephew and namesake of the printer of Savannah's first newspaper, *The Georgia Gazette*, was a close friend of Robert Mackay. These two men had many points in common: both had been born in Augusta, and both enjoyed success in the business and social life of Savannah. By 1795 Johnston was senior partner of Johnston, Robertson and Company, a firm that dealt in general merchandise and engaged in the slave trade (for several of their advertisements, see the *Georgia Gazette*, July 2, 1795, and October 14, 1802, and the *Columbian Museum & Savannah Advertiser*, October 12, 1798). Two years later he married Ann Marion Houstoun, daughter of the Georgia-born baronet, Sir George Houstoun (see below, page 297). Contemporary accounts speak of Johnston as a gracious host. He was made secretary of the Golf Club, of which Robert Mackay was a manager, and civic honors came to him in due course. An alderman of Savannah in 1801 and 1802, and again in 1817 and 1818, he represented Chatham County in the State Legislature, and in 1817 was elected president of the Planters' Bank of the State of Georgia, which he had helped to found.

[A biographical sketch of this prominent Savannahian will appear in Edith Duncan Johnston, *The Houstouns of Georgia* to be published in 1949 by the University of Georgia Press, Athens.]

[27] "M^r. Youngs," in West Broad Street, was the town house of Thomas Young (*c.* 1733–1808), a wealthy planter (see below, pages 288 and 289).

II. CONCERNING THE SHIP *GENERAL OGLETHORPE*

[1] Colonel John Patterson (1753–1801), one of the most capable shipbuilders of his generation, worked for many years in Philadelphia. His yard adjoined that of Joshua Humphreys, the naval architect, and seems to have been taken over by Humphreys in 1794 when the latter received the commission from the Government to construct the frigate *United States*. Patterson then went with his family to St. Mary's, Georgia, where he followed his trade until his death soon after the completion of the *General Oglethorpe*.

["Wreck of the Ship *General Oglethorpe*—1802," *op. cit.*, 44 n.]

[2] John Clark Nightingale (1771–1806) was in his later years a planter of Cumberland Island, Georgia. Born in Providence, Rhode Island, the son of Joseph and Elizabeth (Corlis) Nightingale, he moved to Savannah about 1790 and became a commission merchant. There Nightingale renewed his friendship with fellow Rhode Islanders, the family of Nathanael Greene. This resulted in his marriage in 1795 to Martha Washington Greene (1777–?), the eldest of the General's three vivacious daughters. Nightingale now established himself on Cumberland Island, which his wife's father had bought in 1783, and planted "the Plumb-Orchard" mentioned in Mackay's letter. He died in 1806. His widow married in 1810 Dr. Henry Edmund Turner, a physician from Rhode Island who practiced in St. Mary's, Georgia.

[For genealogical particulars, see Louise Brownell Clarke, *The Greenes of Rhode Island* (New York, 1903), 328. It should be noted that Mrs. Clarke makes the mistake of giving the middle name of Nightingale as Corlis.]

[3] Catherine Littlefield Nightingale was the eldest child and only daughter of John and Martha Washington (Greene) Nightingale. The dates of her birth and death are not given in the Greene genealogy. She married her cousin, Dr. John Littlefield, and after his death a Mr. Black.

[Clarke, *op. cit.*, 328.]

[4] Cornelia Lott Greene (1779–1865) was the second daughter of Nathanael and Catherine (Littlefield) Greene. Possessed of a keen intelligence that had been given direction by the Moravian nuns at their academy in Bethlehem, Pennsylvania, she was a favorite with every one. John McQueen, her father's friend, named the great sand dune on Fort George Island "Mount Cornelia" for her; and his son John, one of her admirers, wrote to his sister: "Your friend Cornelia I always thought lovely, & that she should captivate all Sav^{h}. is not

surprising . . ." (*The Letters of Don Juan McQueen to his Family*, 42). The year after Robert Mackay's visit to St. Mary's, Cornelia Greene married Peyton Skipwith, son of the prominent Virginia baronet. Her husband died of yellow fever on Cumberland Island in 1808. Two years later she married Edward Brinley Littlefield (see below.)

[5] Edward Brinley Littlefield (*c.* 1786–1836) was a common kinsman of the Greenes and of Robert Mackay. His father, William Littlefield, captain in the Rhode Island line and aide-de-camp to General Greene, was a brother of Catherine (Littlefield) Greene. His mother Elizabeth (Brinley) Littlefield (1763–1822), was Robert Mackay's first-cousin, their mothers—Aliph Brinley and Mary Mackay—having been daughters of Godfrey Malbone. Edward Littlefield often visited Georgia; and about 1809 he settled in St. Mary's to practice law. ". . . by a strange coincidence of things," Robert Mackay wrote in a family memoir, "Cap. Littlefield's eldest son is now married to Cornelia the second daughter of Gen. Greene." The marriage took place on Cumberland Island in 1810. Not much is known of Littlefield's later life. He moved to Tennessee, and died in Nashville on February 18, 1836, aged fifty years.

[Clarke, *op. cit.*, 329.]

[6] Dungeness, a great mansion of tabby, four stories high, stood at the south end of Cumberland Island. Begun in 1787 by Nathanael Greene's widow, it was nearly twenty years in building, the delay being generally attributed to a superstition that some dire calamity would befall the family upon its completion. This house was destroyed by fire after the Civil War.

[B. N. Nightingale, "Dungeness," *The Georgia Historical Quarterly*, XXII, 4 (December, 1938), 369–383.]

[7] John McQueen was now living on Fort George Island at the mouth of the St. John's River. The whole island, valuable both for its timber and cotton fields, had been granted to McQueen by friendly Spanish officials soon after his arrival in East Florida.

[*The Letters of Don Juan McQueen to his Family*, xxix, 55–57, 81.]

[8] A picturesque description of St. Mary's, based on travelers' accounts, is in George Gillman Smith, D.D., *The Story of Georgia and the Georgia People, 1732 to 1860* (Macon, Georgia, 1900), 149–151.

[9] ". . . our darling little boy" was Robert Mackay, Junior, two months old when this letter was written. He was born December 11, 1800, and died "of one of the country fevers" in Savannah on October 7, 1804 (see below, page 269).

[10] William Patterson, son of John Patterson the ship-builder, was a well-known ship captain. He commanded several Southern vessels,

including the *General Oglethorpe*, and eventually became master of a constant trader between New York and Liverpool.

["Wreck of the Ship *General Oglethorpe*—1802," *op. cit.*, 44 n.]

[11] Antonio Suarez, a Florida trader, made substantial profits from selling slaves to planters along the St. John's and the St. Mary's Rivers. An opportunist, with possibly a religious side to his nature, he was sponsor to many Anglo-American settlers of this region on their baptism into the Roman Catholic Church.

[Records of Suarez' slave sales are in the Spanish Escrituras, East Florida Papers, transcripts of which are in the Library of the St. Augustine Historical Society, St. Augustine; for the religious obligations he assumed, see *Translation and Transcription of Church Archives of Florida, Roman Catholic Records, St. Augustine Parish: White Baptisms, 1792–1799* (Tallahassee, 1941), index.]

[12] Point Peter is situated on the St. Mary's River in Camden County, Georgia. At the time of Robert Mackay's visit, it was owned by James Seagrove and formed part of his plantation, Newtown. During the War of 1812 a fort was built at Point Peter to protect St. Mary's, but this was seized by the British under Admiral Cockburn, and the town taken.

[13] James Seagrove figured prominently in the affairs of the Georgia-Florida border. During Washington's administration, he served as special agent in Spanish East Florida for the American Government, and in 1796 was appointed superintendent of Indian Affairs. He was present at the conference between the United States and the Creek Nation, held at the town of Coleraine on the St. Mary's, June 29, 1796. This led to the formulation of a treaty of peace and friendship, and to the cession by the Creeks to Georgia of the rich lands across the Oconee River.

A contemporary estimate of Seagrove was made by a young New England physician, Dr. Daniel Turner, recently arrived in St. Mary's: "He is considered the first character in Camden County & very much disposed to befriend the young & enterprizing—I count much on his acquaintance" (Dr. Daniel Turner to Dr. Peter Turner, January 1, 1805; Turner correspondence, in the Division of Manuscripts, Library of Congress, Washington).

[14] The *Georgia Gazette* of March 4, 1802, has the following dispatch from Nassau:

The ship General Oglethorpe of Savannah, William Patterson master, of 530 tons burthen, owned by messrs. Mein and Mackay, was totally lost, on the night of the 15th instant, on the reef N. E. of Whale Key, and 23 persons perished; among whom was mr. Joshua Frazer, of Charleston, 2d mate of the ship, a young man who will be most sincerely lamented by many respectable friends and relations. Capt. Patterson, mr. Robert Mackay, of Savannah, mr. James Broadfoot, of Charleston, and 12 others, were saved, by taking to the boat before the ship went to pieces, and after being 11 days exposed to every hardship were taken up by the schooner Ranger of Charleston, on Tuesday last, about 20 miles to the westward of the Hole in the Wall. Capt. Patterson, mr. Broadfoot, and mr. Mackay, have requested us to mention the obligations they are under to capt. Bennett of the Ranger, for the very hospitable manner in which he received them on board his vessel, and for the great attention and civility they experienced while with him. They arrived here on Wednesday evening [February 17].

III. FROM SAVANNAH

[1] Colonel John McIntosh (1748–1826), member of a Scottish Highland family prominent in the early history of Georgia, served in the Revolution as lieutenant colonel, commandant of the Third Georgia Regiment. It was he who in answer to the British demand for the surrender of Fort Morris made the blunt reply: "Come and take it." This challenge the enemy declined, although they greatly outnumbered the Americans. Soon after the war, McIntosh moved to East Florida and became a planter on the St. John's River. In 1794 he was arrested by the Spanish officials on charges of plotting against the Government and sent to Morro Castle, Havana. His imprisonment attracted international attention, and he was released at the request of President Washington. Returning to Georgia, McIntosh settled on St. Simon's Island. He resumed his military career during the War of 1812. Appointed a major general, he was placed in command of three regiments of infantry and a battalion of artillery, and given the responsibility of defending the coast of Georgia. Crowned with the halo of his military reputation, McIntosh lived to a ripe old age. The general sentiment was expressed by the writer of his obituary: "Noble soul! How the spirit of Washington will greet thee."

[Margaret Davis Cate, *Our Todays and Yesterdays: A Story of Brunswick and the Coastal Islands* (Brunswick, Georgia, 1930), 188, 189.]

[2] Frederica, a fortified town on St. Simon's Island, had been established in 1736 by Oglethorpe as a bulwark against the Spaniards. It developed into a place of considerable importance, but when East Florida passed to the British in 1763, the colonial regiments were withdrawn and Frederica's days as a military outpost were over. In 1768 James Spalding, an extensive trader, bought part of the town site which he converted into a trading-post and plantation.

[3] John McQueen, Eliza Mackay's father, was now in full favor with the Spanish authorities. In 1798 the King of Spain appointed him captain of militia; in 1802 the Governor of East Florida made "Don Juan McQueen" judge of the territory along the St. John's and the St. Mary's Rivers.

[*The Letters of Don Juan McQueen to his Family*, 49, 50, 57, 58.]

[4] ". . . our young traveller" was Robert Mackay, Junior, six months old when this letter was written.

[5] John Caig, a Scottish merchant, moved to Savannah in 1795 from Charleston, where he had been in business for eight years. He formed a partnership with Robert Mitchel and their firm soon acquired that symbol of commercial success, a wharf on the Savannah River. As one of the managers of the Golf Club and a commissioner of the Planters' Bank, Caig took part in the broader interests of Savannah. He died in 1814, aged forty-eight. A phrase entered in the Municipal Mortuary Records, "a merchant of the greatest respectability," attests the esteem in which he was held.

[6] The "Wedding at Waynes," performed in Savannah on June 10, 1801, was that of Richard Montgomery Stites and Mary, daughter of Richard Wayne. The groom, a native of New Jersey, was a lawyer, who on his death in 1813 held the important position of clerk of the Circuit and District Courts of Georgia. The bride, a native of South Carolina, was the daughter of an English-born merchant of Savannah, and the sister of Robert Mackay's friend, Richard Wayne, Junior.

[*Georgia Gazette*, June 11, 1801.]

[7] John Young Noel (1762–1817) had come from New York to practice law in Savannah. He served four terms as mayor of his adopted city. His wife was Sarah Dennis (*c.* 1759–1838), widow of Richard Stites and mother of Richard Montgomery Stites.

[8] George Anderson (1767–1847), at one time a partner of Richard Wayne, Junior, was a wealthy commission merchant. His wife, Elizabeth Clifford Wayne (*c.* 1774–1818), was Wayne's twin sister.

[9] Ann Pooler (*c.* 1758–1815), a native of Limerick, Ireland, was the wife of John Pooler. Her husband was a well-thought-of but improvident resident of Savannah, whose real estate and Negro slaves were sometimes sold for his failure to pay taxes. By an ironic twist of fate Pooler later became receiver of tax returns for Chatham County. The family name was made distinguished by their son, Robert William Pooler (*c.* 1796–1853), graduate of West Point, attorney, member of the Georgia Legislature, and for twenty years clerk of the Superior and Inferior Courts of Chatham County.

[Municipal Mortuary Records, Savannah; *The Georgia Gazette*, August 11, 1791, June 7, 1792, and March 13, 1794; *Columbian Museum & Savannah*

Advertiser, March 14, 1802; George W. Cullum, *Biographical Register of the Officers and Graduates of the U. S. Military Academy at West Point, N. Y.*, I (Boston and New York, 1891), 142.]

[10] When he became one of Robert Mackay's closest friends, Thomas Gibbons (1757–1826) had already gained national prominence, even though Chief Justice Marshall had not yet delivered the famous decision that bears Gibbons' name. The outstanding attorney of Georgia, Gibbons was known for his turbulence and high temper. Both were given full rein in 1791 when he engineered Anthony Wayne's election to Congress. The defeated candidate, James Jackson, claiming that there were "more votes than voters," delivered a memorable philippic in the House of Representatives against "this person Gibbons, whose soul is faction, and whose life has been a scene of political corruption." Wayne was unseated; but Gibbons took his revenge by challenging Jackson to a duel. Now turning to his own affairs, Gibbons was three times elected mayor of Savannah and served as federal judge for Georgia. His wealth and social position enabled him to play an important role in the social life of Savannah. He showed himself a lavish host both at his town house in West Broad Street (the doorway of this dwelling is now in the American Wing of the Metropolitan Museum of Art, New York) and at his plantation, White Hall, on the Savannah River.

About 1810 Thomas Gibbons bought a summer residence in Elizabeth Town, New Jersey. His interest shifting from politics to steam ferries, he contested the right of the State of New York to grant a rival ferry-owner the monopoly of steam navigation in state waters. The case of *Gibbons* v. *Ogden* was carried to the Supreme Court of the United States. In 1824 the verdict was rendered in Gibbons' favor, and the New York monopoly, together with all others of its kind, was declared null and void. In carrying his grievances to the highest tribunal, Gibbons rendered a far-reaching service to the nation. The issue decided in this case has been declared by a competent historian to have "done more to knit the American people into an indivisible Nation than any other one force in our history, excepting only war" (Albert J. Beveridge, *The Life of John Marshall*, IV, 429, 430).

[*Dictionary of American Biography*, VII (New York, 1931), 242, 243; Thomas Gamble, *Savannah Duels and Duellists, 1733–1877* (Savannah, 1923), 41–45, 57–71; *Savannah River Plantations*, 299–312.]

[11] George Whitefield Woodruff (1765–1846), a lawyer, belonged to a distinguished New Jersey family; his brother, Aaron Dickinson Woodruff, was attorney general of that State for twenty-eight years. A graduate of the College of New Jersey, George Woodruff was sent to Savannah by President John Adams as United States district

attorney for Georgia. In 1796, he married Jean Houstoun, daughter of Sir George Houstoun (see below page 297). His intimacy with the Mackay family connections is revealed by the fact that his eldest daughter was named Mary Anne Cowper for Eliza Mackay's first-cousin. In 1808 Woodruff moved to Trenton, and enjoyed a lucrative professional career that enabled him to live on a fine estate outside the town. In his later years he was deferred to as the oldest member of the Mercer County bar.

[Johnston, *The Houstouns of Georgia.*]

[12] George W. Nichols had started business in 1796 with "A FRESH ASSORTMENT OF *Drugs and Medicines*" (*Columbian Museum & Savannah Advertiser*, July 5, 1796); he later became an auctioneer, and disposed of his goods "*on the wharf of Messrs. Mein & Mackay*" (*ibid.*, May 12, 1801). It would seem from Robert Mackay's letters and from other contemporary sources that Nichols took a prominent part in the social life of Savannah. He decided who should have tickets to the "Bachelor's Ball" and was treasurer of the "Dancing Assemblies" (*ibid.*, November 20, 1798, and December 31, 1799).

[13] Jean-Berard Mocquet, Marquis de Montalet (1765–1814), once an officer in the French Army, now a planter of Sapelo Island, Georgia (see below, page 266), had landed in Charleston in 1798, a refugee from the slave insurrections in St. Domingo. Unlike most of these exiled colonists, several thousand of whom fled to the United States, Montalet had managed to save much of his property. It is on record that he brought sixty-seven Negro slaves with him from St. Domingo; mention of his jewels is made in one of Robert Mackay's letters (see above, page 67); and he had sufficient funds to buy the Hermitage plantation near Savannah shortly after coming to Georgia. In Savannah in 1802 he married a refugee from the French Revolution, Angélique-Servanne-Charlotte Picot de Boisfeuillet. The Marquise died three years later, aged eighteen. Montalet then disposed of the Hermitage and moved to the Boisfeuillet holdings on Sapelo Island. There, at his home, Le Châlet, he would receive his friends with Old World courtesy; and, ably assisted by his cook, Cupidon, would offer the dinners of an epicure. His obituary carries a tribute to the gallantry with which he met adversity: "Brought up at Paris, amidst the most fashionable circles of that gay city, he retained to the last hour of his life, the manners of an accomplished gentleman. Poor Montalet!" (*The Republican; and Savannah Evening Ledger*, June 11, 1814.)

[*Savannah River Plantations*, 429–432; Lovell, *The Golden Isles of Georgia*, 97, 98, 110–114; Very Reverend Joseph D. Mitchell, V.G., "Historical Sketches of the Parish of St. John the Baptist, Savannah, Georgia,"

The Bulletin of the Catholic Laymen's Association of Georgia, II, 7 (June, 1921), 12, 13 and 13 (December, 1921), 6.]

[14] James Edmund Houstoun (1776–1819), son of Dr. James Houstoun, a surgeon in the Continental Army, was of the third generation of a family that had much to do with the shaping of Georgia history. For himself, Houstoun was content with a minor role. A representative of Chatham and McIntosh Counties in the State Legislature, he devoted his time to cultivating his rice plantation, Marengo, in McIntosh County.

[Johnston, *The Houstouns of Georgia;* his obituary is in *The Georgian* (Savannah), September 21, 1819.]

[15] Archibald Smith (1758–1830), Eliza Mackay's uncle, was a planter and merchant of Savannah. At his town house in Reynolds Square, Eliza's eighth child, named Robert, was born in 1813 (entry in the Mackay Family Bible). Smith married twice: first, in 1789, Margaret Joyner (1772–1795) of Beaufort, South Carolina; secondly, in 1796, Helena Zubly of St. Mary's, Georgia. "Archy" was a son by his first wife.

[For genealogical data on the Smiths, see *The Letters of Don Juan McQueen to his Family*, 84.]

[16] Isabella Hunter (*c.* 1771–1813) and her sister, Lydia Elizabeth Hunter (*c.* 1774–1813), were intimate friends of the Smiths and McQueens. Daughters of Colonel John Hunter of the British Army and natives of the County Donegal, Ireland, these ladies had come to Savannah about 1795 to join their brother William, an eminent merchant. Their half-brothers were James and Alexander Hunter, also merchants of Savannah.

[Municipal Mortuary Records, Savannah; Joseph G. Bulloch, M.D., "Memoirs of the Hunter Family," in *A History and Genealogy of the Families of Bulloch, Stobo . . .* (Savannah, 1892), 155–158.]

[17] "E. Zubly" was Elizabeth, daughter of David and Elizabeth (Pye) Zubly, and granddaughter of the Reverend John Joachim Zubly, the fearless Tory pastor of the Independent Presbyterian Church of Savannah. Her father also was a Loyalist, and under the new State government he and his family were banished from Georgia. They settled first in East Florida, then in the Bahamas. In 1788 David Zubly's three children—Helena, John Joachim, and Elizabeth—were granted land adjoining his plantation on Cat Island (the original deed is in the Library of the Georgia Historical Society). After Zubly's death in 1792, his daughters returned to Georgia. Helena married Archibald Smith in 1796, and by 1809 Elizabeth had become the wife of a Mr. Magill (see the will of Elizabeth Smith in the Chatham County Court House, Savannah).

["The Will of Dr. John Joachim Zubly," edited by Charles G. Cordle, *The Georgia Historical Quarterly*, XXII, 4 (December, 1938), 384–390.]

[18] Mary Ann Williamson (1786–1854), daughter of John Garnier and Jane (Parmenter) Williamson, married first, in 1804, James Edmund Houstoun (see above, page 265), and secondly, in 1845, Major Jonathan Thomas. She was the sister of John Postell Williamson (see below, page 271).

[From the Williamson family records owned by Mrs. Florence Crane Norvell of Savannah.]

[19] Catherine Bourke, Eliza Mackay's cousin, was the daughter of Thomas and Jane (Smith) Bourke. She married a Mr. Odell.

[20] ". . . the old Gentleman" was Don Juan McQueen.

[21] Belleville in McIntosh County, Georgia, was a small tidewater settlement, the "summer retreat" of the Spaldings, Baillies, and other planters of the region.

[22] Mary Anne Mackay, second child of Robert and Eliza Mackay, was born in Savannah on August 18, 1802. She married in 1825 Benjamin Edward Stiles (whose brother William Henry was to marry her younger sister Elizabeth Anne in 1832), and died in Habersham County, Georgia, in 1862.

[23] Sapelo, one of the richest of the famed "Golden Isles of Georgia," had been the site of a Spanish presidio and mission, and was later a refuge for several French gentlemen exiled by the Revolution. It is likely that Robert Mackay was planning to visit his friend, Thomas Spalding, who the year before, in 1802, had bought the southern half of the island, and was now developing his property into a single plantation.

[For the life of Spalding and an account of his pioneer agricultural experiments on Sapelo, "which should be as much a part of Thomas Spalding's name as Caroline was of John Taylor's or Roanoke of John Randolph's," see E. Merton Coulter, *Thomas Spalding of Sapelo* (University, Louisiana, 1940).]

[24] The "debut" of Joseph Clay (1764–1811) as a Baptist preacher was indeed a startling event to a circle of friends not given to religious enthusiasm. For this distinguished lawyer, at the height of his career before the bar and without peer as an advocate in criminal cases, had forsaken professional honors for the cause of religion. Under the instruction of Henry Holcombe (see below, page 289), he was divested of "Episcopal influence" and prepared for the Baptist ministry. Ordained in 1804, the Reverend Mr. Clay became assistant pastor of the Savannah Baptist Church, of which Doctor Holcombe was pastor. But his ambition was to take him far afield.

Informing his charges that "a door of more usefulness was opened to him to teach in various places," he set forth the next year, preaching as he went, until finally he reached New England. In 1807 Clay became pastor of the First Baptist Church of Boston. This office was not suited to a man of his ardent temperament, and after two disheartening years he resigned. Little is known of Joseph Clay's last years, but it is believed that he returned to Georgia and died there.

[Mabel Freeman La Far, "The Baptist Church of Savannah, Georgia: History, Records, and Register," manuscript in the Library of the Georgia Historical Society, Savannah; Jesse H. Campbell, *Georgia Baptists: Historical and Biographical* (Richmond, 1847), 146–149; Nathan E. Wood, *The History of the First Baptist Church of Boston (1665–1899)* (Philadelphia, 1899), 298, 302–304.]

[25] Ulric Tobler was regarded by his contemporaries as the town wit. Of Swiss descent, nephew of the renowned Savannah clergyman, Doctor Zubly, he was born in South Carolina in 1759, and was brought to Savannah at an early age. He became a hardware merchant and saddler, and served as justice of the peace and alderman. But Tobler was best known for his association with Free Masonry. The recipient of many Masonic offices, including that of Deputy Grand Master of all Masons in Georgia, he was considered "the most zealous advocate of the principles and interests of the craft" (*Columbian Museum, and Savannah Daily Gazette*, December 12, 1820). Dying in 1820, he was buried with full masonic honors by the Grand Lodge of Georgia.

[Benjamin Palmer Axson, "The Lodges and Allied Masonic Bodies of Savannah, Ga., and the Men active in their Organization," manuscript in the Library of the Georgia Historical Society, Savannah.]

[26] Stephen, a Negro slave and house-servant of the Mackay family, was later to fall from favor. In 1807 Robert Mackay informed his wife of his determination to get rid of Stephen "even if I give him away" (see above, page 63).

[27] In the afternoon and evening of September 8, 1804, tidewater Georgia was struck by a hurricane, which by reason of its violence and the damage it caused has found a permanent place in the history of the region. It is interesting to note the similarity between Eliza Mackay's description of the hurricane at the Cottage and Aaron Burr's account of the same storm, written from St. Simon's Island, seventy miles farther down the coast (*Memoirs of Aaron Burr: with Miscellaneous Selections from his Correspondence*, edited by Matthew L. Davis, II, 338–341).

[28] Eliza Mackay's grandmother was Elizabeth (Williamson) Smith

(*c.* 1731–1809). A South Carolinian by birth and early residence, she spent her later years in Georgia, and died in the family home on Oatlands Island May 10, 1809.

[Municipal Mortuary Records, Savannah.]

[29] Richmond was a rice plantation on the Savannah River, ten miles above Savannah. The gift in 1782 of the State of Georgia to General Anthony Wayne, Richmond belonged to William Mein when it was damaged by the hurricane of 1804.

[A monograph on "Richmond Oakgrove Plantation" is in *Savannah River Plantations*, 93–134.]

[30] Oatlands, a small island about a mile from the Cottage, was the only part of John McQueen's estate in Georgia that his family had been able to keep from his creditors. It was here that the younger John McQueen, on his return from Florida, tried his hand at planting Sea Island cotton. The various members of the McQueen and Smith families spent much time in the comfortable dwelling on Oatlands, and took pride in their extensive kitchen garden.

[31] A description of Savannah the day after the storm was published in the *Columbian Museum & Savannah Advertiser* of September 12, 1804:

. . . when the morning came, . . . it was found that busy fancy ever apt to exaggerate, had formed but an imperfect picture of the dreadful scene of havoc and destruction. The trees in every part of the city were prostrated. The chimnies of a great many houses were blown down, and several houses themselves. The steeple of the Presbyterian Meeting, and part of the walls of the Episcopal Church were blown down. The wharves from one end of the city to the other were torn up, and almost every store which was erected at any distance from the foot of the bluff, was either totally destroyed, or much torn to pieces, as to spoil, every thing contained within them. Every vessel in the harbor was thrown upon the wharves, except such as were totally destroyed, and large ships are laying on some of the highest wharves. There was no passing from one wharf to another; lumber, cotton, tobacco, hogsheads of rum, sugar, and in fact every article of domestic and foreign produce, were strewed from one end to the other of them.

In the same issue, under the heading of "Shipping Losses," was further news to dismay Robert Mackay:

At Mein and Mackay's wharf, the ship Magdalen, of Glasgow, upset—the schooner Savannah Packet, of Charleston [,] bilged on the wharf, and sloop Rachel, Brown, upset, since righted.

[32] In 1802 George Scott, formerly a dry goods merchant of Savannah, was taken into partnership by William Mein and Robert Mackay, the firm of Mein and Mackay now becoming Mein, Mackay and

Company (*Georgia Gazette*, February 18, 1802). This association was dissolved "by mutual consent" in 1809 (*Columbian Museum & Savannah Advertiser*, July 10, 1809).

[83] Anne Mein was the sister of Robert Mackay's partner, William Mein. She made her home in Liverpool with her other brother, Alexander Mein.

[84] Robert Mackay, Junior, died in Savannah "11 at night" on October 7, 1804 (from the Mackay Family Bible, owned by Miss Caroline P. Huger of Bluffton, South Carolina).

[85] William Mein Mackay, third child of Robert and Eliza Mackay, was born in Savannah on March 27, 1804. After attending school in New Jersey (see above, page 247), he returned to Georgia and became a rice planter. In 1837 New Hope and Causton's Bluff, valuable Savannah River plantations, were given to him "for love and affection" by his cousin, Mary Anne Cowper. But the next year his wife, Virginia Sarah Bryan, and their two children were lost in the wreck of the steamship *Pulaski*, and William Mackay retired to the home of his mother in Savannah, living there in seclusion until his death August 1, 1859.

[*Savannah River Plantations*, 14, 15; for a survivor's account of the wreck of the *Pulaski*, written by James Hamilton Couper, see Lovell, *The Golden Isles of Georgia*, 156–182.]

[86] Dr. George Jones (1766–1838), in his generation head of the Joneses of Wormsloe, was a man of versatile talents. A physician with an extensive practice, and president of the Georgia Medical Society, he gained a reputation for legal learning that resulted in 1804 in his elevation to the bench of the Eastern Judicial Circuit of Georgia. He later served as United States senator and was mayor of Savannah from 1812 to 1814. Doctor Jones, three times married, and his numerous family connections are frequently mentioned in the letters of Robert Mackay.

[*Biographical Directory of the American Congress, 1774–1927* (Washington, 1928), 1160; *Men of Mark in Georgia*, William J. Northen, editor, II (Atlanta, 1910), 342–344.]

[87] Dr. James Cuthbert (*c.* 1770–1807), a descendant of a cadet branch of the historic Scottish family of Cuthbert, barons of Castle Hill, was the son of Dr. James Cuthbert, a Savannah River planter; through his mother, Anne (Bryan) Cuthbert, he was a half-first-cousin of Eliza Mackay's mother, Anne McQueen. In 1805 he bought Richmond from William Mein and turned planter, the change of profession being duly noted in his will. There was intimacy as well as relationship between the Cuthberts and the Smiths, and for this

reason Doctor Cuthbert, a bachelor, bequeathed his property to his Smith cousins: Mary Cowper, Anne McQueen, Jane Bourke and Elizabeth Smith.

[J. G. B. Bulloch, *The Cuthberts, Barons of Castle Hill and their Descendants in South Carolina and Georgia* ([Washington,] 1908), 36, 37; *Savannah River Plantations*, 125, 126, 149–151; the will of Dr. James Cuthbert is filed in the Court of Ordinary, Chatham County Court House, Savannah.]

[38] Dr. John Irvine (1742–1808), a prominent physician of Savannah, is remembered today as one of the founders of the Georgia Medical Society, of which he was the first vice-president and later president. After the Revolution he was forced into exile because of his loyalty to the Crown. However, Doctor Irvine fared better than most Tories, for, going to London, he found favor at Court. He was appointed physician to George III, and later physician to the Admiralty. About 1790 he returned to Savannah, where he died. By his first wife, Ann Elizabeth Baillie, he had thirteen children, through one of whom, Anne (Irvine) Bulloch, he is an ancestor of Theodore Roosevelt and of Mrs. Franklin Delano Roosevelt.

[J. G. Bulloch, *A History and Genealogy of the Families of Bulloch and Stobo and of Irvine of Cults* (Washington, 1911), 86, 88–92; his obituary is in *The Republican; and Savannah Evening Ledger*, October 18, 1808.]

[39] Miss Jackson was the sister of Doctor Jackson, under whom Robert Mackay studied in Edinburgh. Their friendship was maintained in correspondence over the years.

[40] "Cousin Malbone" was Edward Greene Malbone, the celebrated miniature painter. His father, John Malbone, was a brother of Robert Mackay's mother, Mary (Malbone) Mackay. In 1805 Edward Malbone had gone to Charleston on his way to the West Indies, but was still in that city when Mackay arrived the next year. The "present" that he was "prepareing" for Eliza Mackay may well have been the miniature reproduced as the frontispiece of this book.

[*Dictionary of American Biography*, XII (New York, 1933), 216–218.]

[41] John Bowman, a Scotsman, was before the Revolution a planter on Skidaway Island, Georgia. He later moved to Charleston (see below, pages 301 and 302).

[42] "M^rs M—" was Catherine (Littlefield) Miller, widow of Nathanael Greene and wife of Phineas Miller (see above, page 256). In the spring of 1806 she became ill at her home on Cumberland Island, and was taken to Savannah by Dr. Daniel Turner, who wrote of this trip to his parents: "I left Mrs Miller there in the hands of D^r [Lemuel] Kollock. she was evidently mending—but will never enjoy

health again" (letter, dated April 6, 1806, in the Turner correspondence, Division of Manuscripts, Library of Congress, Washington). Catherine Miller lived another eight years, dying at Dungeness on September 2, 1814, aged fifty-nine.

[43] "Louisa" was Louisa Catherine Greene, youngest child of Nathanael and Catherine Greene. She married James Shaw and died in 1831, in her forty-sixth year. A tombstone to her memory is in the family cemetery on Cumberland Island.

[44] "Mr. Davison" was a member of the firm of Simpson and Davison, London merchants, with whom Robert Mackay had large business dealings.

[45] Robert Mackay's arrival in the Ship *Georgia*, Captain Pierce, "in 55 days from Liverpool," was noted in the *Columbian Museum & Savannah Advertiser* of December 17, 1806.

[46] From early colonial times until the end of the Civil War, Coleraine ranked as one of the great rice plantations on the Savannah River. It was bought in 1804 by William Mein, the purchase including Onslow and Argyle Islands and one hundred Negro slaves. Mein had previously acquired an adjoining plantation, Springfield, and it is on record that he obtained 340 additional slaves to work his combined holdings. Besides rice, Mein raised extensive crops of corn, cotton, and tobacco; and at a kiln on Coleraine thousands of bricks were made from the rich alluvial clay. Before leaving Georgia in 1817, Mein sold "his landed estate together with all the improvements" to John Potter for the considerable sum of $110,000.

[*Savannah River Plantations*, 199–201.]

[47] "Aunt Betsy" was Elizabeth Smith (1756–1823), the sister of Mrs. McQueen, and a member of the household at the Cottage.

[48] John Postell Williamson (1778–1843) was the husband of Sally, Eliza Mackay's sister. Owner of a Savannah River plantation, Brampton, Williamson was a commission merchant of Savannah and a power in local politics. He served on different occasions as justice of the Inferior Court, alderman, and mayor. After the death of Sally Williamson, he married, in 1821, Madeline Julia Dennis. It is evident from several of Robert Mackay's letters that John Williamson was no favorite of the family of his first wife.

[A monograph on Brampton, with much biographical material on John Postell Williamson, is in *Savannah River Plantations*, 391–418.]

[49] The ball described by Robert Mackay was given, in all likelihood, in "The elegant Dwelling House . . . at the corner of Pine and Broughton streets," in one of the western suburbs of Savannah,

from which the Scarbrough family moved in 1819 to the Regency mansion, built for William Scarbrough by the noted architect William Jay.

[The quotation is from a sales advertisement in *The Georgian*, July 27, 1819.]

[50] "The Countess" was Robert Mackay's special name for Julia (Bernard) Scarbrough (1786–1851), daughter of a physician of Wilmington, North Carolina, who had come to Savannah in 1805 as William Scarbrough's bride. Described by a biographer of her husband as "a beautiful wit and belle," Mrs. Scarbrough was fired by the ambition to lead Savannah society. But even with the backing of the Scarbrough fortune, she never achieved that end, for her ways were not Savannah ways. (". . . she is cursed coarse sometimes," Robert Mackay confided to his wife. "I hope she may sink North-Carolina when in the presence of any of our acquaintance—") Yet if she failed to acquire the Savannah idiom ("Mrs. S. gave a *tremendous blow out* to use her own words," a young lady wrote to her brother in 1829), she never lost hope, and as long as her money lasted, would give splendid entertainments to which the élite of Savannah flocked, to dance, feast, and sharpen their wit at her expense. Robert Mackay, a great favorite of Mrs. Scarbrough's, was well placed to glean and pass on many a caustic anecdote about her. But he was not an unkind critic, and Mrs. Scarbrough emerges from his letters as a woman of forceful personality who strongly impressed her generation in the town of her adoption.

[For further references to Mrs. Scarbrough, see below Index; *The Alexander Letters, 1787–1900* (Savannah, 1910), 50; and "The Kollock Letters," edited by Edith Duncan Johnston, *The Georgia Historical Quarterly*, XXX, 4 (December, 1946), 353.]

[51] William Taylor (1769–1840), a native of Scotland, was a prosperous commission merchant. He arrived in Savannah shortly after the Revolution, formed a partnership with Richard Miller, and, as an alderman, took an interest in civic affairs. In his will he made bequests to the two institutions beloved by expatriate Scotsmen in Savannah: the Independent Presbyterian Church and the St. Andrew's Society of Georgia.

[Taylor's will is in the Court of Ordinary, Chatham County Court House, Savannah. His portrait is owned by the Georgia Society of the Colonial Dames of America.]

[52] Dr. Henry Kollock (1778–1819), "the great Jersey preacher," had a reputation for eloquence equalled by few clergymen of his day. In 1806 he resigned the post of professor of Divinity in the College of New Jersey, to which he had been appointed at the age

of twenty-five, and came to Savannah as pastor of the Independent Presbyterian Church. Robert Mackay writes that Doctor Kollock intended to stay only "one Season," but Providence decreed that he retain this pulpit until his death twelve years later. His legacy to Savannah was the beautiful church that was begun at his instigation and completed through his efforts. This structure, designed by the Rhode Island architect, John Holden Greene, after the style of Sir Christopher Wren, was burned in 1889, but was rebuilt according to Greene's plan.

[*Sermons on Various Subjects, by the late Henry Kollock, D.D., with a Memoir of the Life of the Author* (4 vols., Savannah, 1822); Margaret Callaway Axson, "History of the Independent Presbyterian Church," manuscript in the files of the Savannah Historical Research Association, Hodgson Hall, Savannah.]

[53] Before her marriage to Doctor Kollock in 1804, Mehetabel (Hylton) Campbell was the widow of Alexander Campbell, a prominent attorney of Richmond, Virginia.

[54] Ann (Heyward) Gibbons (*c.* 1758–1820), wife of Thomas Gibbons, came of a distinguished South Carolina family, one of whose members, Thomas Heyward, Junior, was a signer of the Declaration of Independence.

[55] Robert Mitchel (1776–1830), a native of Perth, Scotland (or North Britain as that nation is called on his tombstone), emigrated to Savannah as a young man and became a substantial merchant. He was at one time a partner of John Caig (see above, page 262). A founder and the first president of the St. Andrew's Society, Mitchel was considered the leader of the influential group of Scottish merchants in Savannah.

[*The Georgian*, December 28, 1830; *Some Early Epitaphs in Georgia*, compiled by the Georgia Society of the Colonial Dames of America, and edited by Mrs. Peter W. Meldrim, (n.p. [, 1924]), 72.]

[56] Red Bluff, in the Low Country of South Carolina, was a plantation that had belonged to Elizabeth (Williamson) Smith. Mrs. Smith bequeathed to her daughter, Lady Wright, who in turn left to her nephew, the younger John McQueen, a portion of this plantation.

[Red Bluff is mentioned in Lady Wright's will, which is on file in the Chatham County Court House, Savannah.]

[57] Sedgefield was a rice plantation, situated on the south bank of the Ogeechee River, in Bryan County, Georgia. It is probable that the younger John McQueen had secured this property on a short lease, as Sedgefield was often rented on such terms at this period.

[For example, see the *Columbian Museum & Savannah Advertiser*, January 12, 1798.]

[58] Sir James Wright, second baronet, the eldest son of the last royal governor of Georgia, had served during the Revolution as Major in the Regiment of Georgia Loyalists. On the defeat of the British, he retired to England and settled at Little Ealing, County Middlesex. There the relatives of his wife, Sarah Williamson Smith, found a ready welcome. In family tradition, however, Sir James is remembered as a crotchety old gentleman, whose exile was embittered by the contrast with his former prominence in America. Sir James died without issue in 1816, and the title, dating from 1772 and listed in the baronetage as "Wright of Georgia," passed to his grand-nephew.

[*The Letters of Don Juan McQueen to his Family*, xxiii n.; *Debrett's Baronetage of England* (London, 1835), 196.]

[59] Lotteries were much in vogue, both in England and America, at the turn of the century. The "Lottery ticket" mentioned by Robert Mackay was one of many thousands issued by the State of Georgia after 1803, each winning ticket entitling the holder to some two hundred acres in the recently ceded Indian lands beyond the Oconee River. By this policy, western Georgia was reserved for the small freeholders, and saved from the speculators who had perpetrated the notorious Yazoo Fraud.

[60] "Miss C." was Mary Anne Cowper (1776–1856), elder daughter of Basil and Mary (Smith) Cowper. Although apparently encouraging William Mein's suit, she died a spinster.

[61] The "dreadful acco[ts]. of the French successes on the Continent" told of Napoleon's decisive victory over the Prussian Army at Jena October 14, 1806, and of his promulgation the following month of the Berlin Decree by which the coasts of England were declared closed to foreign commerce.

[62] John Mackay, the fourth child and third son of Robert and Eliza Mackay, was born in Savannah, November 30, 1805. Several interesting anecdotes of his childhood are recounted in the letters of his parents. Early attracted to the military life, he entered West Point in 1825 and was graduated four years later, eighth in a class of forty-six. At West Point he formed a lasting friendship with Robert E. Lee, his classmate. Lieutenant Mackay was first attached to the Second Regiment of Artillery and served in the Seminole War; in 1838 he was transferred to the Corps of Topographical Engineers and promoted to a captaincy. He became known for his careful surveys of rivers and harbors. Stricken with tuberculosis, Mackay was granted sick leave from the Army in 1846. Two years later, on May 31, 1848, he died in Savannah and was buried in the family lot in the South Broad Street Cemetery (tombstone).

[Cullum, *Biographical Register . . . of the U. S. Military Academy*, II (New York, 1868), 341; *The Savannah Georgian*, June 2, 1848.]

[63] Sarah Campbell (1784–1843) was the daughter of Macartan and Sarah (Fenwick) Campbell, prominent residents of Augusta, Georgia. In 1795 her mother married Dr. George Jones, and "Miss Campbell" and several of her sisters became members of her step-father's household in Savannah. She was married in 1808 to Noble Wimberly Jones, son of Doctor Jones by his first wife, Mary Gibbons.

Harriet Tattnall Campbell (1790–1862) was the ninth and youngest child of Macartan and Sarah (Fenwick) Campbell. She never married.

[64] Robert Mackay's partner at this "Concert" was one of the four elder daughters of John Wallace, British vice-consul for Georgia, all of whom subsequently married into representative Savannah families: Savage, Howard, Lloyd, and Owens. Their brother, John Wallace (1792–1816), at one time a clerk in the Liverpool office of Alexander Mein, was endowed with a caustic wit that flavors the group of his letters now in the Southern Historical Collection, Chapel Hill, North Carolina.

["The Wallace Letters," edited by Mary Savage Anderson, *The Georgia Historical Quarterly*, XVIII, 2 (June, 1934), 176–193.]

[65] ". . . the Bourke's" were Elizabeth and Catherine, daughters of Thomas Bourke, an Irish-born merchant of Savannah; their mother, Jane (Smith) Bourke, was Eliza Mackay's aunt. Elizabeth Bourke died unmarried; Catherine became the wife of a Mr. Odell.

[66] "Jane" was the two-year old daughter of John and Sally Williamson. She was married in 1821 to Abraham Baldwin Fannin, a Savannah merchant, and died in 1835.

[67] Joseph Welscher, an Englishman by birth and a lawyer by profession, was well-known in the military and political life of Savannah. As a leader of the Republican party, he figured in many factional disputes, one of which led to a sensational duel. Welscher was often elected to the Board of Aldermen, and while representing Chatham County in the Georgia Legislature, died at Louisville, the state capital, in 1806. A contemporary estimate of him shows how high political passions ran in the Savannah of his day: "Capt. Welscher is a man of amiable manners, a truly honorable character, highly beloved by a number of respectable friends and acquaintances—hated by none but Tories—the worst Tories—the enemies of Washington and Jefferson—the enemies of sound order, peace, liberty and happiness."

[Gamble, *Savannah Duels and Duellists*, 91–93, 114–118.]

[68] Cherokee Hill, ten miles from Savannah on the post road to Augusta, rises above the low lands bordering the Savannah River.

In contrast to the river-side plantations, Cherokee Hill in Robert Mackay's day supported a plebian society of Indian traders, tavern-keepers and small farmers who gained a livelihood from the traffic that passed by their doors. A notable event in the religious history of Georgia took place here in 1822: the laying of the corner-stone of "the Church of all Denominations." On this occasion Thomas U. P. Charlton, the distinguished Savannah jurist, delivered "a handsome oration," and Parson Weems, Washington's biographer, preached a sermon.

[Marie E. Reddy, "The History of Cherokee Hill," manuscript in the files of the Savannah Historical Research Association, Hodgson Hall, Savannah; *Mason Locke Weems: His Works and Ways*, edited by Emily Ellsworth Ford Skeel (3 vols., New York, 1929), III, 342, 343.]

[69] John Clark Nightingale died on Cumberland Island, Georgia, September 10, 1806.

[*Columbian Museum & Savannah Advertiser*, September 17, 1806.]

[70] Elizabeth (Fuller) McQueen, widow of Eliza Mackay's uncle, Alexander McQueen, died on her plantation at Montgomery, October 4, 1806, aged fifty-two years.

[Her obituary is in the *Georgia Republican* (Savannah), October 14, 1806.]

[71] François-Didier Petit de Villers (1761–1841), known to his friends as Petit, to others as "Monsieur Petite Devil Ears," was a French aristocrat who after many vicissitudes was now a commission merchant and factor of Savannah. In early youth he had emigrated from France to the colony of St. Domingo, and he was prospering as a notary when the slave insurrections brought an end to French rule in that troubled West Indian island. With a great number of other refugees, Petit fled to the United States. He lived for several years in Baltimore and Philadelphia, and removed to Savannah in 1803. A popular figure at concerts and balls, Petit became an intimate friend of the Mackays. Eliza Mackay was the godmother of his son, William, and Robert Mackay often wrote with affection of Petit's solicitude for the various members of his family.

[Two of Petit's Letter Books, for the years 1798–1799 and 1801, are owned by the Georgia Historical Society, Savannah; the baptism of William Petit de Villers is recorded in the Parish Register of the Church of St. John the Baptist, I, 196, which is in the Archives of the Roman Catholic Cathedral, Savannah.]

[72] "Mrs. Hunter" was Deborah (Malbone) Hunter (1744–1813), Robert Mackay's aunt. On the death of her husband, Dr. William Hunter of Newport, Rhode Island, she went with her son and daughters to England, where she spent her later years. By chance Mrs.

Hunter has attained a measure of celebrity. In 1796, while staying at Walpole House in Chiswick on the Thames, she made the acquaintance of a fellow lodger, Daniel O'Connell. The future Liberator of Ireland was then studying law, but he was much more interested in people than in Blackstone; and he wrote in his journal, since published, such a vivid description of Mrs. Hunter that this lady is assured of a lasting place in literature of the sort:

Mrs. Hunter is about fifty-three years old if I form my judgment from circumstances, if from appearance not within six years of that age. She is tall and well made. Her eyes still retain youthful lustre. When young her beauty must have been uncommonly striking. Her manners are agreeable and genteel, and she possesses a fund of good sense, knowledge of the world, and politeness. She has one foible. Even that is never carried to a troublesome length. She is fond of telling of the rank she very probably did in reality possess in her native country. But to perceive even this foible one must be a considerable time acquainted with her; nay, must almost have gained her confidence.

[Arthur Houston, *Daniel O'Connell: His Early Life, and Journal, 1795 to 1802* (London, 1906), 109, 110.]

[73] Eliza Hunter (1760–1849), Mrs. Hunter's eldest daughter, had once been a celebrated beauty. Tradition affirms that she was engaged to Count Axel von Fersen, an officer in the French forces that occupied Newport during the Revolution; but she became blind and her lover departed, to win fame some years later for his attempted rescue of the Royal Family of France from imprisonment in the Tuileries. Daniel O'Connell believed that the Hunters had come to Europe "for the purpose of consulting oculists on a disorder which had deprived the eldest daughter of sight. I do not now recollect whether this was pointed out to me by some person as the object of the journey, or whether I drew the conclusion myself from circumstances with which I have become acquainted" (Houston, *Daniel O'Connell*, 105).

[Several letters that Eliza Hunter wrote to her cousin, Eliza Mackay, are in the Library of the Newport Historical Society, Newport, Rhode Island.]

[74] ". . . the Bishop" was one of the many French prelates who had fled to England during the Revolution and, resigning their sees when Napoleon assumed power, ended their days in exile. He is often mentioned in the family correspondence, but never by name. In a letter to Eliza Mackay, then in Liverpool, Eliza Hunter writes: "our good Bishop says a thousand kind things on the occasion, and begs to be remembered to the amiable Circle, he comes as usual to Kensington, but he feels there is something wanting, he has had lately some gloomy days, at the loss of his Brother in adversity the Bishop

D'avranche, he officiated at his funeral last Thursday" (letter, dated Kensington Gravel Pits, October 3 [, 1810?], owned by the Newport Historical Society).

[75] ". . . our dear old Hannah," as Margaret Mackay Elliott refers in her memoirs to this faithful Negro slave, had been taken to England as a nurse for the Mackay children. She returned to America with the family in 1811.

[76] Charlotte de Berniere Scarbrough (1806–1861), Robert Mackay's goddaughter, was the daughter of William Scarbrough and "the Countess." Of their several children she was the only one with real claim to distinction. For besides being a woman of rare personal charm, she was also a leading scientist in the field of entomology. A pioneer in the study of insect life associated with the staple crops of the Southern seaboard, she wrote articles on these subjects that were remarkable for their exact information and literary merit. Charlotte Scarbrough traveled widely, married James Taylor, a Savannah merchant, and on the approach of the Civil War left Savannah for England. She was preparing a work about life on Southern plantations when death overtook her on the Isle of Man.

[*Dictionary of American Biography*, XVIII (New York, 1936), 319, 320.]

[77] George Welshman Owens (1786–1856), a Savannahian, had attended Harrow and Cambridge and was now in London, a law student in the office of the celebrated Mr. Chitty. On his return to Georgia, he married Sarah Wallace (see above, page 275) and was soon a successful lawyer, serving as mayor of Savannah and member of Congress. His father, Owen Owens (*c.* 1751–1814), a native of Wales, had arrived in Savannah at the close of the Revolution and had done well as a merchant.

[*Biographical Directory of the American Congress, 1774–1927* (Washington, 1928), 1378.]

[78] It was natural that Savannah, with so many residents of Scottish birth attached to their "Royal and Ancient Game of Goff," should boast one of the first golf clubs in America. Records show that the Savannah Golf Club was in existence as early as 1795: anniversary dinners were held in the various coffeehouses, and mention is made of "their Marquee, on the East Common," where the club's business was transacted. On New Year's Eve, 1811, when Robert Mackay was one of the managers, the Golf Club gave a ball that is memorable in the social annals of Savannah.

[William Harden, "The First Golf Club in America," *Vanity Fair*, V, 1 (January, 1917), 73; *Georgia Gazette*, September 22, 1796; *Columbian*

Museum & Savannah Advertiser, December 30, 1796, March 21, 1797, and October 10, 1797.]

[79] The Exchange, a three-story brick structure, with a clock tower and spire, dominated the Savannah waterfront from its completion in 1802 until it was torn down in 1904 to make way for the present City Hall. Affectionately called "the Faneuil Hall of Savannah," the Exchange provided quarters for the municipal government, the post office, and several mercantile firms; while its Long Room, the scene of assemblies and concerts, was a favorite resort of fashion.

[Thomas Gamble, Jr., *A History of the City Government of Savannah, Ga., from 1790 to 1901* (Savannah [, 1901]), 131–139.]

[80] Richard O'Donnell was a young Irish merchant of Savannah, a member of the firm of Maher and O'Donnell. He died in 1807, in his twenty-fourth year, but his character still lives in his obituary:

"The character of Mr. O'Donnell displayed at once his *nation* and the gentleman: ardent in his feelings, polished in his manners, sincere in his friendship, he became the favorite of every circle. Though not bewailed by family connection, he will long be remembered, and his premature fall regretted by a numerous and admiring acquaintance."—*The Republican; and Savannah Evening Ledger*, September 12, 1807.

[81] Jean-Baptiste Le Roy was the most popular of the several French dancing-masters in Savannah at the turn of the century. In 1802 he opened a school on the Bay, promising to teach his pupils "the gracefulness of the most fashionable dances" (*Georgia Gazette*, November 25, 1802); and in 1811 he found it necessary to employ an assistant, "Mr. FREMON," also a Frenchman, to attend "to the Dancing part, under his care and direction" (*The Republican; and Savannah Evening Ledger*, November 28, 1811). After some months Frémon opened a school of his own. It was there, in "that central stand, Mrs. Leaver's house on Broughton Street," that on January 23, 1813, was born his son, John Charles Frémont, the future Pathmarker of the West.

[For Frémon's stay in Savannah, see *The Republican; and Savannah Evening Ledger*, December 10, 1812; and Allan Nevins, *Frémont: Pathmarker of the West* (New York and London, 1939), 8, 9.]

[82] Ann Gibbons (*c.* 1790–1817), only surviving daughter of Thomas and Ann (Heyward) Gibbons, was married in 1810 to John M. Trumbull (see below, page 291).

[83] Benjamin Burroughs (1779–1837) and Oliver Sturges (*c.* 1777–1824) composed one of the best-known mercantile firms in the South. They owned a third interest in the steamship *Savannah*, and sent a cargo of cotton to Liverpool on the first voyage of that vessel across

the Atlantic. As tangible evidence of their prosperity and of their friendship for each other, the partners built in 1818, on a conspicuous site in Reynolds Square, paired houses of Georgian design; that of Sturges is still standing.

[84] Reynolds Square in Abercorn Street, near the Bay, was commonly called "Bank Square," because of the location there of the Branch Bank of the United States. Robert Mackay was now residing in this square (see below, page 283).

[85] Martha Gadsden Campbell (1789–1820) was a sister of Harriet Campbell and of Mrs. Noble Wimberly Jones (see above, page 275).

[86] Hector Mitchel is an obscure figure in the Savannah scene. His name appears in the local newspapers as plaintiff in several suits (*The Republican; and Savannah Evening Ledger*, May 30, 1809, and February 2, 1811); and in a long letter, first printed in a Jamaica paper, he accused one John G. Johnston of piracy and the theft of the British schooner *Perthshire* off Haiti. He offered to pay Johnston if he surrendered himself "to impartial justice . . . , on his acquittal from the bar, Three Thousand Dollars, a sum more than tenfold adequate to the lost time of a desperate adventurer like himself, during the regular process of law: And I will pay the like sum to any one who will, within a reasonable time, produce the living body of the said Johnston for prosecution" (*Columbian Museum, and Savannah Daily Gazette*, February 11, 1817).

[87] "Miss Telfair" was one of the three daughters of Edward Telfair, a Savannah merchant, member of the Continental Congress, and twice governor of Georgia. Sarah, the eldest, was married in 1815 to Georgia Haig, an army officer (see below, page 313); Margaret, the youngest, became the wife of William Brown Hodgson, the well-known Oriental scholar; while Mary never married and, dying in 1875, bequeathed her considerable fortune to educational and philanthropic uses in Savannah.

[E. Merton Coulter, "Edward Telfair," *The Georgia Historical Quarterly*, XX, 2 (June, 1936), 99–124.]

[88] The Reverend William Best, an Episcopal clergyman, was rector of Christ Church from 1804 to 1807. Much of his time was occupied with rebuilding this "Mother Church of Georgia," for the colonial structure in which Whitefield preached had burned in the great fire of 1796 and the walls of its successor, almost completed, had been leveled by the hurricane of 1804.

Robert Mackay usually attended the Independent Presbyterian Church, but in the Savannah of his day the lines between the Protestant denominations were not strictly drawn; the eloquence of the preacher rather than the form of worship determined the size of his congregation. This was expressed by Margaret McQueen who wrote from Jamaica in 1817 to Eliza Mackay: "Who is the new pastor you speak of at the Episcopal church? I should like a good pew in the Presbyterian Meeting if so good a man & preacher as Mr. K. [Henry Kollock] continues there. Otherwise the Episcopal form with a good minister & preacher w^{d}. be just as welcome to me" (letter owned by Mr. Walter C. Hartridge of Savannah).

[89] James Broadfoot, a Charleston merchant (see below, page 301), had survived with Robert Mackay the wreck of the ill-fated *General Oglethorpe.*

[90] William McLean was the son of Robert Mackay's half-sister, Catherine Chilcott, by her second husband, Andrew McLean. He lived in Augusta, Georgia.

[91] Thomas Gardner was a merchant with interests in Augusta and Savannah. In 1818 he built a handsome brick residence in South Broad Street, on what had once been a part of Savannah's South Common. Commodore Josiah Tattnall spent his last years in this house and died there in 1871.

[92] The Ogeechee River, often the inspiration to Georgia poets, is a stream colored by cypress swamps whose waters flow from the Piedmont to the sea. During the hundred years preceding the Civil War, its tidal reaches were lined with rice fields and plantation homes.

[93] Placentia was a twelve-hundred-acre plantation at Thunderbolt, adjoining the Cottage on the south. It was owned at this time by John P. Williamson.

[*Georgia Republican,* January 7, 1806.]

[94] Mary Johnson Campbell (1794–1889) was the step-daughter and not, as Robert Mackay wrote, in the English usage of his day, "the daughter in Law of Parson Kollock." In 1813 she married James Moore Wayne, a young lawyer of Savannah, whose brilliant career led him in swift stages through the Georgia Legislature, the mayoralty of Savannah, the bench of the Eastern Judicial Courts of Georgia, and the House of Representatives to the Supreme Court of the United States, of which he was associate justice from 1835 until his death in 1867. The promise that Robert Mackay noted in the twelve-year-old girl was amply fulfilled in the woman. Mrs. Wayne enjoyed the reputation of being a delightful hostess, and about her home in Washington lingered the aura of the eighteenth-century salon.

[Alexander A. Lawrence, *James Moore Wayne: Southern Unionist* (Chapel Hill, 1943), 20, 84.]

[95] Peter Henry Morel (1757–1812), a native Savannahian, had spent much time abroad. He studied medicine in Edinburgh, married into a prominent Liverpool family, the Dunbars, and engaged in the East Indian trade. Returning to Georgia, he and his son, John Henry Morel (1780–1834), planted rice at Deerfield on the Ogeechee River. In 1806 his daughter, Tryphena, married Alexander S. Roe, an Irishman, who for some unexplained reason was not acceptable to the Morels. An estrangement followed, and the reconciliation mentioned by Robert Mackay was short-lived. In 1810 Peter Morel announced in the papers that Roe had defaulted on the payment of several notes due him (*The Republican; and Savannah Evening Ledger*, June 19, 1810).

It may be added, however, that Alexander Roe was not as black as he was painted by his in-laws. He was a man of substance in the community, member of City Council, treasurer and secretary of the musical Anacreontic Society; and when he died in 1816, at the age of thirty-seven, he was accorded a funeral "with Military and Masonic honors" (Municipal Mortuary Records).

[For the Morel genealogy, see Harry Alexander Davis, *Some Huguenot Families of South Carolina and Georgia* (n.p., 1926), 60–69.]

[96] "Lee," one of Robert Mackay's Charleston friends, was a frequent visitor in Savannah.

[97] William Bellinger Bulloch (1777–1852), a lawyer, son of Archibald Bulloch of Revolutionary fame, was an important political figure in Savannah. He served at various times as United States district attorney for Georgia, mayor of Savannah, attorney general of Georgia, and, in 1813, United States senator. His interests extended also to banking: he was a founder of the State Bank of Georgia and its president from 1816 to 1843. On January 29, 1807, Bulloch, whose first wife, Harriet De Veaux, had died in 1805, was married to Mary Young, the daughter of Benjamin and Mary (Allston) Young of Georgetown, South Carolina. She survived him, dying in 1868, at the age of eighty-seven.

[*Biographical Directory of the American Congress, 1774–1927* (Washington, 1928), 758; Municipal Mortuary Records, Savannah.]

[98] "MARRIED, in this City, on Wednesday Evening last, by the Rev. Mr. Kollock, Mr. CHARLES HOWARD, Merchant, to Miss JANE WALLACE, both of this city."—*Columbian Museum & Savannah Advertiser*, Saturday, February 21, 1807.

Two interesting children were the result of this marriage: the Reverend Charles Wallace Howard (1811–1876), historical researcher and first pastor of the reorganized French Protestant Church of Charleston; and Mary Wallace Howard, wife of the Reverend Francis Robert Goulding, author of the classic adventure story, *The Young Marooners.*

[Lucy Josephine Cunyus, *The History of Bartow County (Georgia) formerly Cass* (n.p. [, 1933]), 288–290; *Dictionary of American Biography*, VII (New York, 1931), 457, 458.]

[99] "Mendenhall" was one of the three members of that family then living in Savannah: Thomas (1750–1808), cashier of the Branch Bank of the United States; and his sons, Thomas, who succeeded him as cashier of the bank and was mayor of Savannah in 1811, and John, a physician and druggist.

[The elder Mendenhall's obituary is in *The Republican; and Savannah Evening Ledger*, October 8, 1808; and references to his sons are in the *Columbian Museum & Savannah Advertiser*, June 22 and 29, 1809.]

[100] William Bower Williamson, second child of John and Sally Williamson, was born April 23, 1806, and died March 7, 1807. He was buried in the family cemetery at Brampton plantation (tombstone).

[101] ". . . our little Stranger," born at Kensington Gravel Pits, near London, April 25, 1807, was christened Margaret, and grew up to be a woman of distinctive personality. Robert E. Lee, her brother John's classmate and closest friend at West Point, was one of her many admirers. A number of letters that Lieutenant Lee wrote to her while stationed on Cockspur Island near Savannah are in the possession of her family. In 1830 Margaret Mackay was married to Dr. Ralph Emms Elliott, a physician and planter on the Ogeechee River. She died in Savannah on July 31, 1893. Her memoirs, unfortunately never completed, record many interesting incidents in the lives of her parents.

[Family Bible of Robert Mackay; Douglas Southall Freeman, *Robert E. Lee: A Biography* (4 vols., New York and London, 1934 and 1935), I, 55, 83, 100–102.]

[102] ". . . the square" was Reynolds Square, in colonial times the site of public buildings and stores but in which later were grouped many handsome residences. In 1807 Robert Mackay was living in the elegant Georgian mansion fronting "the square" that he bought the next year. It was in this house that his cousin, Edward Greene Malbone, the miniaturist, died on May 7, 1807, having come to Savannah in the vain hope of recovering from consumption. The Mackay family moved in 1813 to Broughton Street and their dwelling in Reynolds Square passed into other hands. When this historic landmark was torn down in 1937, the Adam mantel and graceful arched

recesses from one of the drawing-rooms were installed in the Telfair Academy through the generosity of Mrs. B. F. Bullard; while the unusual screened archway of the hall was presented to the Academy by Mr. Thomas P. Saffold, the last owner of the house.

[103] William McQueen (*c.* 1782–?), youngest of Don Juan McQueen's three sons, spent much time with his father in East Florida. In 1807 he was sent to England for a belated education. "He is a lively giddy Youth," Don Juan wrote of him at this time, "but honourable and will no doubt make a good Member of the community" (*The Letters of Don Juan McQueen to his Family*, 76). On his return to America, William married in 1814 Mary Ann Waight of Beaufort, South Carolina. He bought land that had been a part of George Whitefield's Orphan House tract near Savannah and like his brother, John, tried his hand at planting. But it is evident that William McQueen had inherited his father's roving disposition; for he soon tired of a settled life, went West, and never returned to Savannah.

[For references to William McQueen, see *The Letters of Don Juan McQueen to his Family*, index.]

[104] The former romance between William Scarbrough and Margaret Cowper (see above, page 252) caused this "awkward" situation.

[105] ". . . the Baronet" was Sir James Wright (see above, page 274).

[106] "Mrs De Cadignan," or more correctly, the Comtesse de Cadignan, was the wife of Charles, Comte de Cadignan. The youngest daughter of Dr. William and Deborah (Malbone) Hunter, she was Robert Mackay's first-cousin. Daniel O'Connell considered her "truly beautiful," and declared that he "never was so struck by female beauty as by hers" (Houston, *Daniel O'Connell*, 106).

[107] Causton's Bluff, a plantation on St. Augustine Creek near the Savannah River, was bought by the younger John McQueen in 1802. The name was derived from its first owner, Thomas Causton, one of the early Georgia colonists, foremost in the controversy that caused John Wesley to leave Savannah. McQueen's cultivation of Sea Island cotton led to his borrowing a large sum of money from his uncle, Sir James Wright, who in spite of his exile in England retained an interest in Georgia affairs. After McQueen's death, Causton's Bluff passed to his wife's sister, Mary Anne Cowper, and eventually to his nephew, William Mackay (see above, page 269).

["Causton's Bluff, Deptford, Brewton Hill: Three Allied Plantations," *Savannah River Plantations*, 3–15.]

[108] "On Thursday last was launched at Mr. E. Bolton's ship yard, Messrs. R. & J. Bolton's fine new ship GOSSYPIUM, 264 tons bur-

then. This being the first ship built in this city since the revolution, it drew an immense concourse of spectators to the place—We may with safety venture to assert, that at least nineteen twentieths of the citizens of Savannah, beside numbers who had came [*sic*] from the country for the purpose of gratifying their curiosity, were present. And to the inexpressible satisfaction of all, the launch was so managed as to render it, in the opinion of those who were adequate to judge, as handsome a one as could possibly have been made.

"We understand the Gossypium is intended for the European trade, and that captain JOHN VALENTINE is to command her."—*The Republican; and Savannah Evening Ledger*, Saturday, May 23, 1807.

[109] John Smith (1718–1793), Eliza Mackay's grandfather, is said in a family memoir to have been "a common man only in his name." According to this same source, he was fifty years in advance of his generation "both in refinement and in liberality of feeling" ("Unfinished Memoirs of Margaret Mackay Elliott"). An extensive planter in the Low Country of South Carolina, he moved to Georgia shortly before the Revolution, and by serving on the Council of Safety and in the Provincial Congress of July, 1775, showed himself to be in active sympathy with the Patriots.

[*The Letters of Don Juan McQueen to his Family*, xxii, xxiii, 20 and n., 84.]

[110] Jacob Read (1752–1816) was the owner of Drakies plantation on the Savannah River. A brigadier-general of the South Carolina militia, by profession "Gen.l Read" was a lawyer. He was one of the American colonials admitted to Gray's Inn; and his superior legal learning enabled him to render conspicuous service in the Continental Congress, the South Carolina House of Representatives, of which he was speaker for several years, and in the United States Senate. But planting always remained a vital interest to Read. His family spent part of each year at Read House on Drakies; and the large extent of his Georgia holdings was disclosed by the inventory of his estate made after his death: 265 Negro slaves, live stock valued at $2,720, a rice mill, and 3,600 acres of land.

[*Dictionary of American Biography*, XV (New York, 1935), 425; *Biographical Directory of the American Congress, 1774–1927* (Washington, 1928), 1447; *Savannah River Plantations*, 153–156.]

[111] "Rutledge," a rice planter on the Savannah River, was one of the several sons of John Rutledge (1739–1800), the distinguished jurist and statesman of South Carolina, known as "the Dictator."

[A map of the lower reaches of the Savannah River, drawn in 1825, designates a rice plantation on the South Carolina bank as belonging to the "Este of Genl. Rutledge"; for the Rutledge genealogy, see Mabel L.

Webber, "Dr. John Rutledge and his Descendants," *The South Carolina Historical and Genealogical Magazine*, XXXI, 1, 2 (January and April, 1930), 7–25, and 93–106.]

[112] Robert Scott (*c.* 1775–1845), a native Scotsman, was a prominent merchant of Savannah. In his later years he was senior partner of the firm of Scott and Balfour. Posthumous notice was given him because of the fact that his body was interred in the vault that contained the remains of Nathanael Greene.

[Municipal Mortuary Records, Savannah; *The Remains of Major-General Nathanael Greene* (Providence, Rhode Island, 1903), 217, 218.]

[113] Caroline Dupré Villepontoux (*c.* 1779–1850), daughter of Benjamin and Jane (Dupont) Villepontoux, was descended on both sides from well-known Huguenot families of South Carolina. Her marriage, which took place in Savannah in 1808, to Jacques Rossignol de Belleanse (*c.* 1779–1834) was an unusual event; for the groom, a Catholic, was one of the refugees from the slave insurrections in St. Domingo. These exiles mixed little with Americans in whatever Atlantic port they settled. It is of interest to note that the year after this marriage the bride made her "solemn abjuration of the protestant Religion to embrace the Roman catholic communion," and that her children became leading Catholic laymen in Savannah and Augusta.

[Family records in the possession of Mrs. Charles F. Rossignol of Augusta, Georgia. Caroline Rossignol's "solemn abjuration" is in the Parish Register of the Church of St. John the Baptist, Savannah, I, 180.]

[114] Sutherland's Bluff is in McIntosh County, Georgia. It would seem from this letter and a subsequent one (see above, page 217) that Robert Mackay owned a plantation there.

[115] Savannah, built on a sandy bluff thirty feet above the river of the same name, was affectionately called "the Sandhill" by Robert Mackay. Few travelers of the period failed to mention the situation when writing of Savannah. "Let the *English* reader picture . . . a town erected on the cliffs of *Dover*," John Davis remarked, "and he will behold *Savannah*" (*Travels of Four Years and a Half in the United States of America; During 1798, 1799, 1800, 1801, and 1802*, 100). La Rochefoucauld-Liancourt, the French émigré, was content to describe the city as "bâtie sur un large monceau de sable," and declared that "ses habitans . . . assurent qu'elle est salubre; que l'élévation de sable . . . la préserve de tous les accidens communs dans le Sud des États-Unis aux lieux bas et humides . . ." (*Voyage dans les États-Unis d'Amérique, fait en 1795, 1796 et 1797*, IV, 150). But Jonathan Mason, the New England jurist, expressed a distinctly unfavorable opinion of Mackay's "Sandhill": "It is a wooden town on a sand-heap [he wrote]. In walking their streets you labor as much as if you was wad-

ing through a snow-bank, with this difference only,—you must walk blindfolded, or your eyes will be put out. It resembles my ideas of the Arabian deserts in a hurricane" (*Extracts from a Diary kept by the Hon. Jonathan Mason of a Journey from Boston to Savannah in the Year 1804,*" reprinted from the *Proceedings of the Massachusetts Historical Society* [Cambridge, 1885], 26).

[116] John Garnier Williamson (1756–1814), member of a family long established in the Carolina Low Country, moved to Georgia after the Revolution and in 1792 bought Brampton. He assumed an influential position among his fellow planters of the Savannah River, served in the State Legislature, and was a justice of the Inferior Court of Chatham County. His wife was Jane Parmenter; of their many children, only two reached maturity: John Postell Williamson (see above, page 271) and Mary Ann Williamson, who married James Edmund Houstoun (see above, page 265).

[*Savannah River Plantations,* 404, 407, 408.]

[117] ". . . the fort," a battery at the eastern extremity of Savannah, commanded the harbor. Known as Fort Halifax in colonial times, it was renamed by the Patriots in honor of Anthony Wayne, and was strengthened during the War of 1812 to repel an expected British invasion.

[118] "Miss Jones" was Sarah Gibbons Jones (1789–1834), only surviving daughter of Dr. George Jones by his first wife, Mary Gibbons. She married in 1823 the Honorable Alfred Cuthbert (1785–1856), member of Congress and United States senator from Georgia.

[From family records owned by Mr. G. Noble Jones of Savannah.]

[119] Elizabeth (Farley) Swarbreck (*c.* 1757–1807) seems, from various contemporary accounts, to have been a woman of marked personality. A native of Savannah, the sister of John Farley, cabinetmaker, she married first George Basil Spencer, a merchant, and secondly Edward Swarbreck, a Danish sea-captain, who was profitably engaged in slave-trading. She died on June 19, 1807.

[A eulogy of Mrs. Swarbreck's many virtues and of her fortitude in sickness is in the *Columbian Museum & Savannah Advertiser,* June 23, 1807.]

[120] ". . . little Tom Tatnall" died "of inflammation of the lungs," aged eight years, and was buried on May 15, 1807, from the house of his uncle, Dr. George Jones, with whom he lived after the deaths of his parents (Municipal Mortuary Records). He was the son of the Honorable Josiah Tattnall, United States senator and governor of Georgia; and brother of Commodore Josiah Tattnall, who is remembered for his use of the phrase "Blood is thicker than water" when in 1859 he sent assistance to a British vessel under attack by the Chinese.

Bonaventure, the Tattnall plantation, was on the Wilmington River, a mile north of the Cottage.

[121] Aaron Burr's dream of western empire ended in fiasco. Arrested and charged with treason, he and his associates were brought before a grand jury in Richmond on May 22, 1807. The trial lasted until September, and was followed with close interest all over the country, but in no place more than Savannah, which Burr had visited in 1802 and 1804.

[122] "The Affair of the *Chesapeake* and *Leopard*," as this engagement is known in history, took place on June 22, 1807.

[123] A legacy from colonial and Revolutionary periods, military organizations flourished in Savannah, and vied with one another in the observation of patriotic anniversaries. The Fourth of July, 1807, was celebrated with special honors by the Savannah Volunteer Guards. On the morning of that day the corps assembled to receive from Mrs. James Marshall, a notable Savannah hostess and the wife of their captain, a standard "worked with her own hands, one side of it representing the strength of our [Georgia] Constitution, supported by the pillars of Wisdom and Moderation, and emblematical of Justice and Peace, the other bearing the Spread Eagle, the arms of the United States." Mrs. Marshall then delivered the speech praised by Robert Mackay; this was considered such a model of classic expression that it was published in her obituary seventy years later (*The Morning News*, January 27, 1877). Ensign Reynolds replied for the Guards, and it was he who, as Mackay wrote, "absolutely trembled & for a long time could not remember a word of his speech."

[124] Ann Moodie, Lady Houstoun (*c.* 1749–1821) was the widow of Sir George Houstoun, seventh baronet. Her plantation, Retreat, was at White Bluff on the Vernon River in Chatham County, Georgia.

[125] The dissolution of the firm of Mein, Mackay and Company, though under consideration for some time, did not take place until May 1, 1809 (*Columbian Museum & Savannah Advertiser*, July 10, 1809).

[126] ". . . your Sister" was Sally Williamson (see above, page 254).

[127] ". . . old Tom Young" (*c.* 1733–1808) was a respected planter. A native of Edinburgh, he emigrated to Savannah about 1758, and, marrying into the influential Maxwell family of St. John's Parish, soon acquired much land throughout tidewater Georgia. The Revolution ended his good fortune, as, like many Georgia colonists of British birth, Thomas Young was a Loyalist. He was declared "guilty of Treason" against the State, but his popularity and family connections obtained the removal of his name from the Confiscation Act. Although

records show that he did not regain all of his property, Young was never without funds. In 1795 he bought a rice plantation, Ham, on Hutchinson's Island in the Savannah River; two years later he acquired Rae's Hall on the mainland. Having no children of his own, Young brought his nephew, Thomas Kettle, from Scotland and made him his heir. Kettle took the name of Young, and after his uncle's death he became a leader in the business and social life of Savannah, as well as president of the Georgia Agricultural Society. He died in 1832.

[Municipal Mortuary Records, Savannah; *Savannah River Plantations*, 357–360, 364–368.]

[128] The Reverend Henry Holcombe (1762–1824), a forceful Baptist preacher, was called to Savannah in 1799 as supply minister for the Independent Presbyterian Church. It was he who married Robert Mackay and Eliza McQueen. In 1800 he gathered a flock of ten persons into a Baptist congregation, the first in Savannah. As their pastor he won many converts, published the first religious periodical in Georgia, and railed against pleasures of all sorts, especially the theatre, which he affirmed was manned by "a detachment of his Satanic majesty's forces, called 'stage-players'" (Henry Holcombe, D.D., *The First Fruits, in a Series of Letters*, 96). But in 1810 Doctor Holcombe left for Mount Enon, Georgia, where he had established a seminary, and the religious revival that almost singlehanded he had aroused in Savannah languished.

[Mabel Freeman La Far, "Henry Holcombe, D.D. (1762–1824): Minister, Humanitarian, and Man of Letters," *The Georgia Historical Quarterly*, XXVIII, 3 (September, 1944), 157–175.]

[129] Martha (Fenwick) Gadsden, daughter of Edward and Mary (Drayton) Fenwick, was the wife of Thomas Gadsden. "Mrs Judge Jones" was her sister.

[D. E. Huger Smith, "An Account of the Tattnall and Fenwick Families in South Carolina," *The South Carolina Historical and Genealogical Magazine*, XIV, 1 (January, 1913), 6, 9, 10.]

[130] Sarah (Fenwick) Jones died in Savannah on the evening of January 17, 1810, aged fifty-three.

[Her obituary is in *The Republican; and Savannah Evening Ledger*, January 30, 1810.]

[131] "Mrs Noble Jones (little Sally)" was the daughter of "Mrs Judge Jones" by her first husband, Macartan Campbell (see above, page 275). Her "fine bouncing Girl," Sarah Fenwick Jones, died in 1813 (Municipal Mortuary Records).

[132] James Wallace (*c.* 1754–1825), uncle of Robert Mackay's contemporaries of that surname, was a Scottish-born merchant who settled in Savannah before the American Revolution. A Tory, he went

to Halifax when peace was declared, but soon returned. He succeeded his brother, John, as British vice-consul for Georgia and in 1824 was made consul.

[Municipal Mortuary Records, Savannah. For a list of British consuls in Savannah, see the *Savannah Morning News,* June 19, 1937.]

[133] "Died in Philadelphia, on the 4th of the present month, October, after a long and severe illness, Mrs. MARIA MAGDALEN PETIT DE VILLERS, aged 26 years, the wife of F. D. Petit de Villers, Factor, of this city. She possessed all the virtues and amiable accomplishments that could promote the happiness of her disconsolate husband, and their two infant children; and they will never cease to pay their tribute of love and grief to her memory."—*The Republican; and Savannah Evening Ledger*, October 19, 1809.

[134] Mrs. James Hunter was Eliza, daughter of Leonard Cecil, a Savannah merchant. She died in 1862, aged seventy-three years. Her expected child was a daughter, Harriet, whose life was cut short by whooping cough in December, 1808 (Municipal Mortuary Records, Savannah).

[135] John, Sally Williamson's fourth child, was born on February 3, 1810. He survived to the age of seventy-five, having been in early manhood a rice planter and commission merchant, and in his later years treasurer of Chatham County. Much esteemed by his fellow citizens, he served as chairman of the Board of Aldermen when Savannah surrendered to Sherman in 1864.

[For a biographical sketch of Williamson, see his obituary in the *Savannah Morning News,* September 30, 1885.]

[136] John Bolton (1774–1838), a native of Chestertown, Maryland, spent the greater part of his life in Savannah. In 1796 he went into business with his cousin, Robert Bolton, under the style of Robert and John Bolton (*Columbian Museum & Savannah Advertiser*, April 29, 1796). This firm soon ranked among the most important of Savannah, and for the sake of sentiment, John Bolton retained the name unchanged after the death of his partner (*ibid.*, December 10, 1802). Bolton was elected the first president of the Planters' Bank of the State of Georgia, and received many other tokens of civic regard; but he eventually moved to New York. There he served as president of the Delaware and Hudson Canal Company.

To their "foreign trade" and "domestic produce," Robert and John Bolton added real estate. "Bolton's Brick Buildings" in Market Square were long the most substantial stores in town; and the warehouses that John Bolton erected on the site of Commerce Row in 1810 never lacked tenants, being occupied in the last decades of the century by the well-known firm of Robert Habersham and Sons.

[Robert Bolton, *Genealogical and Biographical Account of the Family of Bolton: in England and America* (New York, 1862), 114–116. A "Day-Book" of the firm of Robert and John Bolton, containing itemized accounts of all articles sold from December 16, 1802, to January 2, 1804, is owned by Mrs. Craig Barrow of Wormsloe; this gives a unique picture of the scope of a Savannah mercantile house of the period.]

[137] It was not until the spring of 1810 that an effort was made to beautify the squares of Savannah. The improvements that Robert Mackay noted were then provided; and City Council paid the firm of Robert and John Bolton $1,024, the largest single appropriation up to that time, for planting Pride of India trees in the downtown squares.

[Gamble, *A History of the City Government of Savannah*, 84.]

[138] It is interesting to compare Robert Mackay's criticism of Doctor Kollock's pulpit manner with the opinion of an English visitor, John Lambert.

"I went one evening [Lambert wrote in his book of travels] to hear a Mr. Conoch [*sic*], the favourite preacher of the Presbyterians. I cannot say that I admired his delivery, which had a fault too common to the clergymen of the United States, viz, *monotony*. His voice, likewise, was so loud, that it became harsh and grating to the ear; but his pronunciation was clear and distinct. This gentleman is allowed, by his congregation, a salary of 3000 dollars per annum, besides the pews in the chapel which bring him in 7000 dollars more; some of the pews being let for upwards of 160 dollars per annum. This enormous sum for one clergyman, in such a small town as Savannah, is rather surprising; particularly as the people are proverbial for oeconomy."—John Lambert, *Travels through Canada, and the United States of North America, in the years 1806, 1807, & 1808* (2 vols., London, 1814), II, 269.

[139] In this letter Robert Mackay refers to the marriages of the two children of Thomas Gibbons. On February 26, 1810, Thomas Heyward Gibbons was married to Molly Dayton; and on March 15, Ann Gibbons was married to John M. Trumbull of Lebanon, Connecticut, both ceremonies being performed by Doctor Holcombe. Ann's marriage so displeased her father that after her death he disinherited her children in his will.

[Marriage Licenses of Chatham County, in the Court of Ordinary, Savannah. The clause in Thomas Gibbons' will relating to the Trumbull children is quoted in Gamble, *Savannah Duels and Duellists*, 71.]

[140] Robert Mackay lost his bet: Mrs. Scarbrough's child, born on April 20, 1810, was a girl. She was christened Julia Henrietta. A woman of many social graces, she married in 1828 Godfrey Barnsley, a Savannah cotton factor, and died in 1845.

[Transcripts of entries in the Scarbrough Family Bible are in the Library of the Georgia Historical Society, Savannah. For a biographical sketch of Godfrey Barnsley, see Cunyus, *The History of Bartow County*, 44, 45.]

[141] Ebenezer Jackson (1763–1837), who served during the Revolution as an officer in the Massachusetts Regiment of Artillery and was an original member of the Society of the Cincinnati, moved to Savannah in 1787 and became a merchant. His firm is said to have established one of the first packet lines between Savannah and New York. In 1792 he married Mrs. Charlotte Pierce, a sister of Mrs. George Jones (see above, page 275); their daughter, Harriette Fenwick, married her cousin, Commodore Josiah Tattnall, the distinguished naval officer (*Dictionary of American Biography*, XVIII, 310, 311). In addition to their home in Savannah and a plantation outside the town, the Jacksons maintained an estate near Middleton, Connecticut.

[Frank Farnsworth Starr, *The Edward Jackson Family of Newton, Massachusetts* . . . (Hartford, 1895), 57, 58.]

[142] Mrs. Thomas Spalding was Sarah Leake, daughter of a Georgia planter, Richard Leake. ". . . celebrated for her beauty, grace, and solid worth" (Coulter, *Thomas Spalding of Sapelo*, 12), she bore her husband sixteen children and died in 1843, aged sixty-five (*ibid.*, 295–297).

[143] Ray Sands, a relative of Mrs. Nathanael Greene, came from Rhode Island about 1798 to make his home with the Greenes on Cumberland Island. He acted as attorney for his cousin after the death of her second husband, Phineas Miller.

[*Columbian Museum & Savannah Advertiser*, April 6, 1798, and March 5, 1806.]

[144] Le Châlet, the plantation of the Marquis de Montalet, was at the north end of Sapelo. The house was destroyed many years ago and the fields have reverted to the forest, but the name survives, corrupted by long usage to "Chocolate."

[Lovell, *The Golden Isles of Georgia*, 97, 115, 116.]

[145] This passage establishes the exact year of the erection of Thomas Spalding's mansion on Sapelo. Built of tabby after Spalding's own plans, "South End Home" was known throughout the region for its functional design and its elegant appointments. The interior was burned soon after the Civil War, but the walls, three feet thick, were used in the construction of the present house.

[For further descriptions of "South End Home," see Coulter, *Thomas Spalding of Sapelo*, 43, 44; and Lovell, *The Golden Isles of Georgia*, 104–106, 274.]

[146] Charles Simpson was a partner of Simpson and Davison, a London firm with which Robert Mackay often dealt.

[147] "MARRIED, at St. James's Church, Liverpool, Eng. JOHN McQUEEN Esq. of this place, to Miss MARGARET COWPER, daughter of the late Bazil Cowper, Esq. of Barron Hill, in the Island

of Jamaica."—*Columbian Museum & Savannah Advertiser*, May 17, 1810.

[148] Pierce Butler (1744–1822), a younger son of a distinguished Irish family, came to South Carolina shortly before the Revolution as an officer in the British Army. On marrying a Carolina heiress, Mary Middleton, he resigned his commission and devoted himself to politics and planting. He was conspicuous in the State Legislature, helped to frame the Federal Constitution, and served in the United States Senate. Following the example of other South Carolina planters, Major Butler, as he was called, bought much land in coastal Georgia. His cotton plantation, Hampton Point, on St. Simon's Island, and his rice plantation, Butler's Island, near the mouth of the Altamaha River, were noted for their efficient management. But in spite of his many admirable qualities, Pierce Butler was not a man to inspire popularity. "In his social intercourse with the island families, Major Butler was stiff and ceremonious. He brought to his new home an overweening sense of his own importance and superiority to all of his island neighbors" (Lovell, *The Golden Isles of Georgia*, 80, 81).

[*Dictionary of American Biography*, III (New York, 1929), 364, 365; *Biographical Directory of the American Congress, 1774–1927* (Washington, 1928), 770.]

[149] Elizabeth Ann Taylor (1802–1882), daughter of William Taylor (see above, page 272) and his wife Mary Elizabeth Miller, was married in 1821 to Robert Morris Goodwin of Baltimore, Maryland.

[Information from Mrs. Charles E. Rieman of Baltimore, Maryland.]

[150] Congress repealed the Non-Intercourse Act on May 1, 1810.

[151] "Carruthers" was either James or John Carruthers, members of a Savannah firm that made a specialty of such diverse commodities as "BILLS ON NEW-YORK" and "Irish LINENS" (*Columbian Museum & Savannah Advertiser*, October 11, 1806, and January 28, 1807).

[152] On Sunday morning, February 11, 1810, as the bells were ringing and the congregation assembling, the spire of the Church of St. Nicholas, Liverpool, fell, breaking through the roof of the church and causing the deaths of more than a score of persons. "Unfortunately the children of Moorfields' Charity School had partly entered the church. The boys being last had not entered and all escaped, but twenty-four little girls were killed, and four badly injured. Singularly enough the men who were in the tower ringing the bells all escaped, except one man and a boy who were buried, but both were extracted alive, although the boy expired soon after" (Henry S. and Harold E. Young, *Bygone Liverpool*, 26). The disaster was caused by the crum-

bling of the foundations of the tower, dating from 1360, upon which a lofty steeple had been built in 1746.

[Thomas Baines, *History of the Commerce and Town of Liverpool, and of the Rise of Manufacturing Industry in the Adjoining Counties* (London and Liverpool, 1852), 542, 543.]

[153] For many years before his removal to Boston in 1803, William Belcher had been a leading merchant of Savannah. About 1797 he built for his wife, Eleanor Brown, the handsome residence in Reynolds Square that Robert Mackay was to buy. In Boston the Belchers kept in touch with their Georgia friends. "We at present stay at Mrs. Belcher's," young John Wallace wrote to his mother in 1809. "We were very much disappointed in her. We thought that they were the first people in Boston" (*The Georgia Historical Quarterly*, XVIII, 179). Possibly the indifference of the Proper Bostonians caused the Belchers to regret Savannah; however that may have been, in 1812 William Belcher announced in the newspaper that he had "returned to reside in Savannah," and offered his services to the public as an insurance broker, auctioneer, commission merchant, and factor (*The Republican; and Savannah Evening Ledger*, July 28, 1812).

[154] "Mr. Gibson" was probably William Gibson, a merchant of Charleston and member of the firm of Gibson and Broadfoot (see below, page 301).

[155] Captain John Smith (*d.* 1815) was in command of the frigate *Essex* when she anchored off Tybee.

[156] The firm of Bacon, Malone and Company (composed of John Bacon, I. Malone, John Malone, and Thomas L. Malone) dealt extensively in timber as well as in "the FACTORAGE and COMMISSION LINE" (*Columbian Museum & Savannah Advertiser*, June 11, 1810). It was dissolved in 1810 (*ibid.*).

[157] Andrew Johnston, eighth of the twelve children of James and Ann Marion (Houstoun) Johnston, was born in Savannah on May 17, 1810, and died on May 30, 1810, four days after Robert Mackay wrote this letter.

[From entries in the Family Bible of James Johnston, Junior, owned by the heirs of Mrs. Macartan C. Kollock.]

[158] "Kollocks children" were the two sons and daughter of Dr. Lemuel Kollock (1766–1823), a Savannah physician and distant cousin of "Parson Kollock." His wife, Maria Campbell, was a step-daughter of Dr. George Jones (see above, page 269). The elder of the boys, Phineas Miller Kollock (1804–1872), became a physician; the younger, George Jones Kollock (1810–1894), a lawyer; their sister, Mary Fenwick Kollock (1806–1885), married the Reverend Edward Neufville, rector of Christ Church, Savannah.

[A group of letters written by members of the Kollock family, and edited by Edith Duncan Johnston, appeared serially in *The Georgia Historical Quarterly* from September, 1946 (XXX, 3), through June, 1948 (XXXII, 2).]

[159] This "most extraordinary report" was true: Mrs. Skipworth and Edward Littlefield had been married on Cumberland Island the previous month.

[Clarke, *The Greenes of Rhode Island*, 309.]

[160] Nathanael Ray Greene (1780–1859) was the only surviving son of General Nathanael Greene. He married Anna Maria Clarke in 1808. Unlike the other members of his family, "Nat Greene" did not take kindly to Georgia ways; and soon after the birth on Cumberland Island of his first child, Nathanael, he moved to Rhode Island, where he remained the rest of his life.

[161] Mossman Houstoun, brother of James Edmund Houstoun (see above, page 265), by profession a lawyer, was now embarked on a military career. Appointed captain of the second company of the Third United States Infantry in 1808, the following year he was placed in charge of the recruiting office at New Orleans. Houstoun rose to the rank of major, later to that of lieutenant colonel, and in 1812 he served as captain of Savannah's historic cavalry company, the Chatham Hussars. But he eventually resigned from the Army and resumed the practice of law. He also held the office of surveyor of Savannah for a number of years. A map of the city, which he drew about 1810, shows that he possessed cartographic talent.

[Johnston, *The Houstouns of Georgia;* (Alexander McCrie Duncan), *Roll of Officers and Members of the Georgia Hussars* . . . ([Savannah] n.d.), 30.]

[162] Benne, a seed-bearing plant better known by the name of sesame, was extensively cultivated throughout the South as food for Negro slaves.

The younger John McQueen was one of the first American planters to realize the commercial possibilities of oil from benne seed (see William Darby, *Memoir on the Geography, and Natural and Civil History of Florida*, iv and n., 37).

[163] Abner Woodruff, brother of George Whitefield Woodruff (see above, page 263), came from the North to Savannah in 1804, and, opening a store on the Bay, sold "China, Glass & Queens Ware" (*Columbian Museum & Savannah Advertiser*, November 21, 1804).

[164] Five Fathoms Hole, a familiar mark on early charts of Georgia, is off the south bank of the Savannah River, several miles below Savannah.

[165] Nichol Turnbull (1756–1824), eldest son of Dr. Andrew Turn-

bull, founder of the New Smyrna colony in East Florida (*Dictionary of American Biography*, XIX, 54, 55), moved to Georgia in 1787 and became a planter on Skidaway Island. He later secured land on Whitemarsh Island where he raised some of the first crops on the American continent of long-staple or Sea Island cotton. In 1792, with his brother-in-law, John Holland, he bought Deptford Hill on the Savannah River; and, acquiring Holland's interest, he spent the remainder of his life in cultivating this plantation.

[*Savannah River Plantations*, 32–36; Coulter, *Thomas Spalding of Sapelo*, 67.]

[166] ". . . my Sister" was Catherine Chilcott (see above, page 256), now the wife of John Course of Augusta, Georgia.

[167] Athelston Dawson Lawrence belonged to a family long associated with St. Simon's Island. In the early colonial period his ancestors had settled the plantation, Lawrence, that he inherited. But Athelston Lawrence ran into debt. When his land was seized by the Sheriff and sold at public outcry, he left Glynn County to try his luck in Savannah.

[Information from Mrs. G. V. Cate, the historian of coastal Georgia; *The Republican; and Savannah Evening Ledger*, March 24, 1808.]

[168] Colonel Edward Harden, Junior, of Oak Grove on the Savannah River, was a planter active in local politics. He served as alderman of Savannah, representative and senator in the Georgia Legislature, and as justice of the Inferior Court of Chatham County.

[*Savannah River Plantations*, 81, 82, 101–103.]

[169] "On the 11th June, after a sudden illness of three days in the 61st year of his age, departed this life at his plantation in Barnwell District, South-Carolina, Mr. WILLIAM SCARBROUGH, long a respectable inhabitant of that quarter. He was a man worthy in all the relations of life—and his death lamented most by those who knew him best."—*The Republican; and Savannah Evening Ledger*, June 21, 1810.

[170] The elder Mrs. Scarbrough (1757–1815), who had been Lucy Sawyer, was proud of her descent from the Reverend John Cotton, an eminent divine of the Massachusetts Bay Colony. Her daughter, Lucy, was the wife of Robert Isaac (see below, page 300).

[Transcripts of entries in the Scarbrough Family Bible are in the Library of the Georgia Historical Society, Savannah.]

[171] Thomas Savage, a planter on the Ogeechee River, and Mary Wallace (see above, page 275) were married by Doctor Kollock on June 19, 1810.

[*Columbian Museum & Savannah Advertiser*, June 21, 1810.]

[172] James Johnston, Junior (see above page 257) held the rank of

lieutenant colonel of the First Georgia Regiment of the United States militia.

[173] Sir George Houstoun, seventh baronet (1744–1795), the father-in-law of Colonel Johnston, was a merchant and planter of Savannah. He inherited the family title on the death of his elder brother, Sir Patrick, in 1785.

[174] Throughout the War of 1812 the citizens of Savannah were on guard against an attack by the British Navy. Fort Jackson, near Deptford Hill (see above, page 296), was occupied by a detachment of the Chatham Artillery, to which Robert Mackay belonged.

[Adelaide Wilson, *Historic and Picturesque Savannah* ([Boston,] 1889), 115, 116.]

IV. FROM ENGLAND

[1] "Mr. Moss" was probably Thomas Moss, a wealthy timber merchant and shipowner, who died in 1805. His son, John Moss (1782–1858), is known as the founder of one of Liverpool's great institutions, Moss's Bank.

[John Hughes, *Liverpool Banks & Bankers, 1760–1837* (Liverpool, 1906), 189–198.]

[2] At the time of Robert Mackay's visit, "the African trade" was the pride of Liverpool. The "African merchants," who were the town's leading citizens, controlled five-eighths of the English trade in slaves and three-sevenths of that of all European nations. Statistics show that from 1783 to 1793 these men enjoyed a profit of fifteen million pounds derived from the sale of some three hundred thousand slaves whom they had transported from Africa to the West Indies. But this traffic was soon to be ended by the growing humanitarian sentiment of the age. The Society for the Abolition of the African Slave Trade was founded in 1787 and within twenty years obtained from Parliament a bill prohibiting the importation of slaves into British colonies.

[Ramsay Muir, *A History of Liverpool* (Liverpool, 1907), 191–206.]

[3] The Theatre Royal, opened in 1772, had been redecorated the year before Robert Mackay's arrival in Liverpool. The leading actors of the day appeared on its boards, and, according to a cherished Liverpool tradition, Mrs. Siddons and John Kemble had once been hissed off this stage by exacting audiences.

[J. A. Picton, *Memorials of Liverpool: Historical and Topographical* (2 vols., London and Liverpool, 1875), II, 167, 168.]

[4] John Fawcett (1768–1837), the well-known actor and dramatist, whose connection with Covent Garden lasted forty years, was at the height of his popularity when Mackay attended his performance in Liverpool. It was generally held that his portrayal of Falstaff surpassed all but one of his contemporaries.

[*Dictionary of National Biography*, VI (New York and London, 1908), 1122, 1123.]

[5] William Thomas Lewis (1748?–1811), the celebrated Welsh comedian, was in his day, according to the actor, George Cooke, "the unrivalled favourite of the comic muse in all that was frolic, gay, humourous, whimsical, and at the same time elegant."

[*Dictionary of National Biography*, XI (New York and London, 1909), 1079–1081.]

[6] Hero, Robert Mackay's manservant, is often mentioned in these letters from England.

[7] "Mr. Leigh" was John Leigh (*d.* 1824), an attorney and one of Liverpool's men of fortune. The "superb seat" that inspired Robert Mackay's admiration tallies with descriptions of his estate, Sandhills House, then in the township of Kirkdale, but later incorporated into the borough of Liverpool.

[Picton, *op. cit.*, II, 171, 403.]

[8] Jean-Louis-Théodore de Palazieu Falconnet (1760–1825), member of a notable Swiss family, was a banker of Naples. He married, in 1790, Anna Hunter (1766–1859), second daughter of Dr. William and Deborah (Malbone) Hunter (see above, page 267).

[From the Malbone family records owned by the Newport Historical Society, Newport, Rhode Island.]

[9] Sullivan's Island, off the coast of South Carolina, was a favored summer retreat for Charlestonians. As the scene of Poe's *Gold Bug*, it has a place in literature.

[10] Mary Esther (Kinloch) Huger, widow of General Benjamin Huger, of Revolutionary fame, was an intimate friend of Mrs. McQueen. In 1784 she had accompanied the McQueens to England, and Eliza had been placed in her care when her mother returned to America.

[11] Michael Grayhurst, a London merchant, acted as agent for Robert Mackay in several business transactions.

[12] William Malcolm was the captain of vessels plying between Savannah and Liverpool.

[13] Alexander Mein (see above, page 252).

[14] Cheltenham, "this gay delightful place" in Robert Mackay's words, was a fashionable watering-place in Gloucestershire.

[15] Elizabeth Billington (1768–1818) has been pronounced by no

less an authority than the *Dictionary of National Biography* "the greatest singer England has ever produced" (II, 499). She is remembered also in Italy: legend asserts that when she sang in Naples on May 30, 1794, the thrill and excitement caused by her voice resulted in the eruption of Mount Vesuvius.

[16] High Change, at the north end of Castle Street, was the favorite meeting place of Liverpool's merchants before the opening of the new Exchange Buildings.

[Richard Brooke, *Liverpool as it was during the Last Quarter of the Eighteenth Century, 1775 to 1800* (Liverpool, 1853), 73.]

[17] This "fine Child" was Anne Williamson, born on December 23, 1807. She was married in 1824 to Jacob Read, nephew of General Read (see above, page 285), and died in 1830.

[18] Don Juan McQueen died at his St. John's River plantation, los Molinos de McQueen, on October 11, 1807. For a picturesque account of his last illness and death, see Branch Cabell and A. J. Hanna, *The St. Johns: A Parade of Diversities* (New York and Toronto, 1943), 146, 147.

[19] Charles Tubman, native of Maryland, was for some years a merchant in Savannah. He died on October 3, 1807, aged thirty-five.

[Municipal Mortuary Records, Savannah; *Columbian Museum & Savannah Advertiser*, October 6, 1807.]

[20] The pathetic end of "Wm. Brailsfords daughter" has all the elements of a romantic novel.

"Died, on the 16th ult. at Potosi, in M'Intosh County, Georgia, Mrs. ELIZABETH WOOD, wife of Major Wood, and daughter of William Brailsford, Esq. of this State, in the 21st year of her age, and the first of her marriage—Her infant Son, 6 days old, expired a few hours before her. This Lady, who was every thing that was estimable in society, and who was surrounded by every blessing, equally the idol of her fond husband as of her doating parents, fell a victim to her love and affection for a brother, who died three weeks before, from a wound he received in a duel."—*City Gazette and Daily Advertiser* (Charleston), December 4, 1807.

[21] "I am much concern'd to hear of the loss of the America—," Lady Wright wrote to her niece, Eliza Mackay, on January 23, 1808, "but quite releiv'd to find by Mr Mackays letter to Sir James that what he was concern'd in, was insur'd [.] We all regret the nice ground nuts &cC that was on board" (*The Letters of Don Juan McQueen to his Family*, 78).

[22] For particulars relating to the younger John McQueen's marriage, see above, pages 295 and 296.

[23] Andrew McLean was the son of Andrew McLean and Robert Mackay's half-sister, Catherine Chilcott. From all accounts he was

the family ne'er-do-well. In 1805 he married Maria Hall of East Florida, but failed to fulfil Don Juan McQueen's hope that "Marriage may be of service to make him more attentive to his concerns" (*The Letters of Don Juan McQueen to his Family*, 68 and n.).

[24] Eliza Augusta Falconnet was married on June 11, 1810, to John Izard Middleton (1785–1849) of South Carolina, called by Charles Eliot Norton "The First American Classical Archaeologist" (*Dictionary of American Biography*, XII, 601, 602). She was Robert Mackay's cousin, her mother having been Anna Hunter (see above, page 298). Her portrait by Sully shows that she inherited the beauty for which her family was noted (for a photograph of this portrait, see *Gardens of Colony and State*, compiled by Alice G. B. Lockwood, II, 244).

[25] Robert Isaac (*c.* 1780–1827), a Scottish-born merchant of Savannah and Liverpool, was a member of the important firm of Andrew Low and Company. His wife, Lucy, was the sister of the younger William Scarbrough (see above, page 253).

[26] ". . . old Mr Tatnall" was Josiah Tattnall, known in Georgia history as "the Loyalist" to distinguish him from his son and namesake "the Patriot." Born in St. Philip's Parish, South Carolina, in 1739, the elder Josiah moved to Georgia soon after his marriage to Mary Mulryne in 1761; and, with his father-in-law, Colonel John Mulryne, he "settled the estate of Bonaventure near Savanna" (letter of his grandson, Commodore Josiah Tattnall, in the possession of Mr. G. Noble Jones of Savannah). At the close of the Revolution, Tattnall was banished from Georgia because of his Royalist sympathies. Going to the Bahamas, he received the appointment of surveyor-general and was elected to his Majesty's Council. In 1801, the bitterness against the Loyalists having subsided, the Georgia Legislature restored Josiah Tattnall "to all the rights of citizenship, with full liberty to remove into this state." His son, then Governor of Georgia, signed this act, writing "with lively impressions of gratitude" above his signature (*The Revolutionary Records of the State of Georgia*, I, 632). But "old Mr Tatnall," now established in London, was indifferent to these overtures. He remained in England until his death in 1813.

V. FROM SOUTHERN PORTS

[1] Alexander Baron (1745–1819) was one of the leading physicians of Charleston. A memorial tablet in the First Presbyterian Church

recites in measured prose the salient points of his career. It informs the reader that he was born in the County of Merns, Scotland, educated in the Marischal College of Aberdeen, and studied medicine in Edinburgh under the celebrated Doctor Gregory; that in 1769 he emigrated to Charleston, became a member of the Charitable and Honorable Society of St. Andrew, of which he was president when he died, and a founder of the Medical Society of South Carolina; and that

"THESE SOCIETIES, WITH A LARGE AND SPONTANEOUS ASSEMBLAGE
OF THE MOST RESPECTABLE CITIZENS OF BOTH SEXES,
TESTIFIED AT HIS OBSEQUIES,
HOW GREATLY THEY HAD BELOVED, AND HOW DEEPLY THEY
DEPLORED THE LOSS OF HIM,
WHOM AS A MAN, A CHRISTIAN, A PHYSICIAN, A FRIEND AND A NEIGHBOUR,
THEY HAD SO LONG REGARDED WITH REVERENCE AND AFFECTION."

[2] The brothers William and James Broadfoot, natives of Whitehorn, County Galloway, Scotland, were merchants in Charleston with whom Robert Mackay often did business (see below, page 302). William Broadfoot was at first copartner of the firm of Gibson and Broadfoot and later a trader on his own account. A solid citizen, he died in 1828, in his fiftieth year. James Broadfoot seems to have taken life less seriously. His business correspondence with Robert Mackay often touches on his private affairs. In a postscript to his letter of September 19, 1805, he makes the curt announcement: "A Lady has sued me because I wont *marry* her."

[Charleston Directories; epitaph of William Broadfoot's tombstone in the burial ground of the First Presbyterian Church. Several letters from the Broadfoots to Mackay are owned by the Georgia Society of the Colonial Dames of America.]

[3] John Bowman (*c.* 1746–1807), a venerable figure in Charleston, brother-in-law of a signer of the Declaration of Independence, Thomas Lynch, Junior, had in his youth participated in many stirring events. These are made known in his obituary:

"This gentleman, an early and ardent friend to the constitutional liberties of Great-Britain, and to their assertion in America, left Scotland immediately after the first struggle against the Stamp Act, and, with ample appointments from his father, settled a plantation in the then young colony of Georgia. His education had been liberal and extensive: for, though admitted an Advocate at Edinburgh, he had also regularly attended Dr. Cullen's Lectures; and the exuberant riches of his conversation discovered an intimacy with every branch of the *literae humaniores*, and with all the pursuits of modern science. But his acquisitions were not those of a pedant. A man, who, during two years residence in Paris, frequented there, circles, to which the Ambassador of his country, (at that time, the late Duke of Richmond) introduced him; who traced in Switzerland, the retreats of Voltaire and Rousseau, with whom he formed a personal acquaintance; and who, in London, was the intimate of *Boyd, Dr. Dodd,* and many other distinguished characters, was not likely to suffer the erosions of Academic rust.

"Having mentioned the Duke of Richmond, and the names of Boyd and Dodd, it will not be improper to introduce a notice respecting each of them. Mr. Bowman was the person, who, by letter, transmitted to the Duke of Richmond, that information concerning the murder of Col. Hayne, which his grace stated to the House of Peers, and which produced a challenge from Lord Rawdon, and this challenge, a retraction from the noble Duke.

"In Campbell's life of Boyd, Mr. Bowman is mentioned as seconding, among others, Mr. Boyd's exertions to procure a pardon for a man, who robbed him (Mr. Boyd) on the highway. The truth is, Mr. Bowman thought Mr. Boyd rather too slack in his efforts; and had he not gone himself to Woolwich, procured testimonials and signatures to a petition, and then pushed it on to Lord Sandwich, the day of execution would have intercepted the coy advance of others.* * *"—*City Gazette and Daily Advertiser* (Charleston), July 10, 1807.

[4] Pierce Butler, the wealthy Georgia planter (see above, page 293), had a town house in Charleston.

[5] The play that Robert Mackay attended at the Charleston Theatre was "*Shakespeare's HISTORICAL PLAY, in five acts, of* KING JOHN; *Or, ENGLAND INVADED.*" By leaving before the end, he failed to see the following pieces that concluded the evening's entertainment: "*a MEDLEYOLIO, or* NEW BROOMS to RUB off the RUST of CARE," and "*the last new OPERA, in two acts, of* Love Laughs at Lock-Smiths" (*City Gazette,* May 31, 1805).

[6] In the latter part of May, 1805, the *Resource,* a British ship, arrived in Charleston from Africa with a cargo of slaves. Of these Robert Mackay bought twenty, probably for resale in the Savannah market. The remainder—"231 prime CONGO NEGROES"—were disposed of in Charleston by the firm of Gibson and Broadfoot (*City Gazette,* May 25, 1805). Slave-trading yielded substantial profits to Mackay and his associates; according to papers among Mackay's business correspondence, they had an interest in another cargo aboard the *Montezuma.* On August 10, 1805, William Broadfoot wrote to Mackay from Charleston: "I am sorry to observe that things are not so well as we expected. I understand from Capt Paine of the Avril that her [the *Montezuma's*] cargo consists principally of *talke,* or *inferior* slaves—The quality is pretty fair if they are in prime order —from the scarcity of provisions and the indisposition of Capt. King I am afraid that they will not be landed in as good order as they ought

to be." The next month he informed Mackay: "I expected before now that you would have heard of the Capture of the Montezuma on the 9th Aug[t] within a days Sail of Charleston by the French Privateer Regulator the Mate & 18 of the Crew are arrived at Norfolk."

[Several letters and memoranda concerning the *Resource* and the *Montezuma* are among Robert Mackay's business correspondence owned by the Georgia Society of the Colonial Dames of America.]

[7] Robert Mackay was planning to visit the Sweet Springs in Virginia.

[8] It was appropriate that Robert Mackay should observe "the Kings birthday" (that of George III, who was born on June 4, 1738) at "M[r] Moodies"; for Benjamin Moodie was the British Consul at Charleston. The honor of this appointment is duly commemorated on his tombstone in the burial ground of the First Presbyterian Church:

Sacred
To the Memory of
BENJAMIN MOODIE Esquire
Consul for many years of his Britannic Majesty
To the United States of America
For North & South Carolina & Georgia.
He was born in Scotland.
And after having long resided here as a Merchant
of eminent Intelligence, Integrity & Enterprize
He was to the gratification of his Friends
and the Inhabitants of Charleston
appointed to the distinguished Station
which, with equal Honor to himself & his Country
He filled, untill his death on the 19th. of April 1823
Aged 68 years.
Combining Firmness with Moderation
Pure Principles, with an enlightened understanding
The strictness of duty
with the manners of the Gentleman.
In private Life
He was Beloved by his Acquaintance
& Devoted to his Family.
His ashes repose here in the ground
of his early & affectionate Friend
ADAM TUNNO.
He has left a Widow & a Son
to mourn their irreparable Loss.
This Stone was erected to his Memory
by his affectionate Son
JAMES GAIRDNER MOODIE.

[9] Robert Mackay's criticism of Norfolk was not more severe than that of other visitors. "C'est une des plus laides, des plus irrégulières, des plus sales villes que l'on puisse rencontrer," La Rochefoucauld-Liancourt wrote in 1796. "Les maisons sont basses et vilaines, presque toutes de bois, construites sans alignement; il n'y en a pas vingt en briques. Les rues ne sont point pavées; la ville est entourée de marais" (*Voyage dans les États-Unis d'Amérique*, IV, 256, 257). The best that Tom Moore, the Irish poet, could say ten years later for Norfolk was that it "abounds in dogs, in negroes, and in democrats" (quoted in Thomas J. Wertenbaker, *Norfolk: Historic Southern Port*, 141).

[10] Robert Maitland, a Scotsman, was for many years an influential merchant of Norfolk. His wife was Elizabeth Sproat Lenox, daughter of Robert Lenox (see below, page 313). Maitland moved to New York in 1815 and formed with his brother, William, with James Lenox, and with David Sproat Kennedy, the great mercantile house of Lenox, Maitland and Company. He was later senior partner of Robert Maitland and Son. His will, which contains many substantial bequests, was probated in New York in 1847.

[Wertenbaker, *Norfolk*, 102; William M. MacBean, LL.D., *Biographical Register of Saint Andrew's Society of the State of New York* (2 vols., New York, 1922 and 1925), I, 331. Maitland's will is in the Surrogate's Court of New York County, Hall of Records, New York.]

[11] Susan (Wheeler) Decatur (1776–1860), wife of Commodore Stephen Decatur, was the daughter of Luke Wheeler, a wealthy merchant and mayor of Norfolk. She is remembered as "the reigning belle of Norfolk" and for her "elegant manners and splendid conversational powers" (William Decatur Parsons, *The Decatur Genealogy*, 16). Jerome Bonaparte is said to have courted her, but she wisely rejected him on the ground that Napoleon would not recognize the marriage of his brother to an American. In 1806 she married Stephen Decatur, then in command of the gunboat flotilla in the Chesapeake. At the time of Robert Mackay's visit, Decatur had charge of the naval forces on the southeastern coast, while his wife was the acknowledged leader of Norfolk society. After the War of 1812, in which the Commodore played a notable role, the Decaturs moved to Washington. Latrobe built a mansion for them in La Fayette Park, and there they entertained the world of diplomacy and fashion for several years. This life came to an end in 1823 when Decatur was killed in a duel by Commodore Barron. Susan Decatur then retired to a small house in Georgetown, and devoted herself to the observance of the Catholic faith, which she had embraced. But, though seldom appearing in public, she was still "a notable figure

to those admitted to her salon" (Charles Hurd, *Washington Cavalcade*, 85).

[For other references to Mrs. Decatur, see Charles Lee Lewis, *The Romantic Decatur* (Philadelphia, 1937), 81–83, 186, 279, 280; *In Memoriam: Benjamin Ogle Tayloe,* edited by Winslow M. Warren (Washington, 1872), 158–160; and Richard P. Jackson, *The Chronicles of Georgetown, D. C.,* . . . (Washington, 1878), 34.]

[12] In 1808 David Montagu Erskine, British minister in Washington, had been instructed by his Government to arrange a treaty with the United States that would remove the differences between those powers that had resulted from "the Affair of the *Chesapeake* and *Leopard.*" But his terms were considered too conciliatory to American interests, and Erskine was recalled. He was succeeded in September, 1809, by Francis James Jackson, "a narrow and obstinate Briton," who, in spite of his hostile attitude toward this country, remained at his post until 1811.

[13] Robert Smith (1757–1842) was the American Secretary of State.

[14] Mary (Wayne) Stites, wife of Richard Montgomery Stites, died in Savannah, October 21, 1809, in her thirtieth year. According to the Municipal Mortuary Records: "This lady . . . had been indisposed several days previous to her death, which happened rather suddenly in the absence of her husband, who was on business in Camden county." The cause of her death is given as "Pregnancy."

[15] Grace (Parker) Farley, widow of Samuel Farley, died in Savannah on October 4, 1809, aged sixty-six. "Her parents were among the first settlers of this state," her obituary reads, "and she one of the first whites born in it" (*Columbian Museum & Savannah Advertiser,* October 9, 1809). That Robert Mackay should have considered her a person "of less consequence" is surprising: her father, the Honorable Henry Parker, had been president of Georgia under the government of the Trustees; and her husband, Samuel Farley, had been a prominent attorney of Savannah. Loyalists, the Farleys went to Nassau at the end of the Revolution. After her husband's death in 1785, Grace Parker returned to Savannah, where "her piety, charity, and benevolence endeared her to all her acquaintance" *(ibid.).*

[From her large collection of material on the Georgia Loyalists, Mrs. Maxfield Parrish of St. Simon's Island, Georgia, has kindly supplied the editor of these letters with information about the Farleys.]

[16] Mary Clay (1790–1867), daughter of the Reverend Joseph Clay (see above, page 266) and his wife, Mary Savage, was married in Newark, New Jersey, on October 19, 1809, to William Rufus Gray. In family records the names of the groom's parents are given as William and Elizabeth (Chipman) Gray.

[*Columbian Museum & Savannah Advertiser*, November 9, 1809; Lawrence Park, "Old Boston Families. III. The Savage Family," *The New England Historical and Genealogical Register*, LXVII, 4 (October, 1913), 321.]

[17] Moses Myers, merchant and director of the Branch Bank of the United States at Norfolk, is best remembered for the handsome brick residence that he built in Freemason Street. This is still standing and is considered by architects to be one of the most graceful examples of the Georgian style in America. Portraits of Myers and his wife, Eliza Judd, were painted by Gilbert Stuart.

[Wertenbaker, *op. cit.*, 137 and n.; Lawrence Park, *Gilbert Stuart: An Illustrated Descriptive List of his Works* (4 vols., New York, 1926), II, 545.]

[18] Decatur was still in command of the *United States* when, at the beginning of the War of 1812, she captured the British frigate *Macedonian* in one of the memorable battles of American Naval history.

[19] "Ancrum" was probably James H. Ancrum, a planter, the only person of that surname in the Charleston Directory of 1809.

[20] "Boyd" was either Benjamin Boyd, "store-keeper," at 134 King Street; or William Boyd, "merchant," whose countinghouse was on Chisolm's Wharf (Charleston Directory of 1809).

[21] Adam Tunno (*c.* 1754–1832), a Scotsman; was one of several brothers who emigrated to Charleston and became merchants. For many years he was a senior partner of a flourishing firm, Tunno and Cox, and he served also as a director of the National Bank. He is buried in the cemetery of the First Presbyterian Church.

[Charleston Directories. Tunno's will is in the Probate Court, Charleston County Court House, Charleston.]

[22] Mrs. Calder and her husband, Alexander Calder, managed the Planter's Hotel, a famous hostelry at the corner of Church and Queen Streets. It was here that Planter's Punch is said to have been first served. In 1936 this building, long abandoned and in ruinous condition, was reconstructed with government funds and part of it was made into the Dock Street Theatre.

[Charleston Directories; *South Carolina: A Guide to the Palmetto State*, compiled by the South Carolina Writers' Project (New York [,1941]), 203, 204.]

[23] Hary Grant appears in only one of the Charleston Directories, that of 1809, in which his occupation is given as "merchant" and his address "2 Savage-st."

[24] Sally Williamson's child, John, was born on February 3, 1810 (see above, page 290).

[25] William Stephens (1752–1819), grandson and namesake of the

first President of Georgia under the Trustees, had a long and distinguished career. The first attorney-general of Georgia, mayor of Savannah, judge of the courts of the Eastern Judicial Circuit, grand master of Masons in Georgia, and president of the Union Society, he was for the last sixteen years of his life United States judge for Georgia. His wife, Margaret De Veaux, died in 1807; and on December 31, 1809, Judge Stephens was married by Doctor Kollock to Charlotte, widow of Francis Levett. His family connections included many prominent Savannahians. In 1818 a "Family Compact" was prepared for Judge Stephens; and in this list of forty-three persons Robert Mackay appears as "[His Honor's] nephew's bro-in-law's cousin's husband" (manuscript in the Library of the Georgia Historical Society).

[Judge Stephens' obituary is in *The Georgian*, August 10, 1819; a notice of his marriage to Mrs. Levett appears in the *Columbian Museum & Savannah Advertiser*, January 4, 1810.]

26 William Heyward died at his plantation in Prince William's Parish, South Carolina, on October 28, 1809. His wife was Charlotte Manby Villepontoux; his sister was Mrs. Thomas Gibbons of Savannah (see above, page 279).

[Heyward's obituary, in which he is given the title of Captain, is in the *City Gazette and Daily Advertiser* (Charleston), November 4, 1809.]

27 Beaulieu, on the Vernon River near Montgomery (see above, page 256), was in colonial times the plantation of William Stephens, president of Georgia. In Robert Mackay's day, it was owned by the Morels.

28 "Mrs. Neyle" was Maria McQueen, the second wife of Sampson Neyle (see above, page 257). A daughter of Alexander and Elizabeth (Fuller) McQueen, she was Eliza Mackay's first cousin.

[*Columbian Museum & Savannah Advertiser*, April 22, 1803.]

29 Owen Owens (see above, page 278) had a plantation on St. Catherine's Island, off the Georgia coast.

30 The tombstone that Pierce Butler placed to the memory of his grandson in the burial ground of Christ Church, Philadelphia, bears a touching expression of his grief:

Here lies entombed the body of
PIERCE BUTLER Junior
Beloved, Lamented.
Beloved for his amiable disposition.
Lamented for his early promise.
And here with Gods permission
will be entombed

the body of PIERCE BUTLER Senior.
An attachment stronger than that which blood gives
united the Grandfather and the Grandson.
July 7th 1810.

[*A Record of the Inscriptions on the Tablets and Grave-Stones in the Burial-Grounds of Christ Church, Philadelphia*, compiled by Edward L. Clark (Philadelphia, 1864). From the date of Robert Mackay's letter, it would seem that Pierce Butler, Junior, died in January, and not July.]

Pierce Butler's wish was fulfilled. He died in Philadelphia on February 15, 1822, and was buried near the grave of his grandson.

[A memorial brass to Pierce Butler and other members of his family has been placed in the vestibule of St. Michael's Church, Charleston. This contains the information that he was buried in Philadelphia. See *Inscriptions on the Tablets and Gravestones in St. Michael's Church and Churchyard, Charleston, S. C.*, copied and arranged by Clare Jervey (Columbia, South Carolina, 1906), 14.]

[81] Cornelia Greene was now the widow of Peyton Skipwith, who had died of yellow fever in the autumn of 1808.

[82] "*Brother Ray*" was Ray Sands, a cousin of the Greenes (see above, page 292).

[83] John Williamson (see above, page 290).

[84] ". . . young Ker" was probably Alexander M. Ker (*c.* 1792–1828), a native of East Florida, who, moving to Savannah with "the whole of the Ker's" in Mackay's phrase, became a clerk in the Planters' Bank. His obituary is interesting because of its unusual wording: "The death of no man, as a citizen, and we would not draw the curtain of domestic grief, has been more generally, nor more sincerely lamented." —*Savannah Georgian*, January 23, 1828.

[Municipal Mortuary Records, Savannah.]

[85] This "Son of Littlefields" was Edward Brinley Littlefield (see above, pages 259 and 295), second child of Colonel William Littlefield. His older brother, Francis, died in 1787, at the age of two.

[From the Littlefield family records owned by the Newport Historical Society, Newport, Rhode Island.]

[86] Don Bartolomé de Castro y Ferrer, a native Spaniard, was one of the prominent residents of East Florida during the Second Spanish Occupation. As administrator of Don Juan McQueen's estate, he earned the gratitude of the McQueen family by saving some property for them from Don Juan's many creditors. His wife, Antonia Seguí, was a daughter of Don Bernardo Seguí, a merchant and official of St. Augustine.

[Several letters from Castro y Ferrer to the McQueen heirs are owned by the Georgia Society of the Colonial Dames of America.]

[37] Andrew Atkinson and his son, George, were planters on the St. John's River. Don Juan McQueen, their neighbor, had business dealings with them, but from his point of view these were not satisfactory. "My prospects are flattering," he wrote to Robert Mackay shortly before his death, "and as I have got rid of Atkinsons tribe I expect in a few Years to make something to pay My Creditors & leave property to My Children" (*The Letters of Don Juan McQueen to his Family*, 77). The Atkinsons were a family to be reckoned with. Although they were Americans, both father and son remained loyal to their Spanish allegiance during the "Patriot Rebellion" of 1812, and took a notable part in the battles of that war.

[38] The Non-Intercourse Act was repealed on May 1, 1810.

[39] "Died on the morning of Sunday last, Mrs. ANN GUNN, wife of Mr. Christopher Gunn, of this city."—*Columbian Museum & Savannah Advertiser*, Thursday, February 15, 1810.

The Municipal Mortuary Records give the further information that Mrs. Gunn, a native Savannahian, died at the age of fifty-four, and had "a large & very respectable funeral." Gunn's Coffee House on the Bay was continued by her husband until his death six years later.

[40] This passage shows that Robert Mackay concurred in the widely-held opinion that modesty was not one of Thomas Spalding's virtues.

[41] The Reverend Theodore Dehon (1776–1817), an Episcopal clergyman, was a Bostonian by birth, a graduate of Harvard College, and had been rector of Trinity Church, Newport, since 1800. His frail health and the necessity of spending his winters in a warm climate caused him to resign that post in 1809 and accept a call to St. Michael's in Charleston. In 1812 he was consecrated Bishop for the Protestant Episcopal Diocese of South Carolina. Bishop Dehon died five years later of yellow fever, and was buried in the chancel of St. Michael's Church.

[Frederick Dalcho, M.D., *An Historical Account of the Protestant Episcopal Church in South-Carolina* . . . (Charleston, 1820), 223–232.]

[42] John Macpherson Berrien (1781–1856), a distinguished member of the Savannah bar, was elected by his fellow-citizens solicitor-general and judge of the Eastern Judicial Circuit of Georgia, member of Congress, and United States Senator. In 1829 he was appointed attorney-general in Jackson's first cabinet, but resigned two years later because of his estrangement from the President in the Eaton affair. Berrien was returned to the Senate in 1841 and served until 1852, during which period he became a commanding leader of the Whig party. For his eloquence in debate he was known as "the American Cicero." He was married twice: his first wife was Eliza Anciaux, his

second Eliza Cecil Hunter, daughter of James Hunter (see above, page 265).

[*Dictionary of American Biography*, II (1929), 225, 226; *Biographical Directory of the American Congress, 1774–1927* (Washington, 1928), 696, 697.]

[43] John O'Reilly was the youngest brother of the Reverend Michael O'Reilly, the parish priest of St. Augustine, and father confessor of Don Juan McQueen after his conversion to Catholicism. In the Spanish Census of 1793, "D. Juan O'Reilly," aged twenty-two, is listed with an older brother, "D. Lorenzo O'Reilly," in the household of Father O'Reilly.

[*The Letters of Don Juan McQueen to his Family*, xxviii n., xxxi, xxxiii, 54 and n., 55; photostats of the 1793 Census are in the Library of the St. Augustine Historical Society, St. Augustine.]

[44] Eleazer Waterman was a planter on the Florida bank of the St. Mary's River, his lands including some five thousand acres in McQueen's Swamp. In 1806 he was authorized by the Spanish Governor to erect and operate a water saw-mill, but the Patriot Rebellion prevented his doing so until several years later.

[*Spanish Land Grants in Florida*, prepared by the Historical Records Survey, Works Projects Administration, (5 vols., Tallahassee, 1940 and 1941), V, 195–202.]

[45] Dr. George V. Proctor (*c.* 1782–1817), a native of South Carolina, was one of the better known physicians of Savannah. Health officer of the port, he served as "hospital surgeon" during the War of 1812. His wife, Harriet Thompson Houstoun, was a daughter of Dr. James Houstoun, and the ward of her uncle, John Houstoun, Governor of Georgia. After the death of Doctor Proctor, she married in 1821 Andrew Brown and died in 1833.

[Doctor Proctor's obituary is in the *Columbian Museum and Savannah Daily Gazette*, March 18, 1817; for his wife's family connections, see Johnston, *The Houstouns of Georgia*.]

[46] Mrs. John Turnbull, a Charlestonian, was before her marriage in 1800 Henrietta Bolton Guerin. Her husband was the youngest son of Dr. Andrew Turnbull and a brother of Nichol Turnbull (see above, pages 295 and 296).

[From a transcript of entries in Doctor Turnbull's Family Bible owned by Mrs. Herbert M. Corse of Jacksonville, Florida.]

[47] Richard, an Italian by birth, was for many years a planter in the French colony of St. Domingo. On the outbreak of the slave insurrections, he and his family fled to South Carolina, but later settled in Spanish East Florida, where his baptismal names were recorded in official documents as Luis Josef Francisco. This "experienced French

Man," as Don Juan McQueen called him, obtained much land along the St. John's, and at one time managed a plantation for McQueen. Richard died at St. Mary's, Georgia, in 1817. Through years of frugal living, he was able to bequeath wealth and an honored name to his descendants.

[Walter Charlton Hartridge, "The St. Domingan Refugees in Florida," manuscript.]

[48] John Houstoun McIntosh (1773–1836), a Georgian, the son of George and Ann Priscilla (Houstoun) McIntosh, was now living on Fort George Island, East Florida. He had bought this island from Don Juan McQueen in 1804. In 1812 McIntosh led the revolt of his American neighbors against Spanish rule and was elected director of the "Republic of Florida." With the defeat of the Republicans, or "Patriots," as they called themselves, McIntosh returned to Georgia and, abandoning politics, cultivated his plantation in Camden County. Historians have confused John Houstoun McIntosh with his cousin, John McIntosh (see above, page 261), who was a planter on the St. John's at an earlier period.

[Johnston, *The Houstouns of Georgia.*]

[49] The Altamaha, one of Georgia's great rivers, has an unenviable reputation in English literature. For it was to those "torrid tracts . . . where wild Altama murmurs to their woe" that Goldsmith consigned the inhabitants of *The Deserted Village.*

[50] Don Fernando de la Maza Arredondo, a native of Spain, was an enterprising merchant of Havana, who settled in East Florida during the Second Spanish Occupation. Conspicuous for his services in repelling the invading "Patriots" from St. Augustine, he was elected the next year, in 1813, delegate from Florida to the Provisional Junta at Havana. Arredondo and his son were rewarded with the grant of 289,645 acres in what is now Alachua County, Florida.

[*Spanish Land Grants in Florida*, II, 87–91.]

[51] Taylor's, Hendrick's, and the Ship Yard were plantations on the St. John's River that Don Juan McQueen owned at the time of his death.

[*The Letters of Don Juan McQueen to his Family*, 82.]

VI. FROM THE NORTH

[1] In 1816, according to the City Directory of New York, Elizabeth Rogers kept a boarding house at 8 State Street. The next year she moved to 15 Cortland Street.

[2] The Tontine Coffee House, at the corner of Wall and Water Streets, was a famous institution of New York. It was built between 1792 and 1794 by the Tontine Association, a company of merchants, founded to provide a center for the discussion of trade. The name was derived from Lorenzo Tontine, a Neapolitan banker of the seventeenth century, who had introduced a similar organization in France. The Merchants' Exchange, later to become the New York Stock Exchange, secured quarters in the Tontine Coffee House; and it was here in 1837 that the modern express system was inaugurated when J. W. Hale sent a messenger to Boston three times a week with a carpet-bag of packages and letters. After a half-century of usefulness, the Tontine Coffee House closed its doors, and the building was finally torn down in 1855.

[Frederic De Peyster, *History of the Tontine Building* (New York, 1855); *Rider's New York City: a Guide-Book for Travelers* (New York, 1924), 161, 164.]

[3] John Forbes, an old friend of Robert Mackay's, was a New York merchant, of the firm of John Forbes and Company. In 1816 his office was at 78 Wall Street.

[New York Directories.]

[4] James Lenox and Robert Maitland (see above, page 304) comprised, with David Sproat Kennedy, the firm of Lenox, Maitland and Company. Lenox, the senior partner, had come from Scotland to New York in 1789, at the age of seventeen, and had enjoyed marked success in business. At one time he was a partner of his brother, Robert (see below, page 313). As a director of the Bank of New York and a manager of the St. Andrew's Society, he was known to the general community. In 1817 he returned to Scotland and bought the estate of Dalskairth in the Stewartry of Kircudbright, where he died, a bachelor, in 1839.

[MacBean, *Biographical Register of Saint Andrew's Society of the State of New York*, I, 300.]

[5] Thomas Brinley (1764–1857), Robert Mackay's cousin, was the youngest child of Francis and Aliph (Malbone) Brinley.

[For an account of the Brinley family and the career of Edward Brinley, brother of Thomas, see Katharine Johnstone Wharton, "An Old Newport Loyalist," *Bulletin of the Newport Historical Society*, no. 32 (April, 1920), 1–14.]

[6] Catherine Marcellin, Robert Mackay's landlady, was the widow of Claudius Anthony Marcellin. He is listed in the City Directories as "professor of the French language in Columbia College" and as proprietor of Mechanic Hall, at 237 Broadway, but his own description

of himself is "Boarding House keeper" (see his will in the Surrogate's Court of New York County).

[7] Robert Lenox (1759–1839), a merchant, is said to have been one of the five richest men in New York. The son of a shoemaker of Kircudbright, Scotland, he emigrated to America shortly before the Revolution to join his uncle, David Sproat. During the war he acted as a clerk for Sproat, who was "Commissary-General of Naval prisoners in North America." Lenox, on the British evacuation of New York, went back to Scotland, but later returned and established himself as a merchant. In 1796, with his brother, James, and with William Maitland, he formed the commercial house of James Lenox and William Maitland. It is recorded that Robert Lenox' individual transactions surpassed in extent and importance those of any other New York merchant of his day. An alderman, Lenox held many civic offices, and at the time of his death was president of the Chamber of Commerce. In 1783 he married Rachel Carmer, daughter of a New York merchant; their son James Lenox (1800–1880), book collector and philanthropist, was the founder of the Lenox Library in New York (*Dictionary of American Biography*, XI, 172, 173).

[MacBean, *Biographical Register of Saint Andrew's Society of the State of New York*, I, 173, 174.]

[8] Hugh McCall (1767–1824), major in the United States Army, later jailer of Savannah, is remembered as Georgia's first historian. His two-volume history (the first volume published in 1812, the second in 1816) covers the period from the beginning of the colony to the close of the Revolution. Although superseded by more scientific works, it is valuable for its account of the Revolutionary campaigns, based on the recollections of veterans.

[A biographical sketch by Otis Ashmore is in the reprint of McCall's *The History of Georgia* (Atlanta, 1909). For a modern estimate of McCall, see E. Merton Coulter, "The Early Historians of Georgia," *The Georgia Historical Quarterly*, XXXI, 3 (September, 1947), 192.]

[9] Sarah (Telfair) Haig (1775–1845) was the wife of Captain George Haig, U. S. A. She was the eldest of three sisters (see above, page 280) whose benefactions to Savannah have assured them grateful remembrance. Among their contemporaries, however, these autocratic ladies were often held up to ridicule. "The Pumpkin faced Telfairs were here a few days since," John Wallace wrote to his sister from Augusta on September 1, 1814. "They cut so many high flourishes, I could not refrain from comparing them to some of the country wenches I have seen in their sunday gowns" (*The Georgia Historical Quarterly*, XVIII, 189).

[10] Sarah Mackay, ninth and last child of Robert and Eliza Mackay,

was born in the Broughton Street house, Savannah, on April 11, 1815 (entry in the Family Bible). She died, unmarried, March 7, 1876.

[11] Thomas Tunno was a merchant of Charleston.

[Charleston Directories.]

[12] Deborah (Brinley) Fogg (1761–1846), daughter of Francis and Aliph (Malbone) Brinley, was the wife of the Reverend Daniel Fogg of Pomfret, Connecticut.

[13] Sarah McQueen Williamson (August 11, 1816–January 31, 1884) was married in 1841 to Edward Clifford Anderson of Savannah. A lieutenant commander in the United States Navy and later a brigadier general of the Confederate States Army, Anderson held many important civic offices: he was mayor of Savannah for eight terms, president of the Ocean Steamship Company, director of several banks, and president of the Board of Education.

[From the Williamson family records, owned by Mrs. Florence Crane Norvell of Savannah. A biography of Edward Clifford Anderson is given in his obituary in the *Savannah Morning News*, January 8, 1883.]

[14] "When Mr. Mackay went to Newport he had been urged to do so by some of his relatives, that he might be present at the opening of a large chest that belonged to his Mother's Father (Godfrey Malbone). This gentleman had been dead for 50 years and his heirs were so scattered that the chest (supposed to contain silver) had remained untouched during that time. Mrs. Mackay had looked forward to this opening with great interest, as it was arranged that all the surviving members of the Malbone family should be present and assist in the division of the contents. There had been great doubt about the contents, it was extremely heavy and no one then living had seen the inside of it. It did contain very valuable silver, which was divided into eight portions. Mrs. Mackay received the portion of her husband and also of his half-sister Mrs. Catherine Course a lady living in Augusta, Georgia, to whom Mrs. Mackay sent her share on her return to Savannah."—"The Unfinished Memoirs of Margaret Mackay Elliott," manuscript, a copy of which is owned by the Georgia Society of the Colonial Dames of America.

[15] Pierce Butler (see above, page 308) spent much time in Philadelphia.

Index

www.ingramcontent.com/pod-product-compliance
Lightning Source LLC
Chambersburg PA
CBHW030655120726
47905CB00001B/218

* 9 7 8 0 8 2 0 3 3 5 3 8 4 *